TIMELINES
The Events That
Shaped History

TIMELINES

The Events That
Shaped History

WITHDRAWN

JOHN HAYWOOD
40 ILLUSTRATIONS

Thames & Hudson

CONTENTS

TRAJECTORIES OF HISTORY

DOES HISTORY HAVE a trajectory? This is different from asking if history has a purpose – a divinely ordained plan, or the inevitable triumph of a particular political or socio-economic system. Nations and empires, cultures and societies, ideologies and religions all rise and fall: history has neither purpose nor inevitability. Yet beneath the distracting film of events, the history of humankind has followed a clear and scarcely interrupted trajectory from the end of the last Ice Age to the present day: there has been an accelerating trend of population, urban and economic growth across the world; closer contacts between cultures and civilizations; and the emergence of greater social and economic complexity.

This book presents the grand sweep of world history in an accessible format through concise introductions to key themes, and timelines pinpointing events on a global scale. Split into four fundamental categories of human endeavour – Politics & Economy, Religion & Philosophy, Science & Technology and Arts & Architecture – the timelines allow unexpected parallels and connections to be made and open up a new understanding of world events. (Asterisks indicate approximate dates.) Maps capture the geopolitical developments of different eras, while galleries of images depict a dazzling spectrum of human creative achievement.

Human history has been marked by a number of turning points that have fuelled social, cultural and political change, and enabled the growth and mass movements of populations that have constantly reshaped the world. For the vast majority of prehistory – the time before the development of writing systems – all humans lived by hunting wild animals and gathering wild plants. The natural productivity of the environment constrained the human population, as for any other animal. As the last Ice Age came to an end around 10,000 years ago, groups of people in different parts of the world independently took up farming as a way to secure their food supplies. It was no accident that the earliest farming societies arose in the Middle East, which benefited from the greatest number of plants and animals suitable for domestication. The advent of farming marked the first turning point in human history: it made possible an enormous increase in the human population.

Farmers' ability to grow more food than they needed for their own subsistence led to a second turning point in human history. Surplus food was the first form of wealth: those who controlled it acquired power over their neighbours, leading to the development of hierarchical societies and political centralization. Surplus food also meant that not everyone had to be a farmer. Some people, although at first only a very small minority, could devote themselves full time to craft production, trade, military training, administration or religion. The first civilizations developed in isolation, but as their influence spread they became linked to each other through trade, diplomacy, war and migration. These connections enabled the spread of both ideas and technological innovations. Certainly, individual civilizations have collapsed, but there has never been a total global collapse of civilization: the trajectory of history has always been towards ever more complex and interconnected civilizations.

From the outset, cities were the main centres of civilization, but the vast majority of people continued to live in rural areas, working on the land. The proportion of people living in cities grew only slowly until the Industrial Revolution of the 18th century. This represented a third turning point in human history, as manufacturing and services, rather than agriculture, became the primary source of wealth. Beginning in Britain, labour migrated from rural areas to towns and cities in search of work, leading to an explosive increase in the urban population. In the 19th century, the Industrial Revolution spread to Europe and North America, and in the 20th century to South America and Asia. Only Africa has yet to feel the full impact of industrialization, but its urban centres are growing rapidly. By 2018 more than half the global human population lived in cities, while hunting and gathering – humanity's original way of life – was all but extinct. By the same year the global population had reached 7.6 billion, more than twelve times greater than at the dawn of the Industrial Revolution three

centuries earlier. However, this rapid population growth is unlikely to continue beyond the late 21st century: by 2010 the world had passed 'peak child' and, with birth rates declining globally, most population growth now is the result of increased longevity.

Industrialization and urbanization have provided humanity with many benefits, from food security and improved health to longer life expectancy and higher living standards. By 2018 the number of people globally living in extreme poverty was falling more rapidly than at any time in history. However, these benefits have come at a high cost to the natural environment. Since the 1990s there has been growing concern about the potential impact on the world's climate of carbon dioxide emissions from fossil fuels. By some estimates, in the early 21st century human activities were playing a greater role in shaping the global environment than natural processes. This has led some geologists to propose that we are now living in a new geological epoch, the Anthropocene (from Greek *anthropos*, meaning 'man', and *kainos*, meaning 'recent'). As humanity enters this new epoch, it remains to be seen what trajectory history will take in the future.

10 MILLION– 100,000 YEARS AGO

THE BIRTH OF HUMANITY

HUMAN HISTORY BEGAN between 8 and 6 million years ago in East Africa. At that time, according to DNA evidence, humans began their separate evolution from the great apes. Between 6 and 4 million years ago, the ardipithecines evolved, also in East Africa. Like modern apes, ardipithecines lived in forests and were good climbers; on the ground, however, they walked upright, albeit inefficiently. Around 4 million years ago, the ardipithecines were succeeded by the australopithecines, who were both omnivores and bipeds – they used two legs to walk. Unlike the ardipithecines, the australopithecines lived in open woodland and savanna, spread across a wide area of Africa. Over half a dozen species of australopithecines are known, but the precise evolutionary relationship between them, and with modern humans, remains uncertain.

Australopithecines possessed brains about the same size as modern apes. The evolution of the large brains characteristic of modern humans began around 2.3 million years ago with the appearance of the first hominin species judged to be human, *Homo habilis*. Anatomically, *H. habilis* closely resembled the australopithecines but possessed a brain that was 50 per cent larger. *Homo erectus*, meanwhile, which appeared roughly 1.8 million years ago, possessed a brain up to two-thirds the size of a modern human's. *H. erectus* became the first human species to live outside Africa, migrating into Europe and as far east as China and Indonesia. In Africa and Eurasia, *H. erectus* evolved seamlessly into *Homo heidelbergensis* (often called *Homo rhodesiensis* in Africa), which had a yet larger brain. In Europe, *H. heidelbergensis* evolved into the Neanderthals, who were physically adapted to a colder climate, while in Africa it evolved into anatomically modern humans, *Homo sapiens*, approximately 200,000 years ago.

The development of behavioural modernity – toolmaking, language, and a capacity for abstract and symbolic thought – took place gradually alongside the evolution of anatomical modernity among humans' ancestors. The earliest evidence is for toolmaking: chimpanzees are known to use naturally occurring objects, often twigs and pebbles, as simple tools, and early hominins may therefore have used similar implements long before the earliest manufactured tools of the Oldowan industry appeared around 2.6 million years ago.

Oldowan tools – typically choppers and scrapers made by flaking (striking) river cobbles to create a sharp edge – probably originated with the australopithecines, and were used to butcher animals. However, it is unclear whether early hominins actively hunted for food, or simply scavenged the kills of other predators. It is not until roughly 500,000–400,000 years ago that unambiguous evidence (such as hunting spears) demonstrates that early hominins hunted animals themselves.

Oldowan tools continued to be created by later human species for more than 1 million years, alongside more complex implements. The evolution of the large-brained *Homo erectus* witnessed the appearance of a new tool type, the hand-axe (actually a leaf-shaped butchery knife). Although both Neanderthals and early *H. sapiens* used a wider range of tools than earlier human species, a variety of hominins appears to have mastered the use of fire at least 800,000 years ago and had begun to cook food by approximately 500,000 years ago.

While language is central to the modern human capacity for abstract and symbolic thought, its origins remain poorly understood. *H. erectus* was the first human species with the physical capacity to speak with a recognizably human voice, and it is generally assumed that both *H. heidelbergensis* and the Neanderthals also had some capacity for language. The earliest evidence for behavioural modernity, however, comes from sites in Africa and the eastern Mediterranean occupied by early anatomically modern humans between 190,000 and 75,000 years ago. The inhabitants exploited a range of land and marine food resources, possessed sophisticated toolmaking skills and engaged in symbolic behaviour, such as wearing shell necklaces, using pigments and creating geometrical designs. We would recognize these people as being like ourselves.

ARDIPITHECUS KADABBA

ARDIPITHECUS RAMIDUS

AUSTRALOPITHECUS ANAMENSIS

AUSTRALOPITHECUS AFARENSIS

AUSTRALOPITHECUS GARHI

AUSTRALOPITHECUS AFRICANUS

CLIMATE CHANGE

10–5mil* The Rift Valley system forms in East Africa

3.5* The Greenland ice cap begins to form

2.6–2.4* The first continental glacial period in the northern hemisphere takes place

6 MILLION YEARS AGO   5   4   3

CULTURAL DEVELOPMENT

6* The last common ancestor of chimpanzees and hominins dies out

4.5* Bipedalism (using two legs to walk) develops in hominins

3.3* Lomekwi, Kenya: The earliest known stone tools are made.

2.6–1.4* The Oldowan toolmaking culture develops in Africa, and spreads across southern Europe and Asia

2.3* The earliest species of the genus Homo (H. habilis) evolves

HOMO ERECTUS

HOMO HABILIS

AUSTRALOPITHECUS SEDIBA

HOMO NEANDERTHALENSIS

HOMO HEIDELBERGENSIS

DENISOVANS

HOMO SAPIENS

2

1

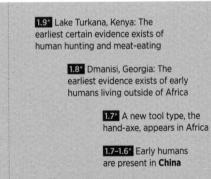

1.9* Lake Turkana, Kenya: The earliest certain evidence exists of human hunting and meat-eating

1.8* Dmanisi, Georgia: The earliest evidence exists of early humans living outside of Africa

1.7* A new tool type, the hand-axe, appears in Africa

1.7–1.6* Early humans are present in **China**

800,000* Gesher Banot Ya'aqov, Israel: The earliest firm evidence exists for humans' controlled use of fire

500,000–300,000* Burnt bone in hearths is evidence that early humans have begun to cook their food

400,000* Schönigen, Germany: The earliest surviving wooden tools (spears) are made

315,000* Jebel Irhoud, Morocco: The oldest Homo sapiens fossils exist

100,000* Qafzeh and Skhul caves, Israel: The oldest evidence exists of anatomically modern humans living outside of Africa

15,000 YEARS AGO

THE JOURNEY OUT OF AFRICA

About 100,000 years ago anatomically modern humans began to migrate out of East Africa. Aided by low sea levels during glacial periods, they had colonized all of the world's continents except Antarctica by 15,000 years ago.

KEY

- ⬚ Modern coastline
- ⬚ Maximum extent of ice caps *c.* 18,000 years ago
- ⬚ Ice caps *c.* 12,000 years ago
- ⬛ Ice caps *c.* 10,000 years ago
- ▦ Area of evolution of anatomically modern humans
- → Migration routes of anatomically modern humans
- **CHINA 50,000** Approximate date of arrival of anatomically modern humans

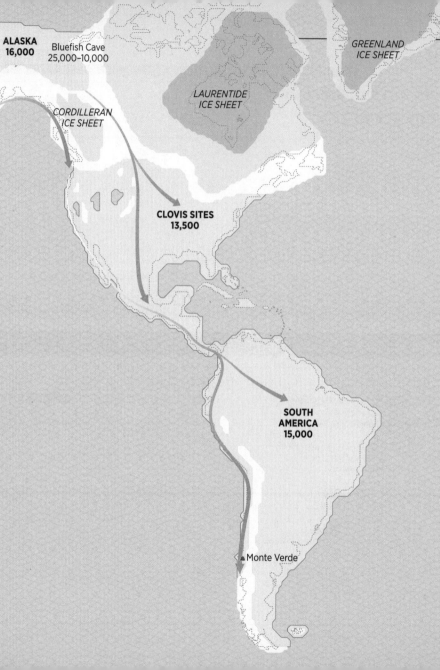

ALASKA 16,000

Bering Strait land bridge

Bluefish Cave 25,000–10,000

CORDILLERAN ICE SHEET

LAURENTIDE ICE SHEET

GREENLAND ICE SHEET

CLOVIS SITES 13,500

SOUTH AMERICA 15,000

▲ Monte Verde

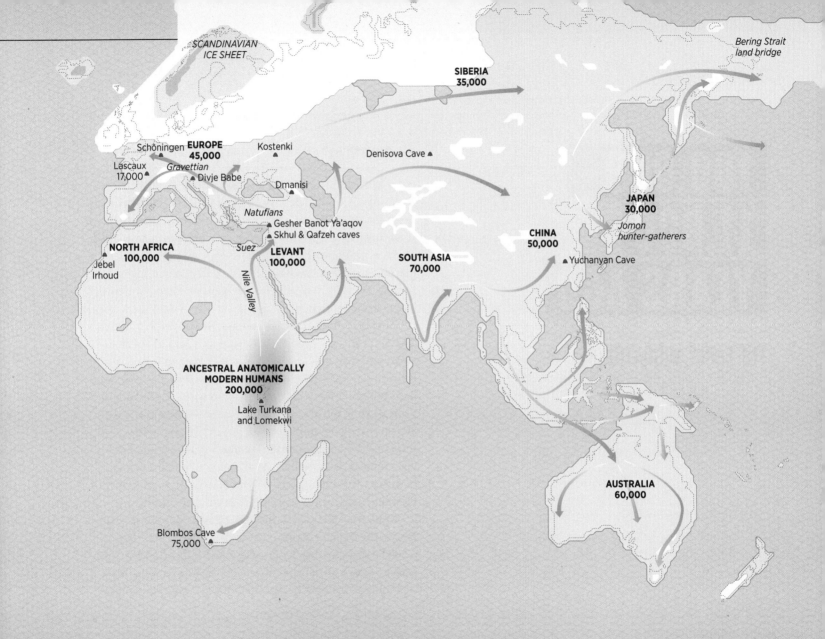

SCANDINAVIAN
ICE SHEET

*Bering Strait
land bridge*

SIBERIA
35,000

Kostenki

Denisova Cave ▲

Schöningen **EUROPE**
45,000

Lascaux
17,000 ▲ *Gravettian*
▲ Divje Babe

Dmanisi

JAPAN
30,000

*Jomon
hunter-gatherers*

Natufians
▲ Gesher Banot Ya'aqov
▲ Skhul & Qafzeh caves

CHINA
50,000

NORTH AFRICA
100,000

Suez **LEVANT**
100,000

SOUTH ASIA
70,000

Jebel
Irhoud ▲

▲ Yuchanyan Cave

Nile Valley

**ANCESTRAL ANATOMICALLY
MODERN HUMANS
200,000**

Lake Turkana
and Lomekwi

AUSTRALIA
60,000

Blombos Cave
75,000 ▲

100,000–11,000 YEARS AGO

THE EARLY MIGRATIONS

ALL MODERN HUMANS are descended from populations of *Homo sapiens* that lived in Africa approximately 200,000 years ago. Around 70,000 years ago, a small group of these *Homo sapiens* left Africa; over the following 50,000 years their descendants colonized all the world's other continents except Antarctica, in the process replacing all other human species. These migrations were enabled by low sea levels during glacial periods (glaciations), which created land bridges linking islands and continents: humans reached most parts of the world on foot.

Modern humans had first migrated out of Africa around 100,000 years ago, probably following the path of the Nile valley and then crossing the isthmus of Suez into modern-day Israel and Palestine. For unknown reasons, however, the descendants of these pioneers died out within a few thousand years, leaving the area to Neanderthals. Nonetheless, some 30,000 years later another small group of *Homo sapiens* migrated out of Africa. In the Middle East, these humans encountered Neanderthals. As all modern humans outside of Africa carry small traces of Neanderthal DNA, relations between the two groups were not necessarily hostile.

From the Middle East, modern humans quickly spread east to the Indian subcontinent and Southeast Asia; by 60,000 years ago, they had reached Australia and New Guinea, which at that time formed a single continent. This was the first over-sea human migration. It was also around this time that the first modern humans arrived in China, before reaching Japan roughly 30,000 years ago. The last continents to be colonized by humans were the Americas. *Homo sapiens* reached Alaska approximately 16,000 years ago from northeastern Asia via the land bridge across the Bering Strait, but further progress was barred until the continental ice sheets began to retreat around 14,000 years ago. Other humans from northeastern Asia, who bypassed the ice sheets by migrating along the Pacific Coast, reached South America by 15,000 years ago.

Early human migrations around the world created a multitude of different cultures as population groups split from one another and adapted to different habitats. Throughout the last Ice Age, all humans lived by hunting wild animals, fishing, and gathering wild plant foods and shellfish, depending on the local environment. Such hunter-gatherers generally lived in bands of no more than twenty to thirty people and migrated seasonally to make the most efficient use of a region's resources. This mobility placed practical limits on humans' cultural and technological development as hunter-gatherers' possessions needed to be easily portable.

With so much water locked up in ice sheets, the Ice Age world was drier as well as cooler. Forests retreated, and vast areas of savanna, open steppe and tundra supported herds of large herbivores. Cultures dependent on hunting large game developed in many parts of the world, most notably in North America and in Europe, where hunter-gatherers created spectacular cave paintings of Ice Age wildlife. New toolmaking technologies were also adopted, as humans used microliths (tiny stone blades) to make composite hunting weapons such as spears, arrows and harpoons.

As the Ice Age began to draw to an end roughly 14,000 years ago, hunter-gatherers in some highly productive environments adopted strategies that allowed them to become partly sedentary. The Jomon culture in Japan appears to have achieved this by exploiting abundant marine resources; freed from the need to constantly migrate, they were among the earliest humans to use pottery. The Natufians in the eastern Mediterranean, meanwhile, built villages formed of permanent huts, and developed sickles and grindstones to harvest and process wild cereals.

Although the global population was still only around 4 million people, humans had already had a considerable impact on the environment by the end of this period. The arrival of *Homo sapiens* in Australia and the Americas was quickly followed by mass extinctions of local megafauna – 'large' animals such as the woolly mammoth – either through hunting or as the result of environmental changes caused by specifically human activities such as lighting bush fires.

HOMO ERECTUS

HOMO NEANDERTHALENSIS

HOMO SAPIENS

HOMO FLORESIENSIS

CLIMATE CHANGE

75,000* The last **glacial period** (Ice Age) begins

100,000 YA	90,000	80,000	70,000	60,000	50,000	40,000

CULTURAL DEVELOPMENT

100,000* Anatomically modern humans colonize the **Levant** (eastern Mediterranean), but die out within a few thousand years

75,000* The earliest evidence exists for anatomically modern humans in **India**

75,000* Blombos Cave, South Africa: **Art** (stone engraved with a simple geometric pattern) and **body ornaments** (shell beads) are both created

60,000* Modern humans reach **Australia**

60,000–50,000* The main **dispersal around the world** of anatomically modern humans begins

45,000* Anatomically modern humans begin to colonize **Europe**

40,000* Kostenki, Russia: The earliest evidence exists for **sewn clothing** (bone needles and awls)

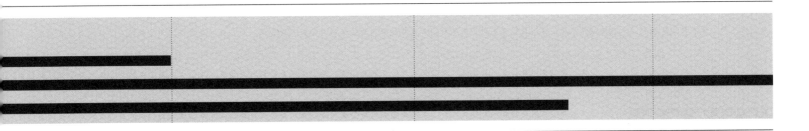

23,000–18,000* The **coldest period of the last glacial period**: sea levels are 100–130 m (328–427 ft) lower than today

14,000* Continental ice sheets begin to retreat as **global warming** sets in

13,500–11,000* Rising sea levels sever the **Bering Strait** land bridge between Siberia and Alaska

11,500* The end of the last glacial period marks the end of the **Pleistocene** and **Palaeolithic** periods

30,000   **20,000**   **10,000**

35,000* Divje Babe, Slovenia: the oldest known **musical instrument**, a simple bone flute, is created

35,000* **Cave art** traditions begin in Europe

30,000* **Neanderthals** become extinct in Europe

29,000–25,000* The **Venus figurines** from Central Europe, the earliest known ceramic objects, are created

28,000* The **Solomon Islands** are first settled

28,000–23,000* The European **Gravettian culture** develops microlithic tool technology

18,300–17,500* Yuchanyan Cave, China: The oldest known **pottery vessels** are created

17,000* Lascaux, France: Famous Palaeolithic **cave paintings** are created

16,000* Humans are present in **Alaska** by this time

12,500* **Cereal cultivation** begins in the Middle East

12,000* The extinction of *Homo floresiensis* leaves ***Homo sapiens*** as the only surviving hominin species

11,600* **Mesolithic** intensive hunter-gatherer cultures emerge in Europe and the Levant

14,500* Humans settle at **Monte Verde**, Chile

14,000* Japanese **Jomon hunter-gatherers** use pottery vessels for storage and cooking

13,500* The **Clovis culture** spreads across the North American Great Plains

11,000 YEARS AGO— 6000 BC

THE FIRST FARMERS

THE END OF the last Ice Age brought far-reaching environmental changes to most regions of the world. The vast amount of water locked in continental ice sheets returned to the seas, inundating coastal lowland areas and severing land bridges before the sea level eventually stabilized around 6000 BC. Large parts of the northern hemisphere, previously under permanent ice, became habitable. The steppes and tundras retreated as forests spread northwards, while changing rainfall patterns caused the greening of the Sahara, desertification in Australia and the spread of rainforests around the Equator.

In many parts of the world, humans adapted to these changing conditions by intensifying their exploitation of small game, wildfowl, fish, shellfish and plants. Areas of great ecological diversity, such as northwestern Europe, could support relatively dense hunter-gatherer populations. In other regions, humans adjusted to the new climate by taking up farming. The first stage was to plant the seeds of preferred wild food plants near regular campsites to ensure a convenient supply. The next step was to domesticate these plants by selectively breeding them for desirable qualities. Cereals, such as wheat, barley, rice and millet, were among the earliest plants to be domesticated, as their seeds are rich in carbohydrates and easy to store. The majority of animal species to be domesticated were herd animals, whose 'follow-the-leader' instincts made them easy to manage.

The first farming societies emerged around 8000 BC in the Fertile Crescent, an area of the Middle East exceptionally rich in plants and animals suitable for domestication. The transition from hunting and gathering to complete dependence on farming lasted two or three centuries. Farming spread from the Middle East to North Africa and southeastern Europe by around 6500 BC, and to South Asia around 6000 BC. In China and New Guinea, meanwhile, farming had developed independently by around 7000 BC. The cultivation of wild plants in the Americas began at much the same time as in other areas of the world, but the transition to full reliance on farming took much longer – over several thousand years. The key challenge was that few animals in the Americas were suitable for domestication and, outside the Andes, livestock farming was of little importance until European contact in the late 15th century.

The growth of farming marked the first great turning point in human history, as it enabled a huge increase in the global population. Hunter-gatherer populations were always strictly constrained by environmental factors: if they rose to an unsustainable level, starvation quickly restored balance. Even in favourable environments, however, hunting and gathering can support a population density of only about one person to 25 square kilometres. In contrast, even the simple techniques employed by the first farming societies could support around 500 people over the same area of land.

In farming societies the productivity of the land is closely related to the amount of work invested in it. For farmers, a high birthrate was thus desirable: a growing population could be used to intensify cultivation or clear new fields, and so further increase food production. Famines resulting from crop failures mainly affected the very young or very old and did little to restrain long-term population growth. Thanks to this numerical advantage, farming societies were able to encroach steadily on the territory of neighbouring hunter-gatherers, who were forced either to adopt farming themselves or to starve.

As settled farmers were not limited to owning portable goods, farming also led to many technological and social changes. The appearance of new tools, such as polished stone axes, hoes, sickles and grindstones, came alongside the invention of looms for weaving textiles and the use of pottery for storage and cooking. In many regions, the kilns used for firing pottery enabled another technological breakthrough: the smelting and casting of copper and gold. Farmers benefited from investing time and effort in building durable houses, and they could accumulate material possessions – developments that ultimately led to the emergence of social distinctions.

SOCIAL ORGANIZATION & ECONOMY

9000–8500 **Sheep** and **goats** are domesticated in the Middle East

8500 **Pigs** are domesticated in the Middle East

8000 **Yams** are cultivated in tropical West Africa

8000–6000 Rising sea levels flood the land bridge linking **New Guinea** and **Australia**

8000–6000* Mexican hunter-gatherers domesticate and casually cultivate **gourds** and **squash**

SCIENCE & TECHNOLOGY

8200–7600 Pesse, Netherlands: The oldest known **boat** (a dugout canoe) is built

7500 Hinds Cave, Texas: The earliest known **basketry** is made

8000* Australian Aborigines invent the **boomerang**

8000 Scandinavia: Polished bone **spear points** are made

8000* Palestine: A walled settlement is built at **Jericho**

9000 BC   8500   8000   7500

RELIGION & PHILOSOPHY

9000 Vasilevka, Ukraine: The earliest known large **cemetery** of human burials is created

7500–5700 Clay figurines of a **'mother goddess'** are made at Çatalhöyük, Turkey

ART & ARCHITECTURE

9000 Palestine: The **Ain Sakhri lovers figurine**, the oldest depiction of humans having sex, is created

8500 **Rock art traditions** begin in the Sahara

7000 China: **Rice** is cultivated in the Yangtze river region

7000 The **cat** is domesticated, probably in Cyprus

6500 The **dog** is first domesticated in the Americas

6500 **Farming** begins in southeastern Europe

6000 **Britain** becomes an island due to rising sea levels after the end of the last Ice Age

6000 **Tasmania** becomes an island: Tasmanian Aborigines remain isolated from contact with other humans until AD 1772

6000 China: **Millet** is farmed in the Yellow river region

6000 Farming villages develop in the mountains of **Baluchistan**, in the Indus valley

6000 **Gourds** are cultivated in eastern North America, probably for use as fishing net floats

7000–6000* **Skis** are first used in northwestern Russia

6500 **Pottery** is in widespread use in the Middle East

6000* **Copper smelting** occurs in the Middle East

7000	6500	6000	5500

6800* Plastered and painted **human skulls** are created at Jericho and other sites, possibly evidence for an ancestor cult

6500–5500 Lepenski Vir, Serbia: Sculptures of **anthropomorphic figures with fish heads** are created

6500 Jordan, Syria and Iran: The earliest known **board games** are played

6000–4000 BC

THE SPREAD OF AGRICULTURE

BETWEEN 6000 AND 4000 BC, farming spread across the Middle East to the Indus river valley, into Western Europe and North Africa, and across most of East Asia. Agriculture spread most readily to regions where environmental conditions closely mirrored its origins in the Fertile Crescent: the Mediterranean, the Sahara (then experiencing a 'wet' phase) and the Indus valley, for example, all benefited from climates naturally suited to cultivating Middle Eastern crops such as wheat and barley. Farming first extended beyond this natural comfort zone by spreading to Central and Western Europe as crop strains developed that could tolerate shorter growing seasons and cooler, wetter summers; European farmers also relied more heavily on stock rearing than their counterparts elsewhere. Genetic evidence increasingly indicates that agriculture spread through Europe mainly through migration: these new farmers appear to have assimilated with, or replaced outright, indigenous hunter-gatherer communities.

In the Middle East, meanwhile, technological innovations like the plough and irrigation allowed farmers to increase their productivity and to colonize regions such as the fertile Mesopotamian flood plain, which did not otherwise enjoy enough rainfall to support agriculture. By 4000 BC Mesopotamia was probably the most densely populated part of the world, and exhibited both the early stages of urbanization and an emerging hierarchical society: small towns dotted the plains, and temple complexes hint at the emergence of a ruling class that combined religious and political authority.

In the Americas, distinct regional variations developed among hunter-gatherers as communities adapted to local environmental conditions. With its rich marine resources, the Pacific coast became relatively densely populated. Farming was not yet established anywhere in the Americas, but in many areas hunter-gatherers cultivated wild plants as supplementary foods, thus unconsciously beginning the process of domestication that would eventually make farming possible. These wild plants included future staple foods such as potatoes in the Andes and maize in Mesoamerica. On the other side of the Atlantic, hunter-gatherers in the West African forests similarly cultivated wild yams as a supplementary food.

By 4000 BC the long-term social and cultural consequences of agriculture were becoming clearer. Population growth was accelerating rapidly: in the 200,000 years before the emergence of the first farming communities around 8000 BC, the number of humans across the world grew from a few thousand to an estimated 5 million. By 6000 BC, the global population had doubled, and by 4000 BC had more than doubled again. Hunter-gatherers were already greatly outnumbered by farmers.

Agriculture also had the power to transform society. Most years, even subsistence farmers are able to produce more food than they need, and this surplus food became the first form of wealth. Cereal crops such as wheat and rice were particularly useful as they can be stored easily, either against later shortages or for exchange. Farmers who succeeded in accumulating surpluses acquired power because they could afford exotic goods and control their distribution, or force other farmers into dependent relationships during food shortages. Distinctions of rank and status emerged, and more intensive agriculture enabled greater surpluses and the development of a more hierarchical society. Food surpluses also fuelled an increase in technological and cultural innovation, since specialists could now be supported in non-agricultural occupations. In 4000 BC this process was most evident on the fertile plains of Mesopotamia.

Beyond the Fertile Crescent, agricultural societies remained relatively egalitarian, as reflected in early farmers' communal megalithic tombs along Europe's Atlantic coast. Equally significant is the Pontic steppe culture, centred on Ukraine, which domesticated the horse at the turn of the 4th millennium BC. Horses would revolutionize transport and warfare, but were initially seen only as sources of meat and milk. In East Asia, widespread and diverse farming societies, such as the Yangshao along the Yellow river, laid the foundations for future Chinese cultural development.

POLITICS & ECONOMY

6000–5000* The farming settlement of Egypt's **Nile valley** begins

5900–4200 The **Ubaid culture**: Urbanization begins in Mesopotamia

5600–4900 The **Bandkeramik culture**: The first farming culture develops in Central Europe

5500 The **cotton plant** is domesticated in the Indian subcontinent

5500* **Cereal farming** spreads to northwestern Africa

5500–5100 Tres Ventanas, Peru: **Potatoes** are possibly cultivated

5400–4800 Ancestors of the **Inuit** and **Aleut** peoples migrate from Asia to Alaska

5400 Domesticated **chickens** are reared in China

5000–3200* The early Chinese **Yangshao culture** flourishes in the Yellow river region

5000 **Olives** are first cultivated in the Middle East

5000* The desertification of the **Sahara** begins

SCIENCE & TECHNOLOGY

5500* **Cosmetics** made from powdered mineral pigments are first used in Egypt

5500 **Irrigation techniques** are developed in northern Iraq

5000 Bulgaria: The earliest known **goldworking** takes place

6000 BC

5500

5000

RELIGION & PHILOSOPHY

5800 The Chinchorro people of Peru make the earliest known **intentionally prepared mummies**

5000 The earliest known **Mesopotamian temple complex** is built at Eridu, probably dedicated to the water god Enki

ART & ARCHITECTURE

6000* Bhimbekta, India: **Rock paintings** begin to record scenes of hunting and communal celebrations

6000* Tassili n'Ajjer, Algeria: **Rock paintings** begin to record scenes of cattle-herding in the central Sahara

5000 Tataria, Romania: **Incised clay tablets** show that a simple system of notation is in use in southeastern Europe

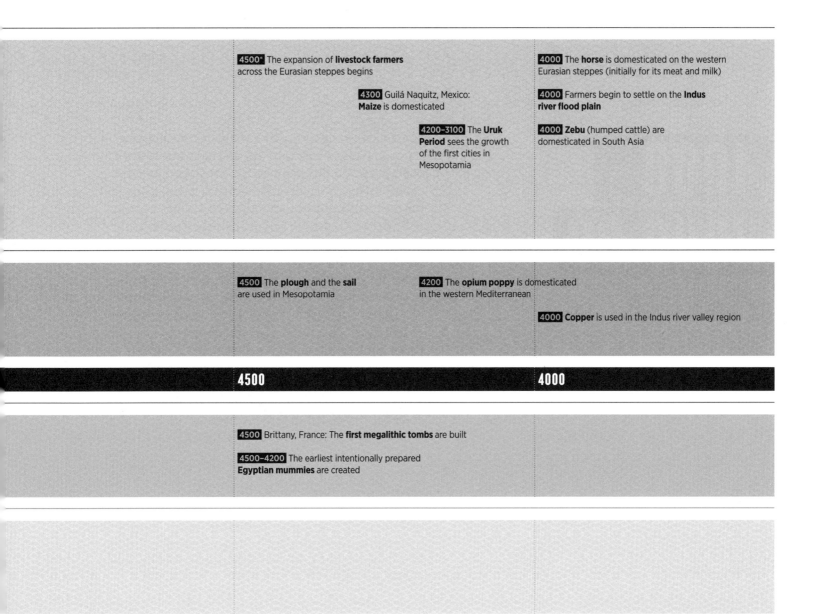

4500* The expansion of **livestock farmers** across the Eurasian steppes begins

4000 The **horse** is domesticated on the western Eurasian steppes (initially for its meat and milk)

4300 Guilá Naquitz, Mexico: **Maize** is domesticated

4000 Farmers begin to settle on the **Indus river flood plain**

4200–3100 The **Uruk Period** sees the growth of the first cities in Mesopotamia

4000 **Zebu** (humped cattle) are domesticated in South Asia

4500 The **plough** and the **sail** are used in Mesopotamia

4200 The **opium poppy** is domesticated in the western Mediterranean

4000 **Copper** is used in the Indus river valley region

4500

4000

4500 Brittany, France: The **first megalithic tombs** are built

4500–4200 The earliest intentionally prepared **Egyptian mummies** are created

4000– 2000 BC

THE RISE OF CIVILIZATIONS

CIVILIZATIONS – complex societies with urban development and state organization – initially appeared during the 4th and 3rd millennia BC. The first, the Sumerian civilization, emerged around 3500 BC in southern Mesopotamia: independent city-states were established, each focused on a temple complex that acted as a centre for craft production, trading, and collecting and redistributing food surpluses. Rulers combined political and religious authority and wars between the city-states were common. Around 2334 BC Sargon the Great, ruler of Akkad, conquered all of Mesopotamia to create the first known empire. After the fall of the Akkadian empire in around 2193 BC, its southern rival Ur grew to dominate the region until its own empire was overthrown in 2004 BC.

Local kingdoms emerged in Egypt's fertile Nile valley towards the end of the 4th millennium BC. United by the king Narmer in around 3000 BC, a tradition of divine monarchy developed that would grow to exercise vast authority over Egyptian society: the enormous pyramid tombs scattered along the Nile valley are testament to its power and organization during the Old Kingdom period (approximately 2649–2134 BC). Further east, the political structure of the Indus valley civilization, which arose in roughly 2600 BC, remains poorly understood, while the Minoan civilization on the island of Crete, dating to around 2000 BC, was ruled from palaces that served similar functions to Mesopotamian temple complexes.

In China, growing social stratification began to develop in the advanced Neolithic Longshan culture, as powerful rulers and skilled artisans established themselves; this may have been the consequence of rapid population growth after rice began to be intensively farmed in the Yellow river region. Livestock farmers also spread across the Eurasian steppes in this period, as far east as the Altai mountains on the borders of modern-day China, Mongolia and Russia. One of these peoples, on the western steppes, spoke a language known to linguists as Proto-Indo-European (PIE). Spread by migration, PIE diversified and evolved into what is now the world's most widespread family of languages. In the Americas, the first farming societies emerged, while marine-mammal hunters began the colonization of the high Arctic.

Writing represented the most important cultural development of the 4th and 3rd millennia BC, effectively marking the beginning of the end of human prehistory. Literacy was an aid to administration in societies that had grown so large and complex that human memory alone could not hold all the information necessary for their efficient government. The earliest writing system, the Sumerian pictographic script, which emerged around 3400 BC, was probably a refinement of a widely used system of clay tokens. Later, in the early 3rd millennium BC, this pictographic script evolved into the more versatile cuneiform system. Hieroglyphic forms of writing developed independently in Egypt and the Indus valley, and by 2000 BC a hieroglyphic script was also being used by the Minoans on Crete, potentially as a result of trade contacts with Egypt.

Equally important alongside writing was the invention of bronze in approximately 3800 BC, probably in Iran. For millennia, copper (and later gold) had been widely employed in the Middle East and Europe to make ornaments, jewelry and small tools, but it was far too soft to supplant stone tools in everyday use. By contrast, bronze – an alloy of copper with arsenic or tin – was much harder, kept a sharp edge longer and, unlike stone tools, could be melted down and recast if worn out. As the technology spread, bronze tools gradually replaced stone implements for most purposes.

Unlike stone, however, the raw materials used to make bronze are relatively rare. A side effect of the invention of bronze was therefore an increase in long-distance trading that in turn enabled new contacts to develop between cultures. More complex goods, made of bronze, copper and gold, could be exchanged in this period thanks to the invention of the lost-wax method of metal casting in the 4th millennium BC. These new connections were further facilitated by the invention of the wheel, which was used for both transport and making pottery.

POLITICS & ECONOMY

4000–3000 **Llamas** and **alpacas** are domesticated in the Andes

3500* **Cities** develop in Sumer, in southern Mesopotamia

3200–1800 China: **Neolithic cultures** see the growth of social and economic complexity in the Yellow river and Yangtze regions

3000–1800 Peru: The growth of a ceremonial city at **Caral** marks early urban development in South America

3000* **Narmer**, a local king, unites Upper and Lower Egypt

SCIENCE & TECHNOLOGY

4000–3600 **Wheeled vehicles** are invented in southeastern Europe or Western Asia

3500* Colombia: **Pottery** is first used in the Americas

3000–2000 Central Asia: **Hemp** is domesticated for use as a fibre and in cannabis

4000 BC	3800	3600	3400	3200	3000

RELIGION & PHILOSOPHY

3000–2300 The stone circle at **Stonehenge** is built in several stages across the Neolithic and early Bronze Age

ART & ARCHITECTURE

3400* **Writing using pictographs** is invented in Sumer

3200–3000 The **Egyptian hieroglyphic script** emerges

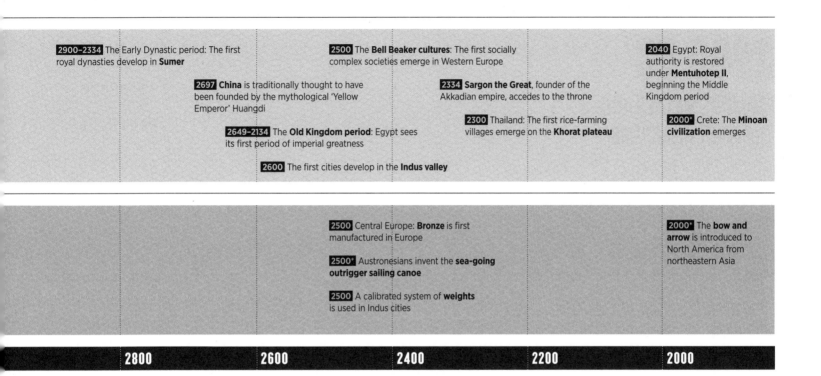

2900–2334 The Early Dynastic period: The first royal dynasties develop in **Sumer**

2697 **China** is traditionally thought to have been founded by the mythological 'Yellow Emperor' Huangdi

2649–2134 The **Old Kingdom period**: Egypt sees its first period of imperial greatness

2600 The first cities develop in the **Indus valley**

2500 The **Bell Beaker cultures**: The first socially complex societies emerge in Western Europe

2334 **Sargon the Great**, founder of the Akkadian empire, accedes to the throne

2300 Thailand: The first rice-farming villages emerge on the **Khorat plateau**

2040 Egypt: Royal authority is restored under **Mentuhotep II**, beginning the Middle Kingdom period

2000* Crete: The **Minoan civilization** emerges

2500 Central Europe: **Bronze** is first manufactured in Europe

2500* Austronesians invent the **sea-going outrigger sailing canoe**

2500 A calibrated system of **weights** is used in Indus cities

2000* The **bow and arrow** is introduced to North America from northeastern Asia

| 2800 | 2600 | 2400 | 2200 | 2000 |

2400–2200 Saqqara, Egypt: The **Pyramid Texts**, the oldest surviving religious writing, are drafted

2350 Sumer: **Urukagina**, king of Lagash, issues the earliest known law code

2900 The **cuneiform writing system** is developed in Sumer

2551–2528* Giza, Egypt: The **Great Pyramid of King Khufu** is constructed

2100 The first **ziggurats** are built in Sumer

2000* Crete: The **Minoan hieroglyphic script** is developed

2000 BC

FARMING, METALS AND THE FIRST KINGDOMS

Farming developed independently in many
different parts of the world between 10,000
and 5,000 years ago. Wherever it appeared,
farming transformed not only the way people
obtained their food but also the nature of
society itself, paving the way for ever greater
social and technological complexity.

KEY

- Hunter-gatherers
- Pastoral nomads
- Settled farming cultures and peoples
- Complex farming societies/chiefdoms
- Urbanized societies/kingdoms
- Empires
- Uninhabited

CARAL

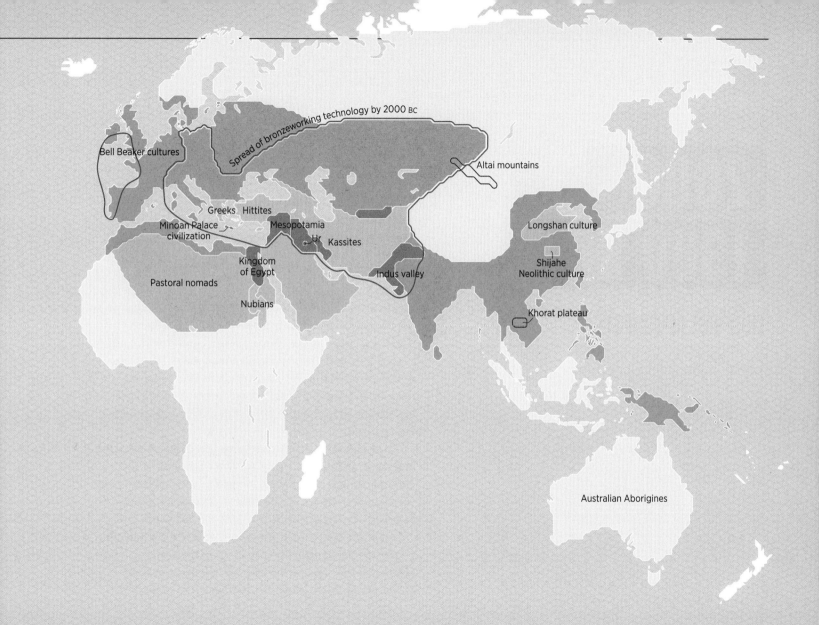

Bell Beaker cultures

Spread of bronzeworking technology by 2000 BC

Altai mountains

Greeks Hittites

Minoan Palace
civilization

Mesopotamia

Ur

Kassites

Longshan culture

Kingdom
of Egypt

Shijahe
Neolithic culture

Pastoral nomads

Indus valley

Nubians

Khorat plateau

Australian Aborigines

2000– 1300 BC

THE FIRST CONQUESTS

THE EARLY 2ND MILLENNIUM BC brought the first sign in history that civilizations can fall as well as rise. The Indus valley civilization, the world's largest in terms of area at the beginning of this period, abruptly collapsed around 1900 BC. Shifts in the course of the Indus river and its tributaries appear to have reduced agricultural productivity so much that the city-states' dense populations could no longer be sustained.

The Minoan civilization on Crete also vanished during this time: in around 1450 BC the Minoans were conquered by the Mycenaean Greek kingdoms, which had emerged about 200 years earlier in the Peloponnese, a peninsula in southern Greece. This period also witnessed the growth of Chinese civilization in the Yellow river region under the Shang dynasty, although by 1300 BC other centres of civilization had also developed in the Yangtze river region, beyond the Shang world.

In the Middle East, Mesopotamia came to be dominated by Assyria and its rival, Babylon, in the first half of the 2nd millennium BC. However, later in this period both were overshadowed by the Hittite empire of Anatolia, which emerged in roughly 1600 BC. The Hittites vied with Egypt – then at the height of its power under the New Kingdom pharaohs – for control over the lands of the eastern Mediterranean. This period also saw the onset of state formation in Nubia, along the southern Nile valley, but this was halted by the Egyptian conquest of the region around 1500 BC.

At about this time, Austronesians of the Lapita culture took a great leap into the unknown by voyaging out into the Pacific Ocean in search of new islands to colonize, reflecting the earlier invention of the stable and seaworthy outrigger canoe. Meanwhile, chiefdoms emerged among the Olmecs and Zapotecs in the middle of the 2nd millennium BC, marking the beginning of state formation in Mesoamerica.

Despite civilizations burgeoning across the world, the cultural links between them were still tenuous at the start of this period. By 1300 BC, however, the civilizations of the Middle East, Egypt and the eastern Mediterranean had developed close contacts through trade, diplomacy and war. The effects of these interactions were most profound in Egypt, which had still not fully entered the Bronze Age when it was invaded in 1640 BC by the Hyksos, a Semitic people from the eastern Mediterranean. By the time the pharaohs expelled the Hyksos in 1532 BC, the Egyptians had acquired the latest technology of the Middle East, most notably the horse-drawn chariot: invented in Western Asia around 1700 BC, the chariot revolutionized warfare by introducing a new element of rapid mobility to the battlefield. This period also witnessed the invention of iron smelting, probably in Anatolia – a development that would ultimately prove crucial to future tool manufacture.

At this time the highly mobile livestock farmers of the Eurasian steppes first emerged as cultural intermediaries between east and west. Although for much of subsequent history, these steppe peoples carried the products of Chinese technology to Europe and the Middle East, initially the flow of ideas went exclusively in the opposite direction. It was from the steppe peoples that the fledgling Chinese civilizations acquired their knowledge of bronze and wheeled vehicles, including the chariot. From this basis, Chinese craftspeople developed astonishing skills in bronze casting, creating intricately detailed vessels using complex piece-moulds.

These early civilizations remained primarily oral cultures, and used writing only for those aspects of administration that could not easily be committed to memory, such as lists of stored goods, tax returns and laws. Only slowly was writing used to record poetry, stories, religious beliefs and history. The first substantial body of 'popular' literature not associated with a burial ritual was produced in Egypt during the Middle Kingdom period (approximately 2040–1640 BC).

1960* Egypt conquers its southern neighbour **Nubia**, a major source of gold

1900* **Ashur**, the capital of Assyria, is founded

1900* Collapse of the **Indus civilization**

1813–1781* The first **Assyrian empire** is created

1700* **Woolly mammoths** become extinct in their last Siberian stronghold

1700* **Knossos** becomes the dominant centre of Minoan Crete

1650* The **Mycenaean civilization** emerges in mainland Greece

SCIENCE & TECHNOLOGY

2000–1500 The **Wessex culture** introduces bronzeworking technology to the British Isles

1750* Pottery is first used in **Peru**

1700* The **horse-drawn chariot** invented in the Middle East or Western Asia

2000 BC   1900   1800   1700

RELIGION & PHILOSOPHY

1800* The *Eridu Genesis*, a Sumerian creation poem, contains the earliest reference to the Flood myth

ART & ARCHITECTURE

1800 The **Etemenanki ziggurat** at Babylon, the probable inspiration for the Tower of Babel, is constructed

1800–1500* Peru: Large **U-shaped ceremonial centres** are built by the people of the El Paraiso culture

1600* The **Shang**, China's first historical dynasty, is founded

1600* Cities in the **Oxus** region of Central Asia are abandoned

1595 The Hittite king **Mursilis** sacks Babylon

1532 The Hyksos are expelled from Egypt, beginning the **New Kingdom period**

1500* **Rice farming** takes place on the Ganges river plain

1500* The Austronesian **Lapita culture** spreads to Samoa, Fiji and Tonga

1500* The **dingo** is introduced to Australia by seafarers from Indonesia

1473 The female pharaoh **Hatshepsut** accedes to the Egyptian throne

1450* The **Mycenaeans** conquer Crete, bringing the Minoan civilization to an end

1363 **Ashur-uballit I**, founder of the second Assyrian empire, becomes king of Assyria

1300* **Assyria** conquers the Hurrian kingdom of **Mitanni**

1500* **Iron smelting** is invented, probably in Anatolia

1500* Extensive **glass production** takes place in the Middle East, Crete and Egypt

1600   1500   1400   1300

1500–1000* The Egyptian *Book of the Dead* contains spells, hymns and instructions to guide the deceased to the afterlife

1400–1000* The *Rigveda*, the earliest Hindu scripture, is composed

1300* **Oracle bones** are used in China for divination and communication with deified ancestors

1600* Germany: The bronze **Nebra sky disc** is created

1600* The **first alphabetic script** (the proto-Canaanite alphabet) develops in the eastern Mediterranean

1323* Egyptian pharaoh **Tutankhamun** is buried with elaborate grave goods

1300* Louisiana: Huge octagonal ceremonial earthworks built at **Poverty Point**

1300–1000 BC

THE COLLAPSE OF DYNASTIES

IN THE MIDDLE EAST and the eastern Mediterranean, the late 2nd millennium BC was a time of severe political instability, from which the main casualties were the Hittite empire and the kingdoms of Mycenaean Greece. Despite the Mycenaeans building new city walls in the 13th century BC as a response to external threats, by around 1200 BC all of their cities had been destroyed by unknown invaders and abandoned. Writing fell out of use, and Greece entered a political and cultural 'dark age'. At almost exactly the same time, the powerful Hittite empire of Anatolia collapsed equally abruptly, most likely destroyed by Phrygian invaders from southeastern Europe.

Mesopotamia also suffered invasions, by the Aramaean and Chaldaean nomads of the Arabian desert, reducing Assyria and Babylon to local powers. Egypt was invaded in around 1180 BC by a Mediterranean coalition labelled the 'Sea Peoples' by modern historians. Though they were repulsed, a powerful priesthood progressively undermined the authority of the pharaohs, and by 1070 BC Egypt's New Kingdom had collapsed. The decline of the Middle East's great powers precipitated the foundation of small kingdoms in the eastern Mediterranean, the most influential of which would be the Hebrew kingdom, founded in approximately 1020 BC. The seafaring Phoenicians also enjoyed growing power at this time as they strove to create a Mediterranean trading network.

Although the foundation of the small Hebrew kingdom went relatively unnoticed by its neighbouring civilizations, it was an event of fundamental importance to the later development of the Jewish, Christian and Islamic faiths: by making Jerusalem his capital, the Hebrew king David ensured its lasting importance as a holy site for all three Abrahamic religions. The Hebrews were closely related to the earlier Canaanites, the first people to write using an alphabetic script; around 1100 BC, the Phoenicians then devised their own alphabet based on the Canaanite original. Thanks to their maritime activities, the Phoenicians gradually disseminated their script around the Mediterranean.

In China, the ruling Shang king was overthrown in 1046 BC by his vassals, led by the Zhou dynasty. While the Shang claimed legitimacy by divine descent, the Zhou justified their seizure of power by claiming that Heaven had transferred its 'mandate' to them thanks to the Shang's corruption and injustice. All later Chinese dynasties would claim legitimacy by the same doctrine. Before the fall of the Shang, a form of writing based on pictographs had come into use in Shang China around 1200 BC; though much modified over the centuries, this system is the direct ancestor of the modern Chinese logographic script. At about this time, the first civilization of the Americas emerged among the Olmec people of Mexico's Gulf coast. As well as inventing their own hieroglyphic script, the Olmecs established many of the features common to later Mesoamerican civilizations, including temple pyramids and a form of sacred ball game. They may also have been the first people to make drinking chocolate and to learn how to cure rubber.

Iron smelting, invented in Anatolia around 1500 BC, had yet to make much impact: by 1000 BC it was still confined to the eastern Mediterranean. In botany, meanwhile, the Assyrian king Tiglath-pileser I appears to have created the first botanic garden in Nineveh at the turn of the 11th century BC. In writing, two documents stand out from this period. One is the earliest known peace treaty, agreed between the Egyptians and the Hittites in 1256 BC after a war lasting over two centuries; remarkably, both the Egyptian and Hittite copies of the treaty survive. The other is the definitive version of what was already an ancient Mesopotamian tale, the *Epic of Gilgamesh*.

POLITICS & ECONOMY

1285 The **battle of Qadesh**: the Hittites block Egyptian expansion in Syria

1256 The **Egyptian–Hittite peace treaty**, The earliest known formal written peace treaty, is agreed

1200* Greek peoples settle on **Cyprus**

1200* The Greek **Mycenaean civilization** collapses

1200* The Phrygians invade Anatolia, causing the collapse of the **Hittite empire**

1184 According to traditional Greek sources, this date marks the **fall of Troy**

1180 The Egyptians defeat an invasion by the Mediterranean coalition of the **'Sea Peoples'**

SCIENCE & TECHNOLOGY

1200* Mexico: The Olmecs begin **chocolate drinking**

1200–900 **Iron tools and weapons** come into common use in the eastern Mediterranean

1300 BC	1250	1200	1150

RELIGION & PHILOSOPHY

1200* Mexico: **San Lorenzo**, the first Olmec ceremonial centre, is established

ART & ARCHITECTURE

1300–1000* The Babylonian priest Sin-liqe-unninni compiles the most complete version of the *Epic of Gilgamesh*

1200* The earliest **Chinese pictographic writing** is used on Shang dynasty bronzes and oracle bones

1200* Olmec carvers begin to create **monumental stone heads** depicting their rulers

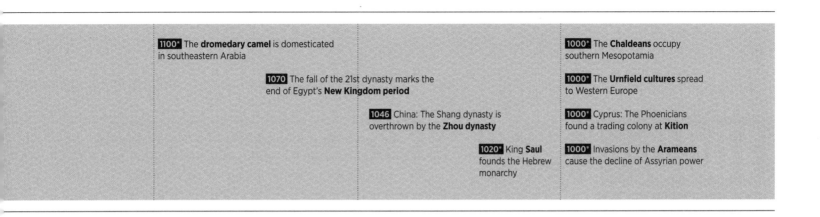

1100* The **dromedary camel** is domesticated in southeastern Arabia

1070 The fall of the 21st dynasty marks the end of Egypt's **New Kingdom period**

1046 China: The Shang dynasty is overthrown by the **Zhou dynasty**

1020* King **Saul** founds the Hebrew monarchy

1000* The **Chaldeans** occupy southern Mesopotamia

1000* The **Urnfield cultures** spread to Western Europe

1000* Cyprus: The Phoenicians found a trading colony at **Kition**

1000* Invasions by the **Arameans** cause the decline of Assyrian power

1100* Assyrian king **Tiglath-pileser I** creates a botanical garden at Nineveh

1100   **1050**   **1000**

1100 Denmark: The creation of the **Trundholm sun chariot** marks evidence of a solar cult

1000 Mexico: San Lorenzo is ritually destroyed and replaced by a new ceremonial centre at **La Venta**

1000* **King David** captures Jerusalem from the Canaanites, making it the capital of the Hebrew kingdom

1100* **Hillfort** construction begins in Western Europe

1100* The influential **Phoenician alphabet**, an evolution of the earlier Canaanite version, is developed

1000* Middle East: The **cupellation process**, to separate silver from lead ore, is developed

1000* Peru: The earliest **bronze** is made in the Americas

1000–771 BC

THE FIRST NOMADS

IN THE LATER 10th century BC, Assyrian power revived under a succession of able military kings. As a consequence, Babylon became a satellite of Assyria in the 9th century BC, but remained Mesopotamia's leading cultural centre. Assyria's growing wealth, and its demand for precious stones, metals, timber, ivory and other commodities, stimulated an economic recovery throughout the Middle East and Mediterranean after the 'dark ages' of the late 2nd millennium BC. In Greece, urban life, which had completely died out after the fall of the Mycenaean kingdoms, began to re-emerge strongly in the 9th century BC.

The seafaring Phoenicians were well placed to take advantage of this economic growth, and by 800 BC they had become the dominant Mediterranean trading power. Phoenician city-states retained their independence, and many founded trading colonies around the Mediterranean. The most successful city-state was Tyre, in present-day Lebanon, whose colonies included Gadir (modern-day Cádiz) in southwestern Spain, and Carthage in North Africa. Through such Phoenician colonies, the influence of Middle Eastern civilizations began to be felt in the western Mediterranean for the first time. In Egypt, the fall of the New Kingdom in 1070 BC had allowed the Nubians to break free of the pharaohs, and around 900 BC they founded the independent kingdom of Kush.

In Central Asia, although early steppe livestock farmers built permanent settlements, they probably practised a form of transhumance, a way of life that involves seasonally migrating to move herds and flocks to fresh grazing land. Ox carts allowed the steppe farmers to transport their belongings, and helped them expand into new territories. Around the beginning of the 1st millennium BC, Iranian steppe peoples, such as the Cimmerians, embraced a fully nomadic lifestyle. This shift is thought to have been caused by the adoption of horse riding, allowing livestock farmers to manage much larger herds that needed regular moving on to avoid overgrazing. This development had far-reaching consequences beyond agriculture, as horses' speed and mobility were as useful in war as in managing livestock. The first recorded cavalry regiment was formed in Assyria in 890–884 BC, and war chariots began to fall out of use.

The nomads' mobility represented a great military advantage over the peoples settled around the steppes, whom they frequently raided: nomad invasions would regularly have drastic and destructive consequences for Eurasian civilizations over the next 2,500 years. China's rulers, for instance, would face the constant headache of providing security for its northern frontier against nomad raids. Indeed, despite the Zhou kingdom's early expansion – extending its power south from the Shang heartlands along the Yellow river into the Yangtze river basin – attacks by neighbouring nomads forced the dynasty to leave its traditional heartland in 771 BC and transfer its capital eastwards to Luoyang.

Very little is known about the thousand years of Indian history that followed the fall of the Indus valley civilization in around 1900 BC. However, new genetic evidence indicates that the sub-continent saw a major influx of populations from Central Asia in this period. In the early 1st millennium BC, a new Indian civilization developed on the Ganges river plain in the north of the subcontinent, with the emergence of around twenty-five tribal kingdoms and republics known as *janapadas* (realms). While the religious beliefs of the Indus valley civilization remain unknown, the inhabitants of the *janapadas* practised an early form of Hinduism based on the *Rigveda*, a collection of hymns and liturgies probably composed in the late 2nd millennium BC. In particular, the beginnings of the Hindu caste system lie in the four *varnas* (classes) of the *Rigveda*. The *Rigveda* also marked a watershed in the literature of Sanskrit, an Indo-European language that is the ancestor to some of the most widely spoken South Asian languages, including Hindi and Urdu.

934 **Ashur-dan II** becomes king of Assyria, precipitating a recovery in the empire's power

928* The Hebrew kingdom is divided into **Israel** and **Judah**

924 Egyptian pharaoh **Shoshenq I** sacks Solomon's Temple at Jerusalem

900* The *janapadas* (realms), early Hindu states, emerge on the Ganges river plain

900* The Nubian kingdom of **Kush** is founded

900* **Indo-Iranian steppe farmers** begin to adopt a fully nomadic way of life

900–800 **City-states** develop in Greece

900–800 The **Medes** and **Persians** migrate to Iran from Central Asia

SCIENCE & TECHNOLOGY

900* **Iron tools and weapons** are in common use in southeastern Europe and Italy

890–884 Assyrian king Tukulti-Ninurta II raises the earliest recorded **cavalry regiment**

1000 BC   950   900

RELIGION & PHILOSOPHY

1000* The formative period of **early Hinduism** begins in northern India

958* **King Solomon** constructs the Temple in Jerusalem

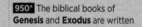

950* The biblical books of **Genesis** and **Exodus** are written

ART & ARCHITECTURE

1000–900* Mexico: **Writing** is first used in the Americas, at the Olmec site of El Cascajal

1000–900 The earliest Chinese book of poetry, the *Shi Jing* (Book of Songs), is compiled

853 **Babylon** becomes an Assyrian protectorate

828 **Egypt** begins to break up into five rival kingdoms

800* **Turkeys** are domesticated in Mexico

800* The Phoenicians establish a trading post at **Gadir** (Cádiz) in southern Spain

800* The **Etruscan civilization** emerges in Italy

800* The **Hallstatt** (Celtic) Iron Age culture begins to spread across Central and Western Europe

820* Phoenician colonists from Tyre found **Carthage**

771 China: The Zhou dynasty capital is moved east to **Luoyang** to escape nomad raids

850

800

850* The prophets **Elijah** and **Elisha** defend the Hebrew religion against Phoenician and Aramean beliefs

850* Peru: A major ceremonial centre is founded at **Chavín de Huántar**

776 The earliest recorded **Olympian games**, held in honour of Zeus, take place

825 The **Black Obelisk of Shalmaneser III**, depicting the Assyrian king receiving tribute from five conquered rulers, is created

800* Mexico: The **Zapotec hieroglyphic script** is developed

770– 480 BC

THE STIRRINGS OF CLASSICAL CIVILIZATION

THE EARLY MESOPOTAMIAN empires expanded and declined according to the military capabilities of their rulers as they were based on tributary relationships: if a weak ruler acceded to an imperial throne, its vassals could easily reassert their independence. The Assyrian emperor Tiglath-pileser III (reigned 742–727 BC), however, embarked on a new chapter in imperialism by imposing centrally appointed provincial governments on conquered areas, underpinned by a standing army. Removing vassals from the equation led Assyria to enjoy a century of unparalleled dominance; yet soon the empire became overextended, and it quickly collapsed after Babylon rebelled in 626 BC. Magnificently rebuilt by its king Nebuchadnezzar (ruled 604–562 BC), Babylon dazzled contemporaries, but this was the last time a Mesopotamian power would dominate the Middle East.

In 539 BC, the Babylonian empire was conquered by Cyrus the Great, king of the Persians, former steppe nomads who had settled in southern Iran three centuries earlier. Under Cyrus, Persia had already conquered its neighbours the Medes (another former nomad people) and the wealthy Anatolian kingdom of Lydia. By the end of the 6th century BC, Cyrus's successors had created the world's first superpower by conquering Egypt – which had already experienced periods of Nubian and Assyrian rule – the Indus valley, and a large part of Central Asia.

Further east, China's Zhou kingdom had broken up into a patchwork of feudal states during the so-called 'Spring and Autumn' period (770–481 BC). In the face of nomad threats, the dynasty became increasingly unable to maintain its authority: eventually, feudal aristocrats in the provinces asserted their independence, prompting the breakup of the kingdom. In Mesoamerica, the first Maya city-states emerged in modern-day Guatemala, while in Africa, Bantu-speaking peoples began to migrate out of their homeland in the west of the continent.

Beyond the political sphere, the 7th and 6th centuries BC were among the most important ever in the history of religion and belief. Early in this period the Hebrew kingdoms had been conquered first by Assyria and then by Babylon, leading to large numbers of Jews (as Hebrews came to be known) to be deported to Mesopotamia. It was among these Jewish exiles that the main books of the Old Testament were first written in approximately their present form, and that Judaism emerged as a definitively monotheistic religion. The Old Testament reflects an understanding of Mesopotamian mythology, and was probably also influenced by the Iranian prophet Zoroaster's embrace of both monotheism and cosmic dualism.

In India, the composition of the philosophical *Upanishads* marked a major step in the development of classical Hinduism. At the same time, Hindu ritualism was being challenged by the religious ascetic Mahavira, the founder of Jainism, and Siddhartha Gautama the Buddha, who established Buddhism. In China, the same period saw the life of the philosopher Confucius. In the face of the Zhou kingdom's collapse, his emphasis on respect for legitimate authority, social order, family, ancestors, tradition and education became integral to Chinese thought. In later eras, it was also thought that Laozi, the mythical founder of Daoism, lived during this time.

In Europe, the 6th century BC witnessed the beginning of the Greek scientific tradition in the mathematical works of Thales of Miletos and Pythagoras of Samos. The foundation at Athens of a drama festival in honour of the god Dionysus constituted a key moment in the development of Western theatre. From this basis, Greek culture spread widely across the Mediterranean and Black Sea through colonies founded by the flourishing Greek city-states. In 509 BC, when Athens attempted to deal with its internal social tensions by introducing a form of democracy (*demokratia*), it gave birth to one of history's most potent political ideas.

POLITICS & ECONOMY

770 The Nubian king **Kashta** conquers southern (Upper) Egypt

770–481 The **'Spring and Autumn' period** in China: the Zhou kingdom breaks up into rival states

750–550 **Sparta** emerges as the most powerful Greek city-state

753 According to traditional sources, **Rome** is founded

729 Assyria under King Tiglath-pileser III conquers **Babylon**

700* The **Scythians** begin to dominate the Eurasian steppes

700* The emergence of the northern Vietnamese **Dong Son** culture marks the beginning of chiefdoms in Southeast Asia

674–671 The Assyrians conquer **Egypt**, expelling the Nubians

650* Anatolia: Lydia becomes the first state to mint **coins** for use as currency

640* The kingdom of **Macedon** is founded

SCIENCE & TECHNOLOGY

750* The **ram-equipped war galley** is developed in Greece

800 BC	750	700	650

RELIGION & PHILOSOPHY

750–500* The 'primary' *Upanishads* of Hinduism are composed

ART & ARCHITECTURE

750* Greek poet **Homer** composes the *Iliad* and the *Odyssey*

668–627 Assyrian king **Ashurbanipal** creates a library of around 10,000 texts at Nineveh

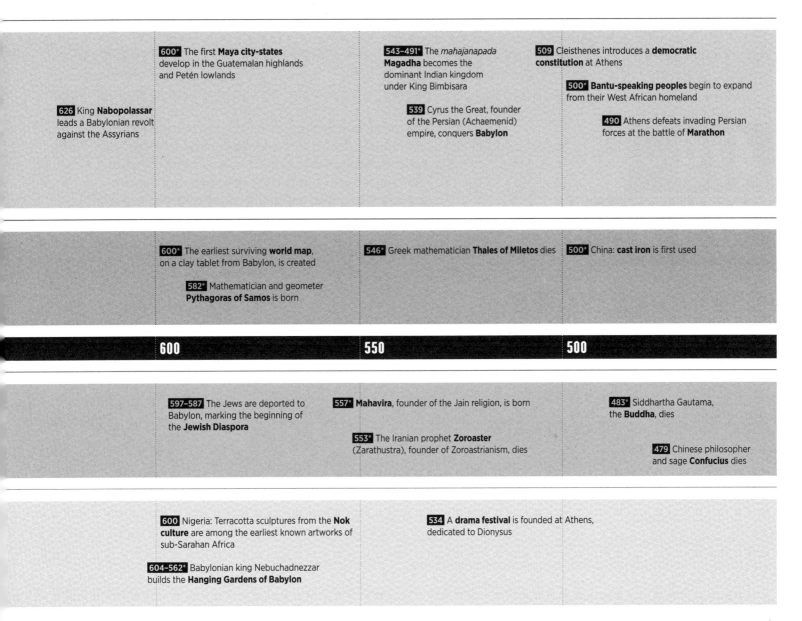

600* The first **Maya city-states** develop in the Guatemalan highlands and Petén lowlands

626 King **Nabopolassar** leads a Babylonian revolt against the Assyrians

543–491* The *mahajanapada* **Magadha** becomes the dominant Indian kingdom under King Bimbisara

539 Cyrus the Great, founder of the Persian (Achaemenid) empire, conquers **Babylon**

509 Cleisthenes introduces a **democratic constitution** at Athens

500* **Bantu-speaking peoples** begin to expand from their West African homeland

490 Athens defeats invading Persian forces at the battle of **Marathon**

600* The earliest surviving **world map**, on a clay tablet from Babylon, is created

582* Mathematician and geometer **Pythagoras of Samos** is born

546* Greek mathematician **Thales of Miletos** dies

500* China: **cast iron** is first used

600   **550**   **500**

597–587 The Jews are deported to Babylon, marking the beginning of the **Jewish Diaspora**

557* **Mahavira**, founder of the Jain religion, is born

553* The Iranian prophet **Zoroaster** (Zarathustra), founder of Zoroastrianism, dies

483* Siddhartha Gautama, the **Buddha**, dies

479 Chinese philosopher and sage **Confucius** dies

600 Nigeria: Terracotta sculptures from the **Nok culture** are among the earliest known artworks of sub-Saharan Africa

604–562* Babylonian king Nebuchadnezzar builds the **Hanging Gardens of Babylon**

534 A **drama festival** is founded at Athens, dedicated to Dionysus

479– 323 BC

THE ERA OF ALEXANDER THE GREAT

THE EXPANSION OF the Persian empire ground to a halt in the early 5th century BC, stopped in its tracks by the usually quarrelsome Greek city-states. Faced with a common enemy, however, the Greeks united for just long enough to inflict exemplary defeats on the Persians at the battles of Salamis (480 BC) and Plataea (479 BC), before renewing their traditional rivalries. Most Greek cities were forced to ally with either Athens or Sparta as they vied for the leadership of Greece in the two Peloponnesian Wars (457–445 BC and 431–404 BC).

Yet ultimately, no Greek city could achieve lasting dominance and, worn out by their conflicts, they were defeated by Philip II of Macedon in 338 BC. In 334 BC, Philip's son Alexander the Great invaded the Persian empire in the hope of uniting the Greeks behind him. A prodigious military genius, Alexander conquered the Persian empire in only five years; but his death at Babylon in 323 BC, without a viable heir, left the future of his own imperial project in doubt. When he died, Alexander was planning to conquer the western Mediterranean, where the main power was the newly independent Phoenician trading city of Carthage. Its ally, the Roman republic, was establishing itself as the most powerful state on the Italian peninsula, while much of Western and Central Europe was dominated by the Celts.

Greece in the 5th and 4th centuries marked the height of one of the most inventive and influential civilizations in world history. Socrates, Plato and Aristotle together laid the foundations of Western philosophy. Aristotle's thought was equally fundamental to the development of scientific method, and Hippocrates was one of the first physicians to eschew the idea that diseases were caused and cured by supernatural forces. The works of Herodotus and Thucydides, meanwhile, demonstrate the beginning of a critical analytical approach to the study of history.

Athens was Greece's greatest cultural centre, producing not only some of the finest art and architecture of the Classical age, but also staging the first great plays at its annual drama festival dedicated to Dionysus. Alexander's conquests extended Greek influence as far east as India, in particular by the foundation of new cities: most were named Alexandria after himself, and were populated with Greek and Macedonian settlers. Most successful was the Alexandria he established in Egypt: strategically sited close to the mouth of the Nile, it grew rapidly into a great trade centre.

Beyond the Classical Mediterranean, the Warring States period (5th–3rd centuries BC) engulfed China, as rival powers controlled their populations both through bureaucratic structures, and by mobilizing them for total war against each other. Such interstate conflict led to competition between prominent political and military theorists: during this period, Sun Tzu wrote his classic work on strategy, *The Art of War*, while the dominant Legalist school advocated total state power over society.

In India, the *janapadas* (realms) of the early 1st millennium BC had coalesced into a smaller number of *mahajanapadas* (great realms) by the beginning of this period, the most powerful of which by 323 BC was Magadha, which expanded from its heartland in the northeast to encompass much of the Ganges plain. The vast Hindu epic, the *Mahabharata*, also began to take shape in this period, but did not achieve its final form until around AD 400; it popularized worship of the new deity Krishna. In Mesoamerica, the Olmec civilization was declining, but the younger Zapotec and Maya societies were beginning to flourish. They shared the use of a 52-year ritual calendar cycle, first used at the Zapotec site of Monte Albán in Oaxaca. Further south, in the Peruvian Andes an art style that first developed at the ceremonial centre of Chavín was adopted over a wide area, most probably through the spread of a religious cult, rather than by conquest.

The invention of the outrigger canoe in Southeast Asia around 2500 BC made possible the settlement of the western Pacific archipelagos by Austronesian peoples. It was among these pioneers in Tonga, Fiji and Samoa that the Polynesian culture emerged around 400 BC. Over the next thousand years or so, the Polynesians would go on to settle almost all the remaining uninhabited islands of the Pacific.

480–479 Greek forces defeat the Persian empire at **Salamis** and **Plataea**

457–445 The **First Peloponnesian War** breaks out between Athens and Sparta

480–221 The **Warring States period**: China enters an era of intense warfare and competition between its states

450–350* **Polynesian culture** develops from the earlier Lapita culture on Tonga, Samoa and Fiji

450* Mexico: The foundation of Monte Albán in the Oaxaca valley marks the birth of the **Zapotec** state

450* The **Law of the Twelve Tables**, the basis of Roman law, is compiled

431–404 Athens and Sparta renew their conflict in the **Second Peloponnesian War**

SCIENCE & TECHNOLOGY

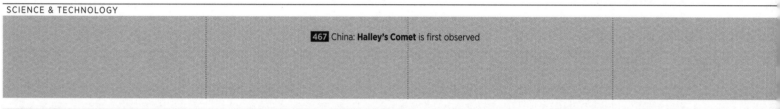

467 China: **Halley's Comet** is first observed

| 500 BC | 475 | 450 | 425 |

RELIGION & PHILOSOPHY

ART & ARCHITECTURE

450* Chinese general Sun Tzu writes **The Art of War**, a treatise on warfare

430* Herodotus completes **The Histories**, the first major narrative historical work

450–400* **Greek drama** flourishes under tragic playwrights Aeschylus and Sophocles, and comic playwright Aristophanes

420–400* Thucydides writes his **History of the Peloponnesian War**, the first critical analytical history

404 The **Egyptians** rebel against the Persian empire and restore the rule of the pharaohs

396 Roman expansion begins with the capture of the Etruscan city of **Veii**

361–338* **Qin** becomes the most powerful Chinese state

350* The first **Maya city-states** emerge

338 The battle of **Chaironeia**: Philip II of Macedon wins control of Greece

336–323 The reign of **Alexander the Great** sees Macedon expand across the eastern Mediterranean

332 Alexander the Great conquers Egypt and founds the city of **Alexandria**

331 Alexander the Great defeats the Persian king **Darius III** at Gaugamela

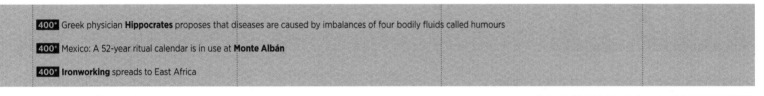

400* Greek physician **Hippocrates** proposes that diseases are caused by imbalances of four bodily fluids called humours

400* Mexico: A 52-year ritual calendar is in use at **Monte Albán**

400* **Ironworking** spreads to East Africa

400   **375**   **350**   **325**

400* The earliest version of the Hindu epic, the *Mahabharata*, is composed, popularizing the worship of Krishna

400 The destruction of the ceremonial centre of **La Venta** marks the increasing decline of the Olmec civilization

399 Athenian philosopher **Socrates** is condemned to death for impiety

388 The philosopher Plato founds the **Academy** at Athens

384 The philosopher and scientist **Aristotle** is born

350* Shang Yang, chief minister of the Chinese Qin kingdom, formulates the absolutist political philosophy of **Legalism**

400* **Chavín art styles** are at their most influential in the Peruvian Andes

322– 200 BC

UNIFICATION AND DISINTEGRATION

CHINA'S WARRING STATES period reached its climactic conclusion during the 3rd century BC. Qin, the strongest of the states, destroyed the last remnant of the Zhou kingdom in 256 BC. Subsequently, in nine years of brutal campaigning, the Qin king Zheng (reigned 246–210 BC) conquered the remaining states, completing the unification of China in 221 BC. Zheng celebrated his achievement by adopting the ruling name Shi Huangdi (First Emperor). He destroyed all vestiges of the old states, ruthlessly suppressed challenges to Qin power, and imposed cultural and economic uniformity over the empire, ruling through professional, non-hereditary bureaucracies. Oppressive Qin rule was hated, and rebellions across the former states overthrew the dynasty after Shi Huangdi's death. Its Han successors (206 BC–AD 220) gradually re-established central authority, retaining many of the legal and administrative structures created by the Qin, but initially ruling with a lighter hand.

Alexander the Great's empire disintegrated immediately after his death in 323 BC as his generals carved out kingdoms for themselves. The most powerful were the territories established by Seleucos, based in Babylon, and Ptolemy, based in Egypt. The sprawling Seleucid empire immediately descended into instability, and was in decline by 200 BC. In contrast, Ptolemy and his successors (all also called Ptolemy) won acceptance from their Egyptian subjects by adopting the trappings of the pharaohs' rule. Meanwhile,

Rome and Carthage fell out over their respective spheres of influence in Sicily: Carthage's power was eventually broken during the bitter Punic Wars, leaving Rome to dominate the western Mediterranean.

Alexander's conquests left Greece itself almost at the margins of the newly Greek world, and his various successors continued to found new cities and encourage Greek colonization throughout his former empire. Greek became the common language of trade, diplomacy and culture across the whole Middle East: the region became a vast melting pot where Egyptians, Jews, Persians and Indians all borrowed and adapted Greek culture, creating a new multinational Hellenistic civilization. Even the remote kingdom of Bactria in Central Asia, to the northeast of the Seleucid empire, remained part of the Greek cultural mainstream. In this period, Alexandria in Egypt and Pergamon in Anatolia grew to overshadow Athens as cultural centres, though it retained its primacy as a centre of philosophical study. Nonetheless, Greek cultural leadership was evident even in areas never conquered by Alexander, such as the rapidly expanding Roman republic, where Greek literary forms were freely adapted by Latin poets and playwrights.

The 3rd century BC saw most of India united under the Mauryan dynasty of Magadha, recently transformed from a *mahajanapada* (great realm) into a fully-fledged empire. It reached its height under the emperor Ashoka, but lacked internal unity and went into decline immediately following his death. Despite this, the memory of a pan-Indian empire remained influential in later times. During his reign, Ashoka converted to Buddhism, supposedly horrified by the suffering caused by one of his military campaigns. He actively promoted Buddhism in India and supported Buddhist missionary activity abroad, helping to turn it into a major global religion. Asoka may have seen Buddhism as a way of uniting a population otherwise divided by caste and cultural diversity. In this ambition he failed: Hinduism remained the majority religion in India. But Buddhism did gain greater prominence during his reign, for example with the building of the first stupas: these distinctive monuments house relics of the Buddha and his disciples.

The invention of stirrups in this period, possibly in India, allowed a horse rider to sit more securely in the saddle (thus greatly improving the effectiveness of cavalry), although the innovation first became widespread among the steppe nomads only two or three centuries later. Far to the east, the Polynesians' invention of the ocean-going double-hulled canoe opened up the furthest reaches of the Pacific to human settlement.

322-301 The **Wars of the Diadochi** (successors): Alexander the Great's empire breaks up as his generals seize power

321 Chandragupta Maurya seizes power in Magadha, founding the Mauryan empire

312 Seleucos, one of Alexander's generals, captures Babylon, founding the **Seleucid kingdom**

304 Ptolemy, the Macedonian governor of Egypt, adopts the title 'pharaoh'

300* Japan: The **Yayoi period**, which saw hunting and gathering replaced by farming, begins

300* **Rice farming** is introduced to Japan, probably from Korea

268-233 Ashoka becomes Mauryan emperor

279 The **Celts** invade Greece and Anatolia

300* Greek mathematician **Euclid** compiles a comprehensive geometry textbook

340 BC   320   300   280

312 Zeno, the first Stoic philosopher, begins teaching at Athens

306 The philosopher **Epicurus**, founder of Epicureanism, begins teaching at Athens

300* The **Daodejing**, the fundamental text of Daoism, is compiled

300 Egyptian pharaoh Ptolemy I founds the **Museum** (a library) at Alexandria

275 The **Pharos of Alexandria** (a lighthouse) is completed

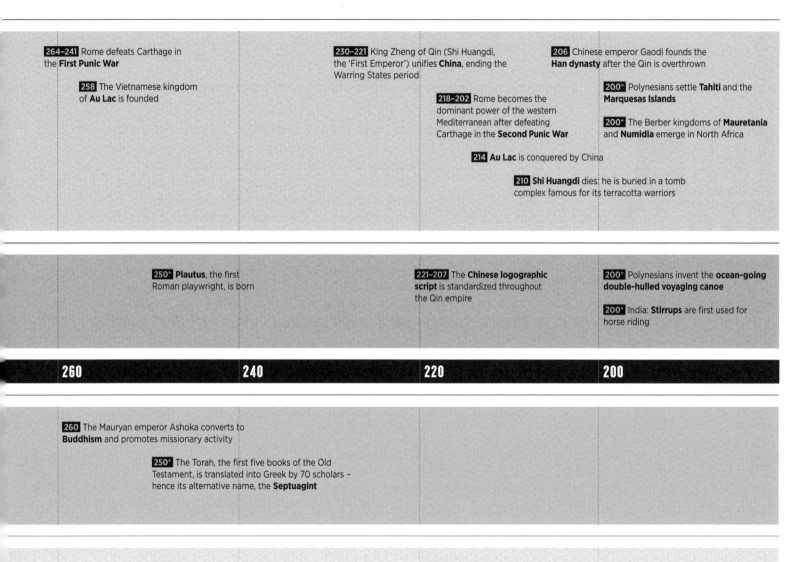

264–241 Rome defeats Carthage in the **First Punic War**

258 The Vietnamese kingdom of **Au Lac** is founded

230–221 King Zheng of Qin (Shi Huangdi, the 'First Emperor') unifies **China**, ending the Warring States period

218–202 Rome becomes the dominant power of the western Mediterranean after defeating Carthage in the **Second Punic War**

214 **Au Lac** is conquered by China

210 **Shi Huangdi** dies: he is buried in a tomb complex famous for its terracotta warriors

206 Chinese emperor Gaodi founds the **Han dynasty** after the Qin is overthrown

200* Polynesians settle **Tahiti** and the **Marquesas Islands**

200* The Berber kingdoms of **Mauretania** and **Numidia** emerge in North Africa

250* **Plautus**, the first Roman playwright, is born

221–207 The **Chinese logographic script** is standardized throughout the Qin empire

200* Polynesians invent the **ocean-going double-hulled voyaging canoe**

200* India: **Stirrups** are first used for horse riding

260   **240**   **220**   **200**

260 The Mauryan emperor Ashoka converts to **Buddhism** and promotes missionary activity

250* The Torah, the first five books of the Old Testament, is translated into Greek by 70 scholars – hence its alternative name, the **Septuagint**

250* Sanchi, India: The **Great Stupa** is built to house relics of the Buddha

220* Shi Huangdi creates a continuous line of **fortifications** to protect China's northern frontier

199– 27 BC

WAR AND EMPIRE

AFTER ITS VICTORIES over Carthage in the 3rd century BC, Rome continued to expand for more than 200 years. Neither the warlike Celts of Western Europe nor the wealthy Hellenistic kingdoms of the eastern Mediterranean proved capable of withstanding Rome's disciplined armies of legionary infantry. As slaves and the spoils of war flooded into Roman territory following its military success, social divisions increased. In the aftermath of civil war, victorious general Julius Caesar proclaimed himself dictator for life, effectively destroying the Roman republic; his murder in 44 BC provoked further conflict. Caesar's nephew Octavian, the eventual victor, introduced imperial government and adopted the ruling name Augustus (revered one).

With the bloodless annexation of Egypt in 30 BC, Rome's domination of the entire Mediterranean world was complete. Despite their conquest by Rome, the Greeks remained the cultural leaders of the Mediterranean world. Nonetheless, the turbulent final years of the Roman republic and the early period of the empire saw Latin literature flourish as well: much of this writing celebrated Rome's achievements, none more so than Virgil's epic poem, the *Aeneid*, which recounts the adventures of the Trojan prince Aeneas, the Romans' legendary ancestor.

In China, the main foreign rival to the Han empire was the Xiongnu nomad confederation to its north: in response, the Han extended the Qin border wall system westwards and tried to outflank the Xiongnu in Central Asia. The confederation began to break up in 36 BC after a succession of defeats at the hands of the Han, who also expanded into parts of Korea and Vietnam during this period.

To the southwest, the collapse of the Mauryan empire in India was complete by around 185 BC, and the subcontinent was divided among rival dynastic states, which rose and fell depending on the abilities of their rulers. Like China, India suffered nomad invasions during the 2nd century BC: the Sakas, an Indo-Iranian steppe people, established their own kingdom in around 94 BC. This period also witnessed the emergence of the Moche kingdom in the coastal valleys of Peru, the first state to develop in South America, while the neighbouring Nazca culture created enormous geoglyphs (patterns produced in the ground) for use in ritual practice. To the north in Mesoamerica, the city of Teotihuacán became the dominant regional power.

Systematic timekeeping is important in most civilizations – for administrative purposes, to record major events, and to ensure that important religious rituals are regularly performed. The 1st century BC saw the introduction of two important calendars in different parts of the world. In the Roman empire, the Julian calendar (named after Julius Caesar, who introduced it) established a regular year of 365 days divided into 12 months, with a leap day added to every fourth year. Far from Rome, the Mesoamericans had previously used a ritual calendar that repeated itself every 52 years, but this did not allow for accurate historical dating. To solve the problem, a Long Count calendar was therefore devised, probably by the Olmecs, based instead on a cycle of 5,125 years.

Differential gears, watermills and glassblowing were important technological developments in the eastern Mediterranean region at this time, although Babylon's abandonment in approximately 140 BC marks the effective extinction of ancient Mesopotamian civilization after centuries of foreign rule. Though not impossible to cross, the Sahara desert presented a major obstacle to trade and other cultural contacts between West Africa and the Mediterranean world. With the introduction of the dromedary camel to the Sahara around 100 BC, however, this began slowly to change. Long used for desert transport in the Middle East, camels made travel in the Sahara easier and led to regular caravan routes opening between North and West Africa.

POLITICS & ECONOMY

200* The city of **Teotihuacán** is founded in the Valley of Mexico

190–130 Rome conquers the **Iberian peninsula**

185* The **Shunga dynasty** deposes the Mauryan dynasty of Magadha in northern India

149–146 The **Third Punic War**: Rome conquers and destroys Carthage

134 The **Kushan nomads** destroy the Graeco-Bactrian kingdom

128–36 China: The Han dynasty fights a series of campaigns against the **Xiongnu nomads**

111 The Vietnamese **Nanyue kingdom** is conquered by China

SCIENCE & TECHNOLOGY

200–100 China: **Paper**, made from plant fibres, is invented

105* A **school of technology** is established at Alexandria

200 BC · 180 · 160 · 140 · 120

RELIGION & PHILOSOPHY

200 Peru: The **Nazca** lay out huge geoglyphs of animals and patterns, for use as ritual pathways

200–100 The **Hebrew Bible** (the Old Testament) reaches its present form

160* The biblical **Book of Daniel**, written in Babylonia, predicts the overthrow of the Seleucid kingdom

ART & ARCHITECTURE

196 The **Rosetta Stone**, the key to deciphering Egyptian hieroglyphs, is created

140* **Babylon** is abandoned and falls into ruins

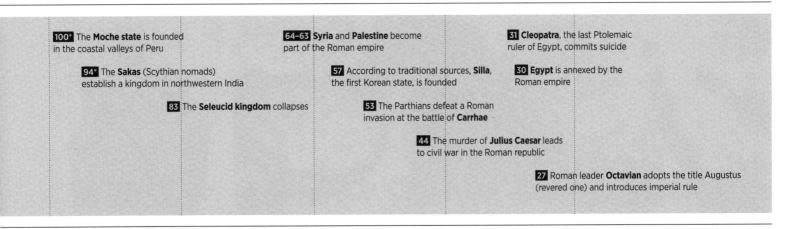

100* The **Moche state** is founded in the coastal valleys of Peru

94* The **Sakas** (Scythian nomads) establish a kingdom in northwestern India

83 The **Seleucid kingdom** collapses

64–63 **Syria** and **Palestine** become part of the Roman empire

57 According to traditional sources, **Silla**, the first Korean state, is founded

53 The Parthians defeat a Roman invasion at the battle of **Carrhae**

44 The murder of **Julius Caesar** leads to civil war in the Roman republic

31 **Cleopatra**, the last Ptolemaic ruler of Egypt, commits suicide

30 **Egypt** is annexed by the Roman empire

27 Roman leader **Octavian** adopts the title Augustus (revered one) and introduces imperial rule

100* The **dromedary camel** is first introduced to the Sahara desert

50* A technique for **glassblowing** is invented, probably by the Phoenicians

46 Julius Caesar introduces the **Julian calendar**

32 The earliest known inscription using the Mesoamerican **Long Count** calendar is created

100   **80**   **60**   **40**   **20**

45 In *On the Nature of Gods*, the Roman orator Cicero questions the literal existence of the pagan Roman gods

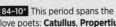

84–10* This period spans the lives of the major Latin love poets: **Catullus**, **Propertius** and **Tibullus**

29* Virgil begins writing his epic poem the *Aeneid*

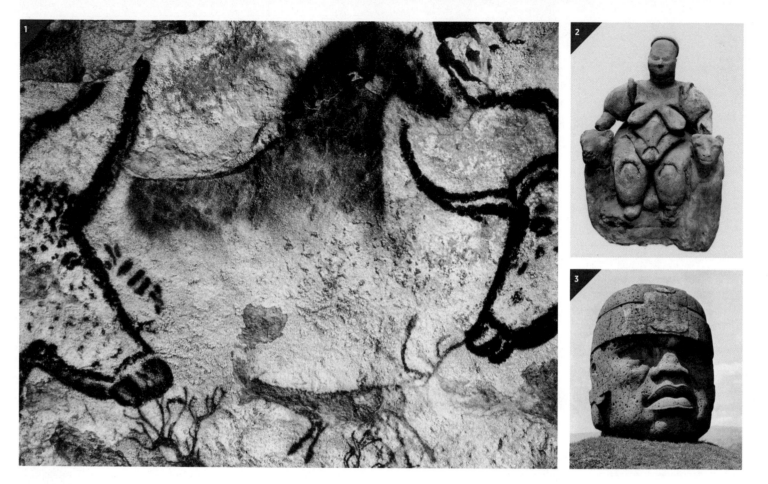

15,000 – 30 BC

1 *Cave painting of aurochs, horses and deer*, Lascaux Cave, *c.* 15000 BC, p. 15

2 *Seated Woman of Çatalhöyük (Mother Goddess)*, *c.* 7500–5700 BC, p. 19

3 *Colossal Head from San Lorenzo*, Olmec civilization, *c.* 1200 BC, p. 37

4 *Relief of Nebhepetre Mentuhotep II and the Goddess Hathor*, Middle Kingdom Egypt, *c.* 2010–2000 BC, p. 29

5 *Alexander Mosaic*, Roman civilization, *c.* 100 BC, p. 48

6 *Seated male figure*, Nok culture, 500 BC–AD 500, p. 47

7 *The Toilette of Cleopatra*, Benedetto Servolini & Frederick Stibbert, 1869, p. 59

8 *Kneeling Archer*, Qin dynasty, *c.* 210 BC, p. 52

26 BC– AD 184

THE BIRTH OF CHRISTIANITY

BETWEEN AD 25 AND 75, the nomadic Kushan people created a vast empire in Central Asia and northern India. Their empire was notable for its cosmopolitan culture that blended Indian, Persian and Graeco-Roman influences, reflecting its role as a key intermediary in east–west trade routes across Eurasia. The Kushan empire was, however, highly decentralized, and by the end of the 2nd century its power was already in decline.

Superficially the other empires established by this time had scarcely changed, but in fact all faced serious problems. The prestige of the Parthians, always regarded as outsiders by their Persian subjects, was severely dented after a series of defeats at the hands of both Rome and the Kushans. Believing that the Roman empire was overextending itself, the emperor Hadrian (reigned AD 117–38) brought a halt to Roman expansion and fortified the northern imperial frontiers, which increasingly well-organized Germanic tribes were putting under ever greater pressure. Earlier in this period, the eruption of Mount Vesuvius on the western coast of the Italian peninsula had famously destroyed the Roman city of Pompeii, burying and preserving it in a layer of volcanic ash.

In China, the Han dynasty lost power to local warlords, on whom it had previously relied to suppress the Yellow Turban peasant revolt in AD 184. The warlords promptly began fighting between themselves. Further south, Funan

– the first kingdom in Southeast Asia – emerged thanks mainly to the stimulus of international trade. In the 1st century AD trade between the Roman empire and India similarly increased greatly, as a result of Graeco-Roman mariners discovering how to exploit the monsoon winds to sail directly from Egypt to India and back in a single season. To meet Roman demand, Indian mariners in turn increased trade with Southeast Asia, taking with them not only goods but also Hindu and Buddhist practice. In southwest North America during this period, the Basketmaker cultures' adoption of maize cultivation around the end of the millennium began a gradual transition to dependence on farming.

The most significant cultural development of the first two centuries AD was the birth of Christianity. Based on the teachings of Jesus of Nazareth, crucified at Jerusalem in around AD 30, the religion spread first among the Jewish diaspora of the Roman empire. Under the influence of Paul of Tarsus (approximately AD 5–67), Christianity transformed from a Jewish sect into a universalist religion, winning converts among non-Jewish populations despite official hostility and occasional persecution. A parallel thread of Jewish radicalism led to the Zealot revolt against Roman rule in AD 66; its bloody suppression witnessed the destruction of the Temple in Jerusalem and the expulsion of many Jews from Palestine.

Religious developments in this period were not confined to Judaism and Christianity. In the Roman empire the latter was rivalled in popularity by another eastern religion, the cult of the Persian god Mithras, which attracted many converts in the army. In India, the Mahayana (Great Vehicle) school of Buddhism emerged under the tolerant and eclectic Kushan rulers, and is now the largest branch of the Buddhist faith. The first representations of the Buddha were also made under the Kushans. In China, Confucianism remained the state ideology, but at the same time the Daoist school of philosophy became assimilated with traditional religion and its supposed founder Laozi was deified.

Important technological developments of this period included the spread of watermills in the Roman empire – otherwise not usually considered to have been interested in labour-saving technology – the discovery of the magnetic compass in China (not used for navigation for another 800 years, however), and the invention of cast steel in India. The codex (a book of sewn pages) began to replace the scroll in the Roman empire, and paper grew to supersede bamboo strips as the main medium for writing in China. The Polynesians, however, serve as a reminder that constant technological progress is never guaranteed, losing the skill of pottery manufacture in this period.

POLITICS & ECONOMY

20–15 BC The Roman frontier is advanced to the **Danube**

2 The first **Chinese census** gives the population as over 57 million people

30* Prince **Kujula Kadphises** founds the Kushan kingdom in Bactria

40* Graeco-Roman merchants begin sailing directly from Egypt to **India**

43 The Roman conquest of **Britain** begins

50–75 The nomadic **Kushans** conquer the Parthian kingdom of Suren

50–100* The **Funan kingdom** is founded in Southeast Asia

66–73 The **Zealot revolt** against Roman rule occurs in Palestine

SCIENCE & TECHNOLOGY

1 BC* The emergence of the **Basketmaker II culture** marks the beginning of farming in North America

36 The earliest known **Maya calendrical inscriptions** appear

50* **Watermills** are first used in the Roman empire

79 Italy: **Mount Vesuvius** erupts, covering Pompeii in a blanket of ash

83 The **magnetic compass** is described in a Chinese book on divination

| 20 BC | 0 | AD 20 | 40 | 60 | 80 |

RELIGION & PHILOSOPHY

6 BC* **Jesus of Nazareth** is born

1–100* **Mahayana** (Great Vehicle) **Buddhism** emerges in India

30* **Jesus** is crucified at Jerusalem

34–156* Religious **Daoism** develops in China

47–62 **St Paul** undertakes missionary work across Asia Minor and the Mediterranean

64 The first **persecutions of Christians** take place at Rome

75–100* **Mithraism** spreads to the Roman empire from Persia

ART & ARCHITECTURE

6* Roman poet Ovid writes his narrative ***Metamorphoses***

72–80 The **Colosseum** is built at Rome

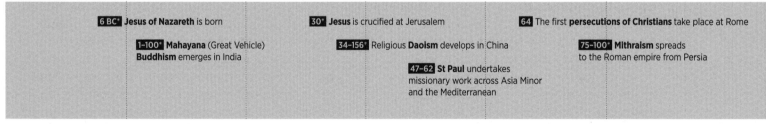

100* The **Tiwanaku Kingdom** is established in the Andes

132–35 The Romans defeat the **Bar Kochba revolt** against Roman rule in Palestine

184 The **Yellow Turban peasant revolt** takes place in northern China

116 The **Roman empire** reaches its greatest extent under the emperor Trajan

120–30* The **Kushan empire** is at its peak under the emperor Kanishka

122 The Roman emperor **Hadrian** begins a defensive wall across northern Britain

100* Indian metallurgists invent **cast steel**

105* **Writing paper** is invented in China

150* The Greek astronomer **Ptolemy of Alexandria** writes his *Almagest* and *Guide to Geography*

| 100 | 120 | 140 | 160 | 180 | 200 |

100 The first **Chinese dictionary** lists over 9,000 characters

150* Mexico: The **Pyramid of the Sun** is built at Teotihuacán

AD 184

AGE OF EMPIRES

By AD 200 the Old World's most densely populated and economically developed regions were dominated by a handful of powerful, urbanized and increasingly interconnected, multi-ethnic empires. Humanity's ancestral way of life, hunting and gathering, was increasingly marginalized.

Basketmaker cultures

TEOTIHUACÁN

Maya city-states

Moche

TIWANAKU

Nazca

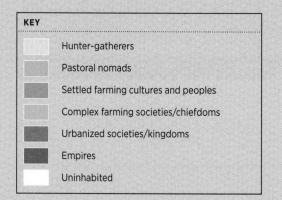

KEY

Hunter-gatherers

Pastoral nomads

Settled farming cultures and peoples

Complex farming societies/chiefdoms

Urbanized societies/kingdoms

Empires

Uninhabited

Celts

Germanic
peoples

ROMAN EMPIRE

Rome

Alexandria

KUSHAN
EMPIRE

PARTHIAN
EMPIRE

SAKA
KINGDOM

MAGADHA

SATAVAHANA

CHOLAS

HAN
EMPIRE

Yayoi Chiefdoms

FUNAN

Polynesians

Australian Aborigines

185–391

INVASIONS AND CONVERSIONS

PERSIA, UNDER FOREIGN rule since the time of Alexander the Great, underwent a strong resurgence in the 3rd century when the indigenous Sasanian dynasty overthrew the Parthian empire in 224–26. The Sasanians were aiming to restore Persia's ancient glory and came to pose a formidable threat to the Roman empire, which was already struggling with a destructive combination of inflation, Germanic invasions and political instability. Nevertheless, Rome survived the crisis and, under its emperor Diocletian, was divided into eastern and western halves, each with its own emperor. In 324, Constantine the Great founded Constantinople as the new capital of the eastern empire, and Rome was reduced in importance. By the end of this period, the Romans were again struggling. The nomadic Huns had invaded Eastern Europe, completely destabilizing the Germanic tribes; the Romans admitted the Goths as refugees in 376, but they soon rebelled and proved impossible to pacify.

Despite these upheavals, the culture of the Roman empire was transformed by the spread of Christianity in the 4th century. At the beginning of this period, Christians were a persecuted minority. In 312, this changed dramatically: the emperor Constantine, ascribing his victory in civil war to the Christian god, converted to and legalized the religion. Under Constantine's patronage, Christianity won converts among the imperial ruling classes, and the first great

Christian architecture was commissioned. In 325 Constantine convened the Council of Nicaea, which agreed the first uniform Christian doctrines.

An attempt by the emperor Julian to revive paganism in 360–63 failed completely; three decades later Theodosius proscribed pagan beliefs and established Christianity as the empire's official religion. Despite this, knowledge of pagan Roman myths and literature still commanded respect as the sign of good education, and there were fruitful connections between Christian theologians and pagan Neoplatonist philosophers. Christianity was strongest in the eastern empire, and it was in Egypt that the Christian monastic tradition developed. It was similarly from Egypt that Christianity reached the East African kingdom of Axum – the dominant trading power of the Red Sea after defeating its neighbour Meroë – representing the origin of the Ethiopian church.

From the late 180s onwards, China was divided into rival states, apart from a brief period of unity between its unification by the Jin state in 280 and the outbreak of the Rebellion of the Eight Princes in 291. After 304, non-Chinese nomad leaders fought for control over the north, while the south stayed under Chinese rule. In contrast, India became increasingly unified when the Magadha kingdom experienced a strong revival under the Gupta dynasty: by the end of this period, all of northern India was under Gupta rule. The construction of enormous earth burial mounds (*kofun*) around 300 in the Yamato region of Japan marked the foundation of the Japanese state. In Mesoamerica, the Maya civilization entered its most brilliant era from the turn of the 4th century (the Classic period). Further south, the Tiwanaku state in the Lake Titicaca basin began around 375 to create what would be the first great Andean empire.

Alongside Christianity, other religions also expanded during this period. In Persia, the Sasanians made Zoroastrianism the state religion; an offshoot, Manichaeism, won converts in spite of official persecution, and spread widely across the Roman empire to rival Christianity. In India, the Gupta dynasty was a generous patron of Hinduism and Buddhism, whose influence was further growing in China, Tibet and Korea. Buddhism brought books, art, medicine, music and ideas from India and Central Asia to China, provoking the biggest cultural changes there until the 19th century. During this time, tea drinking also became an important part of Chinese culture for the first time.

192* The kingdom of **Champa** is founded in Southeast Asia

220 The **Han dynasty** collapses: China splits into three rival states

224–26 **Ardashir I** overthrows the Parthian kingdom to found the Persian Sasanian dynasty

280 China is reunified by the state of **Jin**

286 **Diocletian** divides the Roman empire into eastern and western halves

291–306 The **Rebellion of the Eight Princes**: northern China breaks away from Jin control

SCIENCE & TECHNOLOGY

190* The **abacus** is first used in China

200* The **Roman road network** is completed

250* **Diophantus of Alexandria** writes a treatise on equations

180　　**200**　　**220**　　**240**　　**260**　　**280**

RELIGION & PHILOSOPHY

224–40* Ardashir I establishes **Zoroastrianism** as the Persian state religion

253 Chinese Daoist philosopher **Ge Hong**, who advocated alchemy as a way to achieve immorality, is born

276 The Persian mystic **Mani**, founder of Manichaeism, dies in prison after being accused of heresy

ART & ARCHITECTURE

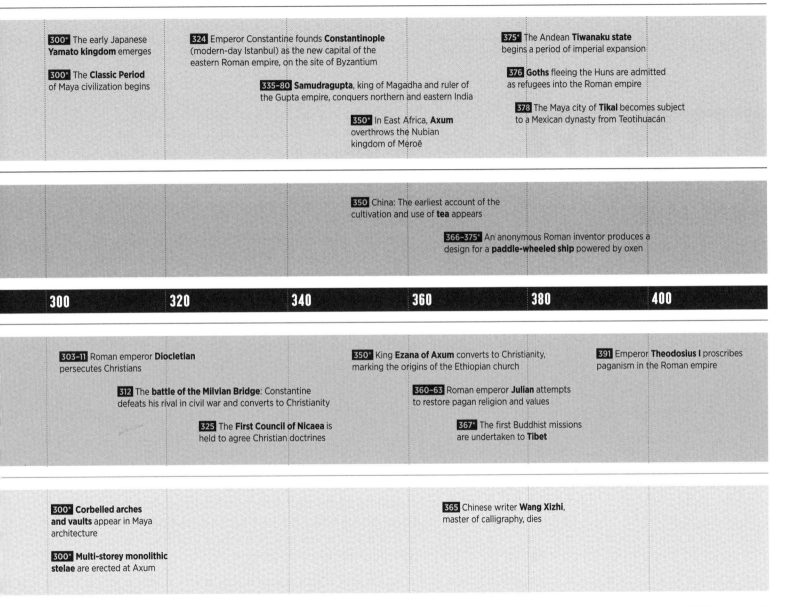

300* The early Japanese **Yamato kingdom** emerges

300* The **Classic Period** of Maya civilization begins

324 Emperor Constantine founds **Constantinople** (modern-day Istanbul) as the new capital of the eastern Roman empire, on the site of Byzantium

335–80 **Samudragupta**, king of Magadha and ruler of the Gupta empire, conquers northern and eastern India

350* In East Africa, **Axum** overthrows the Nubian kingdom of Meroë

375* The Andean **Tiwanaku state** begins a period of imperial expansion

376 **Goths** fleeing the Huns are admitted as refugees into the Roman empire

378 The Maya city of **Tikal** becomes subject to a Mexican dynasty from Teotihuacán

350 China: The earliest account of the cultivation and use of **tea** appears

366–375* An anonymous Roman inventor produces a design for a **paddle-wheeled ship** powered by oxen

300	320	340	360	380	400

303–11 Roman emperor **Diocletian** persecutes Christians

312 The **battle of the Milvian Bridge**: Constantine defeats his rival in civil war and converts to Christianity

325 The **First Council of Nicaea** is held to agree Christian doctrines

350* King **Ezana of Axum** converts to Christianity, marking the origins of the Ethiopian church

360–63 Roman emperor **Julian** attempts to restore pagan religion and values

367* The first Buddhist missions are undertaken to **Tibet**

391 Emperor **Theodosius I** proscribes paganism in the Roman empire

300* **Corbelled arches and vaults** appear in Maya architecture

300* **Multi-storey monolithic stelae** are erected at Axum

365 Chinese writer **Wang Xizhi**, master of calligraphy, dies

392–502

DECLINE AND FALL

IN THE EARLY 5TH CENTURY Rome found itself under attack: in 406 a coalition of Germanic tribes crossed the Rhine, invading the western empire, while four years later a Visigothic army sacked Rome and made the empire's declining power shockingly obvious. Poorer and less populated than its eastern counterpart, the western empire struggled to contain the invasions. By 476 it had dissolved, its territory partitioned between different Germanic peoples. By the end of this period, the main victors seemed to be the Goths, who had founded two kingdoms in Spain and Italy, but the Franks under King Clovis were a rising power. Anglo-Saxon tribes from northern Germany had also established a number of small kingdoms in eastern Britain over the 5th century.

By contrast to the chaos engulfing the western empire, the eastern empire survived the 5th century with its territory intact, although it bore the brunt of attacks by the Huns under their ruler Attila. The eastern emperors were helped by their Persian Sasanian rivals having to fend off the powerful Ephthalite branch of the Huns. Although the Sasanians repelled the Ephthalites, the Gupta empire of northern India was less fortunate, losing its northwestern territories to them around 475. After Attila's death in 453, the Huns broke up; in the aftermath, the Slavs emerged as the dominant peoples of Eastern Europe, occupying much of the territory inhabited by Germanic tribes before the Hun invasions.

In Africa, the Bantu migration was nearing an end after a millennium of expansion: Bantu-speaking peoples now dominated most of central and southern Africa. At this time, the first towns in tropical West Africa began to develop in the fertile inland delta of the river Niger. In South America, the central Andes were divided between the Tiwanaku empire to the south and the Wari empire to the north. Further, the power of the Mexican city of Teotihuacán was at its height, extending throughout Mesoamerica: even the most powerful Maya city, Tikal, was ruled by a Teotihuacán dynasty.

Christianity continued to transform the culture of the Roman world in this period. Theological debate was shaped by disputes concerning the relationship between Christ and God. Traditional doctrine on the Trinity – to this day accepted by Roman Catholic, Orthodox and Protestant churches – was challenged by monophysite ('one nature') ideas that had many followers in Egypt and Syria. Unable to find agreement, the church split after the Council of Chalcedon in 451, and monophysite beliefs would go on to influence the Coptic and other Oriental Orthodox churches to varying degrees.

Monophysite Christians frequently suffered persecution by the Roman imperial authorities, who sought to impose doctrinal uniformity on their territories. In Western Europe, conventional teaching on the Trinity was also challenged by Arianism, which spread widely among the Germanic peoples, notably the Goths and Vandals. This became a serious obstacle to the tribes being accepted by their new Roman subjects, who regarded Arians as heretics. The Germanic peoples were not hostile to the Romans, however, and ultimately the two cultures would assimilate. Yet in the short term, the invasions caused major economic disruption to Western Europe and a corresponding decline in cultural activity.

Nonetheless, the church became the main patron of art, architecture and book production in this period. Roman culture remained most vibrant in the Ostrogothic kingdom of Italy, whereas in the eastern empire, growing intolerance of pagan culture resulted in the works of Classical philosophers and scientists being neglected. In Asia, Buddhism steadily increased in importance in China, aided by major Buddhist texts being translated into Chinese for the first time. Buddhism continued to enjoy success in India: the Gupta empire founded a Buddhist university at Nalanda, and some of the finest Buddhist frescoes were painted at Ajanta. It was also under Gupta rule that the Sanskrit playwright Kalidasa founded Indian theatre traditions.

POLITICS & ECONOMY

400* Polynesians from the Marquesas Islands settle **Hawaii**

400* Mali: **Jenne-jeno** becomes the earliest known city in West Africa

406 A coalition of the **Vandals**, **Sueves** and **Alans** crosses the Rhine and invades the western Roman empire

410 The **Visigoths** sack Rome

420 The southern Chinese Jin dynasty is overthrown by Wudi, founder of the **Liu Song dynasty**

439 The **Xianbei Northern Wei** unify northern China

440–50 The **Huns** under Attila overrun the Balkans

450* State formation in **Indonesia** begins

451 **Atilla the Hun** is defeated at the battle of the Catalaunian Plains by the Romans and Visigoths

SCIENCE & TECHNOLOGY

400* Gallic author **Marcellus Empiricus** compiles *De medicamentis*, a collection of medical prescriptions

450* **Ironworking technology** spreads to southern Africa

400　　410　　420　　430　　440　　450

RELIGION & PHILOSOPHY

400* Indian merchants and seafarers introduce **Hinduism** to Southeast Asia

400* Sanskrit writer Vatsayana writes the *Kamasutra*

413 North African bishop **Augustine of Hippo** writes *The City of God*, a major source for medieval theology and political thought

414 Monk **Fa Xian** translates Buddhist texts into Chinese

415–55* King Kumaragupta of the Gupta empire founds a **Buddhist university** at Nalanda

433* The **Nestorian church** emerges in the Middle East

451 The **Council of Chalcedon** leads to a schism between the Catholic and eastern Monophysite churches

ART & ARCHITECTURE

400* Influenced by the Sanskrit playwright **Kalidasa**, Indian theatre traditions develop

413 Constantinople: The **Theodosian Walls** are constructed

450* The Chinese **shan shui** (mountain-water) school of landscape painting emerges

462-78 The Visigoths conquer **Spain**

475* The **Ephthalites** (knows as the Hunas in India) conquer northwestern India from the Gupta empire

488-93 Italy is conquered by **Theodoric**, king of the Ostrogoths

500* The **Wari** state emerges as a rival to **Tiwanaku** in the Andes

500* **Scots** from Ireland begin settling in northern Britain

502 The short-lived **Qi dynasty** is overthrown in China

499 Indian astronomer **Aryabhata** publishes his treatise *Aryabhatiya*

460   **470**   **480**   **490**   **500**   **510**

480* India: Buddhist frescoes are created in the rock-cut temples at **Ajanta**

500* Deogarh, India: The earliest surviving Hindu temple, the **Temple of Vishnu**, is built

503–632

RELIGIOUS AND IMPERIAL EXPANSION

IN THE 530s, the eastern Roman empire reconquered much of the territory previously held by the western Roman empire. A catastrophic plague outbreak shortly afterwards, however, severely weakened the eastern empire, and by the turn of the 7th century, it was on the defensive against attacks from all sides: it lost northern Italy to the Germanic Lombards, while the Persian Sasanian empire acted in concert with the Slavs and Avar nomads to attack Constantinople in 622–27. After the emperor Heraclius defeated this alliance, he reformed the empire and made Greek its official language; as a result, the eastern Roman empire is known as the Byzantine empire from this time on.

By this time, the Franks were the main power in Western Europe, while in Britain the Anglo-Saxon settlers had occupied most of what would become known as England. Previously pagan, both were converted to Christianity in this period, marking the faith's expansion in Northern Europe. Elsewhere, the Nubians in northeastern Africa adopted Christianity under Byzantine influence, and Nestorian Christians began to win converts in China.

While Byzantium fought the Sasanians, Muhammad's migration to Medina in 622, to escape persecution for his religious teaching at Mecca – the *hijra* – marks the beginning of the Muslim era in world history. Before the spread of Islam, most Arabs were polytheists, but many were Jews, Christians, Zoroastrians or Hanifs (monotheists who were neither Christian nor Jewish), and all these faiths may have influenced Muhammad's religious ideas. Muhammad did not see himself as founding a new faith so much as restoring the original religion of Abraham, which he believed Jews and Christians had misunderstood. At Medina, Muhammad established a theocratic Muslim state where he exercised both religious and political authority. On Muhammad's death, his father-in-law Abu Bakr was elected as the first caliph (successor); the institution of the caliphate was intended to unite all Muslims in a single community.

Further east, the power of the Gupta empire was broken after defeat by the Central Asian Ephthalites in the 5th century, and by 550 it had collapsed entirely. Harsha, king of Kannauj, reunited northern India in the first half of the 7th century, but his empire would not long survive his death in 647. Around 550, the Chalukya dynasty replaced the Vakatakas as the main power of southern India. Buddhist influence, meanwhile, began to decline in the face of the Bhakti Hindu revival movement. In Mesoamerica, the previously dominant city of Tikal was superseded in importance by Calakmul.

After centuries of division and dynastic instability, China was reunited by the Sui dynasty in 589; after the Tang succeeded in 618, China built on this unity and expanded far into Central Asia under the emperor Taizong. Japan emerged fully from prehistory in this period, following Prince Shotoku's introduction of a form of imperial government similar to China's. This was just one element of the burgeoning Chinese influence on Japanese culture at this time: in 552, Korean monks introduced Chinese schools of Buddhism to Japan, while the Chinese script and calendar, Chinese literary and legal forms, and Chinese crafts were also all adopted and adapted to Japanese needs. While the peoples of Vietnam were unsuccessful in their uprisings against Chinese rule, elsewhere in Southeast Asia the Mon Dvaravati kingdom was founded in what is now Thailand.

This period saw Christian Byzantine artists produce dazzling mosaics for the vast dome of the Hagia Sophia cathedral at Constantinople, and Chinese engineers construct both the first suspension bridges and the 1,770-km (1,100-mile) Grand Canal. In India, mathematicians formulated the decimal number system early in the 7th century; around fifty years later is the first record of the strategy game *chaturanga*, the ancestor of modern chess.

POLITICS & ECONOMY

511 **Clovis**, king of the Franks and founder of the Merovingian dynasty, dies

533–54 Italy: The eastern Roman empire conquers the **Ostragothic kingdom**

534 The **Northern Wei** kingdom of northern China breaks up and collapses

541–42 **Bubonic plague** kills up to one third of the population of the eastern Roman empire

541–47 Unsuccessful revolts occur in **Vietnam** against Chinese rule

550* Collapse of the **Gupta empire** in northern India

550* The **Mon Dvaravati kingdom** in Southeast Asia is established

550* The **Chalukya dynasty** replaces the Vakatakas in southern India

562 **Calakmul** replaces Tikal as the dominant Maya city

SCIENCE & TECHNOLOGY

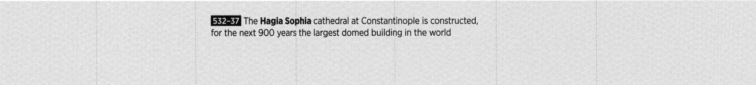

510 **520** **530** **540** **550** **560** **570**

RELIGION & PHILOSOPHY

545* The Nubian kingdom of **Nobatia** converts to Christianity

552 **Buddhism** is introduced to Japan

ART & ARCHITECTURE

532–37 The **Hagia Sophia** cathedral at Constantinople is constructed, for the next 900 years the largest domed building in the world

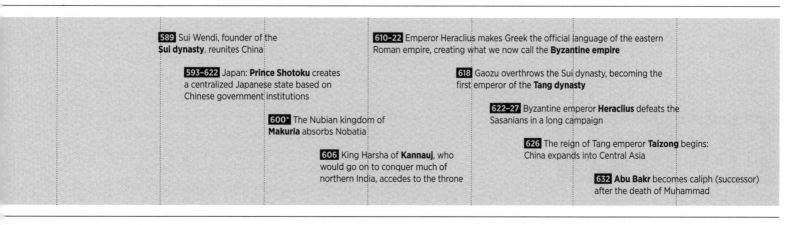

589 Sui Wendi, founder of the **Sui dynasty**, reunites China

593–622 Japan: **Prince Shotoku** creates a centralized Japanese state based on Chinese government institutions

600* The Nubian kingdom of **Makuria** absorbs Nobatia

606 King Harsha of **Kannauj**, who would go on to conquer much of northern India, accedes to the throne

610–22 Emperor Heraclius makes Greek the official language of the eastern Roman empire, creating what we now call the **Byzantine empire**

618 Gaozu overthrows the Sui dynasty, becoming the first emperor of the **Tang dynasty**

622–27 Byzantine emperor **Heraclius** defeats the Sasanians in a long campaign

626 The reign of Tang emperor **Taizong** begins: China expands into Central Asia

632 **Abu Bakr** becomes caliph (successor) after the death of Muhammad

600* China: **Porcelain** is invented

630* China: Texts are first reproduced by **woodblock printing**

628 Indian mathematicians devise the **decimal** ('Arabic') **system of numerals**

| 580 | 590 | 600 | 610 | 620 | 630 | 640 |

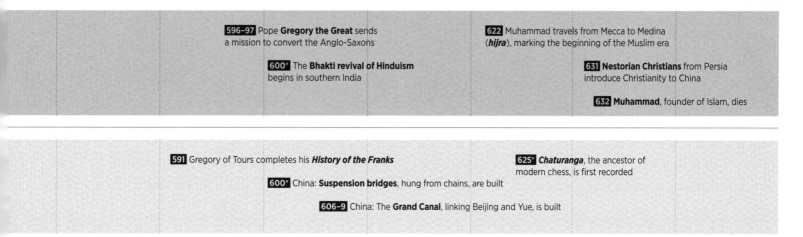

596–97 Pope **Gregory the Great** sends a mission to convert the Anglo-Saxons

600* The **Bhakti revival of Hinduism** begins in southern India

622 Muhammad travels from Mecca to Medina (**hijra**), marking the beginning of the Muslim era

631 **Nestorian Christians** from Persia introduce Christianity to China

632 **Muhammad**, founder of Islam, dies

591 Gregory of Tours completes his *History of the Franks*

600* China: **Suspension bridges**, hung from chains, are built

606–9 China: The **Grand Canal**, linking Beijing and Yue, is built

625* *Chaturanga*, the ancestor of modern chess, is first recorded

633–711

THE RISE OF ISLAM

ON MUHAMMAD'S DEATH in 632, his father-in-law Abu Bakr was elected as the first caliph (successor). It was intended that the institution of the caliphate would continue to unite all Muslims in a single community. But in 656 the third caliph, Uthman, was murdered. When Muhammad's son-in-law Ali was chosen to succeed him, civil war broke out between Ali's supporters and those of Muawiya, a member of Uthman's Umayyad family. Muawiya finally became caliph in 661, after Ali's murder, and became the first of the Umayyad dynasty of caliphs that would rule for nearly a century. Under Muawiya, the caliphate suffered its first serious setback when the Byzantine empire defeated their attack on Constantinople in the 670s using Greek fire incendiaries.

On Muawiya's death in 680, Ali's son Husain claimed the caliphate, causing another civil war with the Umayyads. After Husain was killed in battle at Karbala, a schism erupted in Islam between the majority Sunni and minority Shi'a (from *shi'atu Ali*, 'party of Ali') branches. As political stability gradually returned to the caliphate, it resumed its expansion with the conquest of the Berbers and Byzantine territories in North Africa, the Indus valley, and the Visigothic kingdom of Spain. By 712 the Umayyad caliphate was the largest empire the world had so far seen.

The Arab conquests completely transformed the culture of the Middle East and North Africa through the spread of Islam. Islam was not imposed by force, but unbelievers were subject to *jizya* (tribute) and other restrictions, providing a strong incentive to convert. Moreover, because translation of the *Qur'an* – Islam's holy book – was forbidden, converts were required to learn Arabic, which was also useful for commerce and government employment. Islamic expansion led to the acculturation of conquered populations to Arab identity: Mesopotamia, Syria, Palestine, Egypt and most of North Africa eventually became fully Arabic in language and culture.

The Arabs were in turn influenced by the cultures of the peoples they conquered, especially Persian art and literature, and Greek science and philosophy. While the Persians accepted Islam, they resisted the full sweep of Arab culture. In former Byzantine territories, elite communities fled to unconquered areas, but the complete collapse of the Sasanian state left the Persian elite nowhere to go; by reaching an accommodation with the new rulers, however, they retained substantial cultural and political influence in the caliphate.

Arab conquests also affected the early Christian church: though the bishops of Antioch, Alexandria and Jerusalem had previously been accorded special respect as patriarchs (along with the bishops of Rome and Constantinople), they now saw their influence diminish as Islam expanded across the Middle East. By contrast, the bishops, or popes, of Rome asserted their own claims to exercise supreme authority over the church as God's representatives on earth; yet while papal claims came to be accepted in Western Europe, Rome's new assertiveness caused increasing friction with the Greek church.

In Asia, the Chinese Tang dynasty reached its peak in the later 7th century with the conquest of the West Turk khanate in Central Asia and the Korean kingdom of Koguryo; these conquests, however, overextended the empire and were soon lost. By 712 the Tang had powerful neighbours in Korea to the east, and Tibet and the expanding Umayyad caliphate to the west, but was still the world's wealthiest and most urbanized state. In Indonesia, the Malay kingdom of Srivijaya created the first of a series of maritime trading empires that would successively dominate the region until the 16th century.

Economic expansion was not limited to Southeast Asia: the growth of trans-Saharan trade contributed to the emergence of Ghana, the first kingdom in West Africa. New societies also developed in the American Southwest, with the emergence of the early Ancestral Pueblo culture; on the other hand, in Mesoamerica, the great city of Teotihuacán was violently destroyed and abandoned around 650, leaving a yawning power vacuum. In the Pacific, the turn of the 8th century marked the Polynesian discovery and settlement of Easter Island: for over a millennium it would remain the world's most remote inhabited place.

634–44 The reign of the caliph **Umar** sees the beginning of Arab expansion

650* **Teotihuacán** is destroyed by unknown invaders and abandoned

638 The Arabs capture **Jerusalem**

656 Caliph **Uthman** is murdered: civil war breaks out following the succession of Muhammad's son-in-law Ali

640–42 The Arabs conquer **Egypt**

661–80 Caliph Muawiya founds the **Umayyad dynasty**

642 The Sasanian empire collapses after its defeat by the Arabs at **Nehavend**

668 The Tang empire destroys the Korean kingdom of **Koguryo**

SCIENCE & TECHNOLOGY

643 The first reference appears to the **heavy two-wheeled plough** being used in Western Europe

672* Byzantine chemist Kallinikos invents **Greek fire**, an early form of flamethrower

630   **640**   **650**   **660**   **670**

RELIGION & PHILOSOPHY

645 Chinese monk **Xuanzang** returns from India with Buddhist scriptures

656 The text of the *Qur'an* is first written down

664 The **Synod of Whitby**: British churches accept the authority of the papacy and its method of calculating the date of Easter

ART & ARCHITECTURE

671–87 Chinese monk **Yijing** writes accounts of his extensive travels in India and Indonesia

678 The **first Arab siege of Constantinople** is defeated

680 Iraq: Ali's son Husain is defeated and killed by the Umayyads at the **battle of Karbala**

682 The **Srivijaya kingdom** begins a period of maritime expansion in Indonesia and the Malay Peninsula

682–702 The Arabs conquer the Berbers of the **Maghrib**, completing their conquest of North Africa

700* The first West African kingdom, **Ghana** (in present-day Mali), is founded

700* Polynesians from Tahiti settle on **Easter Island**

700* The **early Ancestral Pueblo culture** emerges in the American Southwest

705 Chinese Zhou dynasty empress **Wu Zetian** dies

708 The first **Japanese coinage** is issued

711 The Arabs and Berbers conquer most of the **Visigothic kingdom** in Spain

711 The Arabs conquer **Sindh** and **the Indus valley** in western India

680   **690**   **700**   **710**   **720**

680 The death of Ali's son Husain leads to schism between the **Sunni** and **Shi'a** traditions of Islam

703 The **Taiho laws**: Japanese penal and civil law is codified

683 Maya king **Pakal** is interred with a jade burial mask under a giant sarcophagus lid

684* **Caedmon**, the earliest known English poet, dies

691–92 Jerusalem: The Islamic shrine of the **Dome of the Rock** is completed

711

THE RISE OF ISLAM

In the 7th century, the culture of the Mediterranean and Middle East was transformed by the rapid rise of the Arab Islamic empire, the largest that the world had yet seen. Large areas of the New World were now also dominated by empires.

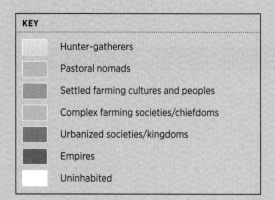

KEY

- Hunter-gatherers
- Pastoral nomads
- Settled farming cultures and peoples
- Complex farming societies/chiefdoms
- Urbanized societies/kingdoms
- Empires
- Uninhabited

Ancestral Puebloan culture

MAYA CITY STATES

WARI EMPIRE

TIWANAKU EMPIRE

Easter Island

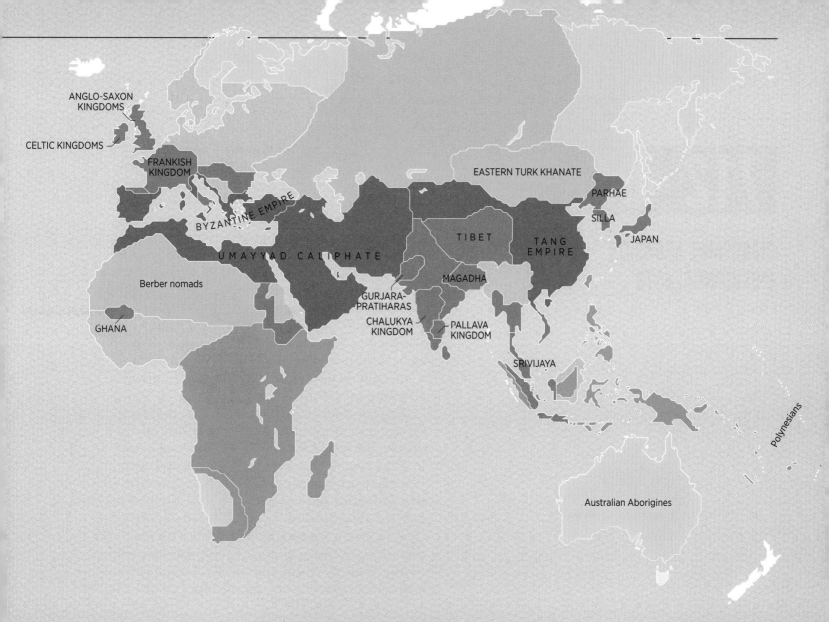

ANGLO-SAXON
KINGDOMS

CELTIC KINGDOMS

FRANKISH
KINGDOM

BYZANTINE EMPIRE

EASTERN TURK KHANATE

PARHAE

SILLA

TIBET

TANG
EMPIRE

JAPAN

UMAYYAD CALIPHATE

Berber nomads

GHANA

GURJARA-
PRATIHARAS

MAGADHA

CHALUKYA
KINGDOM

PALLAVA
KINGDOM

SRIVIJAYA

Polynesians

Australian Aborigines

85

712–800

UMAYYADS, ABBASIDS AND ICONOCLASTS

DECISIVE VICTORIES BY the Byzantine empire (716–17), the Franks (732) and the Gurjara-Pratiharas (738) brought the years of Arab conquests to an end in the first half of the 8th century. The ideal of Islamic unity – in which all Muslims belonged to a single community, recognizing the religious and political authority of the caliph – did not survive long after these defeats. The Umayyads saw Islam primarily as a symbol of Arab racial superiority, viewing the caliphate as their own private empire: they treated non-Arab converts as inferiors and excluded them from government office. Unsurprisingly, this bred resentment among these new Muslims, who believed that the caliphate existed to spread Islam, rather than to further Arab interests. Part of the reaction against these policies came in the development of the mystical Sufi tradition.

Umayyad authority was similarly undermined by the simmering split between the Sunni and Shi'ite branches of Islam, and by renewed feuding among the Arab tribes. In 747 an uprising broke out in Persia and quickly spread: the rebels proclaimed Abu al-Abbas caliph in 749, and a year later he defeated the Umayyads at the battle of the Zab and captured Damascus. Only one significant member of the Umayyad dynasty survived the bloodbath that followed – Abd al-Rahman, who fled to Spain and founded a breakaway state with its capital at Córdoba. Compared to Umayyad rule, non-Arab converts enjoyed greater equality under the Abbasids.

This both removed the remaining barriers between the Arabs and their subjects, and also sharpened the distinction between Muslims and non-Muslims in their territories.

Although the Abbasids had also lost control over Islamic lands in North Africa by 800, their caliphate remained the world's wealthiest state. Under Harun al-Rashid (ruled 786–809), the rapidly growing new Abbasid capital at Baghdad became the world's leading cultural centre, where Greek science and philosophy, alongside Persian literature, became assimilated with Islamic beliefs. Harun's opulent court became the stuff of legends, and was the setting for the stories of the *One Thousand and One Nights*.

In East Asia, the Chinese Tang empire was in decline by 800 as a result of both military rebellions and attacks by the Tibetan empire and Uighur nomads. Despite, or because of, the political turmoil, this was also one of the great ages of Chinese poetry, most notably the works of Du Fu and Li Bo. The removal of the Japanese imperial court to Kyoto marked the beginning of the classical Heian age. Though exquisitely refined, Japanese culture during this period remained focused on Buddhist monasteries and the court itself, where the emperors became increasingly isolated from their subjects. Buddhism's dominant influence on the culture of Tibet, meanwhile, was assured in 791, when it was adopted as the established state religion. Across the Pacific, the Mesoamerican Maya civilization reached its peak in the 8th century, as rulers commissioned ever more ambitious buildings and commemorative stelae (stone monuments).

Under the domination of the Frankish emperor Charlemagne (reigned 768–814) and his Carolingian empire, Western Europe enjoyed greater peace and prosperity than at any time since the fall of the western Roman empire three centuries earlier. Further east, in 726 the Byzantine emperor Leo III abolished all religious images, bitterly dividing the Orthodox church and causing a split with the papacy that persisted until iconoclasm was formally renounced in 842. It was a sign of the popes' increasing spiritual authority in the Catholic West that Pippin III ('the Short'), who had held a senior palace position among the Franks as their mayor, sought papal blessing for his seizure of the Frankish throne from the Merovingian dynasty in 751. Monasteries were Western Europe's main cultural centres; however, being rich and undefended, they proved attractive targets for Viking raiders from Scandinavia, who began to appear along the coasts of Europe in the 790s.

717 The **second Arab siege of Constantinople** is defeated

732 **Charles Martel**, mayor of the Franks, defeats the Arabs at Tours

738 The **Gurjara-Pratihara** dynasty defeats the Arabs at the battle of Rajastan

750 The **battle of the Zab**: the Abbasids seize control of the Islamic caliphate from the Ummayads

751 Pope Zacharias authorizes the deposition of the last Merovingian king by the Carolingian **Pippin III** ('the Short')

755–63 The **An Lushan rebellion** begins the decline of China's Tang dynasty

756 The **Rashtrakuta dynasty** becomes the dominant power of central India

SCIENCE & TECHNOLOGY

720* Indian doctor Madhav describes a method of **inoculation against smallpox**

725 Chinese monk and astronomer Yi Xing builds an **armillary sphere** (model of the heavens)

710   **720**   **730**   **740**   **750**

RELIGION & PHILOSOPHY

720* The **Sufi mystical tradition** of Islam begins to develop

726 The **Iconoclastic Controversy**, regarding the veneration of religious images, causes a split between the Byzantine Orthodox and Roman Catholic churches

ART & ARCHITECTURE

715 The **Umayyad mosque** at Damascus is completed

715* Northumbrian monks produce the illuminated *Lindisfarne Gospels*

756 The Classical Arabic poet **Abu Nuwaz** is born

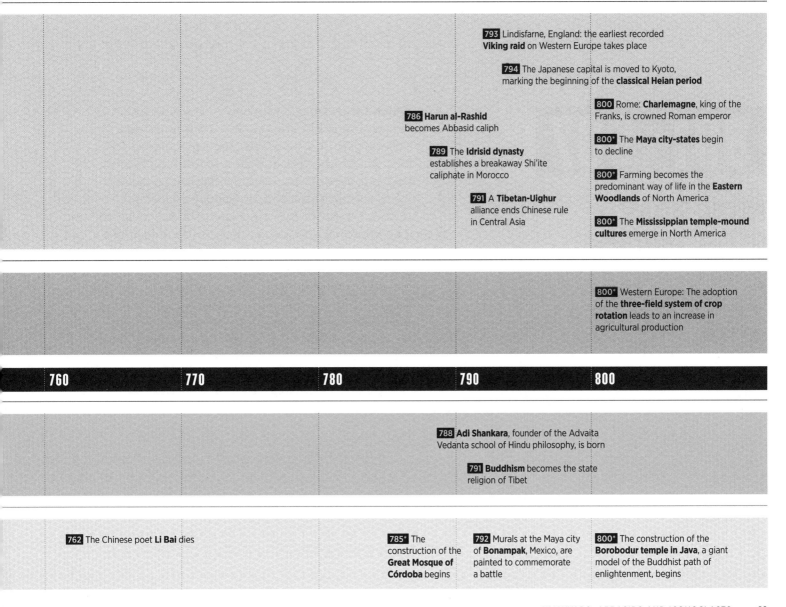

793 Lindisfarne, England: the earliest recorded **Viking raid** on Western Europe takes place

794 The Japanese capital is moved to Kyoto, marking the beginning of the **classical Heian period**

786 Harun al-Rashid becomes Abbasid caliph

789 The **Idrisid dynasty** establishes a breakaway Shi'ite caliphate in Morocco

791 A **Tibetan-Uighur** alliance ends Chinese rule in Central Asia

800 Rome: **Charlemagne**, king of the Franks, is crowned Roman emperor

800⁺ The **Maya city-states** begin to decline

800⁺ Farming becomes the predominant way of life in the **Eastern Woodlands** of North America

800⁺ The **Mississippian temple-mound cultures** emerge in North America

800⁺ Western Europe: The adoption of the **three-field system of crop rotation** leads to an increase in agricultural production

760   **770**   **780**   **790**   **800**

788 Adi Shankara, founder of the Advaita Vedanta school of Hindu philosophy, is born

791 Buddhism becomes the state religion of Tibet

762 The Chinese poet **Li Bai** dies

785⁺ The construction of the **Great Mosque of Córdoba** begins

792 Murals at the Maya city of **Bonampak**, Mexico, are painted to commemorate a battle

800⁺ The construction of the **Borobodur temple in Java**, a giant model of the Buddhist path of enlightenment, begins

801–907

IMPERIAL DECLINE, CULTURAL AWAKENINGS

DURING THIS PERIOD, China's Tang empire continued its decline in the face of frequent attack by its neighbours – Tibet and Nanzhao in the west, and steppe nomads to the north. Foreign religions, including Christianity and Buddhism, faced official persecution. Peasant rebellions fatally undermined the dynasty's authority, allowing warlords to seize power in the provinces in the second half of the 9th century. At the same time, the Daoist search for an elixir of immortality created a strong interest in alchemy, an unintended consequence of which was the invention of gunpowder around the middle of the 9th century. In 907 the Tang were finally overthrown and China fragmented into several independent kingdoms. To the south, in the early 9th century the Khmer empire emerged as the great power of Southeast Asia, and later in the century the first Burmese kingdom was founded at Bagan. In Japan, the emperors' authority began to deteriorate as power passed to the Fujiwara clan of hereditary regents.

In Western Europe, dynastic disputes led to the break-up of Charlemagne's empire after his death in 814, from which both the French and German kingdoms emerged. Raids by the Scandinavian Vikings were especially frequent in this period, reaching as far as the Mediterranean: they founded colonies in Ireland, Scotland and Normandy, and became the first inhabitants of Iceland and the Faroe Islands. The kingdoms of Anglo-Saxon England escaped total conquest only thanks to the military leadership of the king of Wessex, Alfred the Great. Swedish Vikings, known as Rus, penetrated the river systems of Eastern Europe to forge trade routes to the Byzantine empire and the Abbasid caliphate; they founded the first Russian state at Kiev, which preyed on the surrounding Slav peoples for tribute and slaves.

Vikings were not the only raiders in the 9th century: Muslim pirates and Magyar nomads also attacked strongholds and monasteries, reducing cultural life to a low ebb. The break-up of the Frankish empire stemmed both from its rulers' failure to prevent Viking assaults, and from persistent dynastic disputes and civil wars. This decline in royal authority led to the emergence of highly decentralized kingdoms with weak monarchies and powerful feudal aristocracies. Nonetheless, it is also from the end of this period that the first examples of polyphonic music are known.

In the Americas, the Maya city-states collapsed one after another, most probably because of an ecological crisis created by deforestation and soil exhaustion. Maya civilization survived in the north of the Yucatán peninsula in a somewhat reduced form. The power vacuum in Mexico left by the fall of Teotihuacán in the seventh century was finally filled by the expanding Toltec state. On the other side of the world, the political fragmentation of the Muslim world continued in this period: the peoples of Persia began to throw off Abbasid domination, founding independent emirates under the Samanid and Saffarid dynasties.

Yet despite its political decline, the Abbasid caliphate presided over a golden age of Islamic culture in the 9th century. Baghdad's House of Wisdom became a centre for translating Greek, Persian and Hindu works into Arabic. Many works of Classical Greek science and philosophy, neglected by Byzantine Christians because of their pagan associations, were preserved as a result: when these texts were rediscovered in Western Europe in the 12th century, they often owed their existence to Arabic translations originally undertaken in Baghdad. Astronomy and mathematics also flourished. Influenced by Greek philosophy, the Mutazilist school of Islamic theologians attempted to reconcile faith and reason, but could not overcome the opposition of *hadith* scholars, who believed it was not the role of humans to question God's will or explore it intellectually.

POLITICS & ECONOMY

802 King Jayavarman I institutes a divine monarchy, beginning the **Khmer period** of Cambodian history

810* **Trading towns** begin to grow on the East African coast

814 **Charlemagne** dies, leading to dynastic disputes over the succession to the imperial throne

843 The **Treaty of Verdun**: The Frankish empire is divided between Charlemagne's grandsons

850* The **Tamil Chola dynasty** becomes the dominant power of southern India

850–900* The Itzá Maya found the city of **Chichén Itzá** in Yucatán

SCIENCE & TECHNOLOGY

813 A **school of astronomy** is founded at Baghdad

825* Persian scholar al-Khwarizmi writes a treatise on **algebra**

850* China: **gunpowder** is used for the first time

854 Persian physician and alchemist **Razi**, who would discover kerosene and alcohol, is born

| 800 | 810 | 820 | 830 | 840 | 850 |

RELIGION & PHILOSOPHY

833 Abbasid caliph al-Ma'mun attempts to impose **Mutazilist beliefs** on his subjects

842–45 The **Tang dynasty** orders the persecution of non-Chinese religions, including Buddhism and Christianity

ART & ARCHITECTURE

813–33* Abbasid caliph al-Ma'mun founds the **House of Wisdom** at Baghdad

856* Java: The Hindu **Prambanan temple** is completed

858 Japan: the aristocratic **Fujiwara clan** seizes control of the government

870 Norse Vikings colonize **Iceland**

874 **Bagan** becomes the capital of the first Burmese kingdom

874 The Persian **Samanid emirate** in Central Asia becomes independent of the Abbasid caliphate

874–84 Provincial warlords seize power as peasant rebellions undermine the authority of the **Tang dynasty**

882* **Kiev** becomes the capital of Rus

889 King Yasovarman I founds **Angkor** as a new capital for the Khmer empire

896–907 The **Magyar nomads** invade Europe and settle on the Hungarian plain

899 **Alfred the Great**, king of Wessex, who led the Anglo-Saxons against the Vikings, dies

900* Irrigation-based farming is practised by the **Hohokam culture** in the American Southwest

903 The Persian **Saffarid emirate** of Seistan gains independence from the Abbasids

907 The Tang dynasty collapses, beginning the **Five Dynasties and Ten Kingdoms period**

900* The **lost-wax method** of gold casting is introduced to Mesoamerica from South America

| 860 | 870 | 880 | 890 | 900 | 910 |

860–900 The *hadith*, the basis of Islamic law, are collected in their final form

868 The **oldest surviving dated printed book**, a Chinese copy of the Buddhist *Diamond Sutra*, is published

900* The musical treatise *Musica enchiriadis* contains the earliest examples of **polyphonic music**

900* New Mexico: The **Great House** at Pueblo Bonito, Chaco Canyon, is constructed

908–1004

FROM CÓRDOBA TO KORYO

IN THE MIDDLE EAST, the Abbasid caliphate's long decline as a political power came to an end in 945, when the Persian Buwayhid dynasty captured Baghdad. The Buwayhids were Shi'ites, but they permitted the Sunni Abbasid caliphs to continue as religious figureheads. The Abbasids' religious authority was, however, more explicitly rejected by the powerful Shi'ite Fatimid dynasty that seized power in Tunisia in 909 and continued its expansion eastwards: in 941, the Fatimids conquered Egypt and made Cairo the capital of a Shi'ite caliphate to rival the Buwayhids.

Abd al-Rahman III, the Umayyad ruler of Spain, similarly rejected Abbasid religious authority, and reclaimed the title of caliph for his own dynasty in 929. The Umayyads ruled Córdoba, Europe's most important cultural centre, and its largest and wealthiest city. The library of al-Hakim, Abd al-Rahman's successor as caliph, was probably the largest in the world at the time, with over 400,000 volumes. In Central Asia, meanwhile, Islam began to spread among the Turkic peoples following the conversion of the Oguz Turks around 970. By the end of this period, Arab merchants had begun to establish Islam in their trading bases in West Africa, and along the East African coast.

Western Europe became a less turbulent place in the 10th century. Viking raids declined and stable kingdoms emerged in Scandinavia. The Viking settlements in Normandy were brought under the nominal sovereignty of the French kings, while Alfred the Great's successors conquered Viking territories in England, uniting the whole country under a single crown. Otto I, king of Germany, celebrated his annexation of Italy and his victories over the Magyars with an imperial coronation in Rome in 962: his Holy Roman empire ambitiously saw itself as the legal successor to both Charlemagne's Carolingian empire and the Roman empire. Under Basil II, the Byzantine empire, a more genuine successor to the Roman empire, emerged from centuries of territorial decline.

During this period, Christianity began to expand quickly into Northern and Eastern Europe, as Roman Catholic and Greek Orthodox missionaries competed for influence over possible converts. Scandinavia, Poland, Bohemia and Hungary accepted conversion by Roman Catholic missionaries, and thus recognized the authority of the papacy and began using the Latin alphabet. By contrast, Serbia, Bulgaria and the Kievan Rus were converted by Greek missionaries, and so accepted the traditions of the Greek Orthodox church; they also developed alphabets derived from Greek. This split created a major cultural and political fault line through Europe, which exists to this day. In Catholic Europe, an influential monastic reform movement also emerged in the 10th century, dedicated to faithfully observing the 6th-century Rule of St Benedict. The movement was supported by the Holy Roman emperors, who cultivated the church as a counterbalance to the feudal aristocracy, and who relied on bishops and abbots to fill the highest offices of state.

In East Asia, the Song dynasty reunited most of China in 960 but remained hemmed in by powerful states and nomadic peoples, leaving it unable to expand beyond areas of ethnic Chinese settlement. In terms of territory, Song emperors presided over a markedly small empire, but it is remembered as one of the most humane Chinese dynasties, ushering in a period of extraordinary prosperity and inventiveness: Song innovations included both the chamber lock and the first known gunpowder weapons. Vietnamese victory over Chinese forces in 939 led to the establishment of the Dai Viet state, while in this period Korea emerged as a unified kingdom under the Koryo dynasty. In South America, the Andean Tiwanaku and Wari empires collapsed around 1000, beginning a long period of political fragmentation in the region. The main culprit is thought to have been prolonged drought caused by a succession of El Niño events – climatic variations that lead to warmer sea temperatures in the Pacific.

POLITICS & ECONOMY

909 The Shi'ite **Fatimid** dynasty overthrows the Aghlabids in Tunisia

927 **Athelstan** becomes the first king to rule all of England

945 The Persian **Buwayhids** capture Baghdad, ending the Abbasids' political power

914* The earliest records of **samurai warriors** appear in Japan

936 Wang Geon, founder of the Koryo dynasty, unifies **Korea**

939 Vietnam: The independent kingdom of **Dai Viet** is founded

941 The Fatimid dynasty conquers **Egypt**

SCIENCE & TECHNOLOGY

950* Simple **gunpowder weapons**, such as 'fire lances' and rockets, are used for the first time in Chinese warfare

900	910	920	930	940	950

RELIGION & PHILOSOPHY

911 **Cluny abbey** is founded in Burgundy, initiating a period of monastic reform based on the Rule of St Benedict

ART & ARCHITECTURE

900* The earliest records appear of the *One Thousand and One Nights* collection of stories

950* The first **stone castles** are built in France

956* Arab traveller, geographer and historian **al-Masudi** dies

960 Song Taizu becomes emperor of the Five Dynasties state, marking the beginning of the imperial **Song dynasty**

975 Pagan invaders destroy the East African kingdom of **Axum**

997 Afghanistan: **Mahmud of Ghazni** rebels against the Samanids, founding the Ghaznavid emirate

961 Umayyad caliph of Córdoba **Abd al-Rahman III** dies

962 Otto I, king of Germany, is crowned emperor in Rome, founding the **Holy Roman empire**

969 Cairo becomes the capital of the Fatimid caliphate

1000* Collapse of the Andean **Wari** and **Tiwanaku empires**, thought to be due to climate change

1000* Viking **Leif Eriksson** travels to Vinland, the first European landing on the American continent

1004 The Song agree to pay an annual tribute to the **Khitans**

965* Dry docks are invented in Song China

984 Chamber locks are built on Chinese canals

| 960 | 970 | 980 | 990 | 1000 | 1010 |

970* The **Oguz Turks** convert to Islam

988 Vladimir, grand prince of Kiev, converts to Greek Orthodox Christianity

1000* Pilgrimage becomes an important part of Hindu devotional practice

1000* Arab traders spread **Islam** to West Africa and the East African Swahili coast

970 Cairo: The **al-Azhar mosque** is completed

1000* The Song school of **landscape painting** emerges

1005–1099

THE AGE OF INVADERS

BEFORE THIS PERIOD, the Turks were known in the Middle East mainly as a source of *mamluks* (slave soldiers). One such *mamluk* was Mahmud of Ghazni, who had overthrown his master and created his own emirate in Afghanistan at the end of the 10th century. A militant Muslim, Mahmud spent his reign (997–1030) sacking the Hindu temples of northern India, and conquered the Punjab in 1021. Firdawsi's *Shahnameh* (*The Book of Kings*), meanwhile, marked a watershed in the revival of Persian cultural identity: written in a pure Persian, excluding Arabic influences that had crept into the language, this legendary history of the kings of Persia quickly established itself as the national epic.

Between 1037 and 1086 the Seljuk Turks, a branch of the nomadic Oguz Turks, invaded and subjugated almost all of the Middle East; the Seljuk sultanate, however, broke up into rival emirates in 1092. The lasting legacy of the Seljuk invasion was that previously Greek-speaking Anatolia, seized from the Byzantine empire after the latter's defeat at Manzikert in 1071, became culturally and linguistically Turkish. The loss of the region's resources seriously weakened Byzantium.

The Seljuk conquests provoked a military response from Catholic Western Europe. In 1095, Pope Urban II proclaimed the First Crusade, which captured Jerusalem four years later and established small Christian territories (the crusader states) in Syria and Palestine. The First Crusade's success owed much to the disunity of its Muslim opponents, but was also an important sign of growing prosperity and confidence in the Catholic West. Elsewhere in Europe, the Normans, descendants of Viking settlers in France, conquered Muslim and Byzantine lands in southern Italy and Sicily, conquered Anglo-Saxon England, and also joined the crusades.

The popular response to Urban II's call for an expedition to free the Holy Land from Muslim control was a sign of the papacy's unchallenged spiritual leadership in Catholic Europe. Its power stemmed from reforms begun in 1046 under Pope Clement II that aimed to free the church from lay control. His successor Gregory VII's decree abolishing the investiture of bishops by lay rulers led to open conflict with the Holy Roman emperor Henry IV, whose government depended on control of the church. The dispute – labelled the Investiture Controversy – caused a civil war that severely damaged the emperor's authority and started the empire's progression into a looser confederation of princely states. Earlier in the period, the newly assertive papacy had already caused a permanent schism between the Roman Catholic and Greek Orthodox churches in 1054.

Around 1000, the North American Thule Inuit began to spread east from the Bering Straits towards Greenland: one of the most sophisticated hunter-gatherer cultures, it was superbly adapted to the Arctic environment. Around the same time, Vikings became the first Europeans to reach the Americas. Their settlement in Greenland survived for 400 years, but their attempts to settle on Newfoundland failed. Further south, by 1100 North America's first towns were emerging in the Mississippi basin. In Southeast Asia, Tai peoples began migrating southwards into present-day Thailand, while in the first half of the 11th century, the region was also raided by the powerful Chola dynasty of southern India.

At the beginning of the 10th century, China's Song rulers had been forced to pay tribute to their powerful northern neighbours, the Khitan and the Tangut, in return for peace. China was easily able to afford this: the introduction of new rice strains from Vietnam made growing two crops a year possible, greatly increasing the prosperity of the countryside and allowing peasant farmers to support larger families. In this era, Chinese technology was the most sophisticated in the world: Song innovations included the use of the magnetic compass for navigation; water-powered mechanical clocks; and the earliest movable type printing, using clay type. The thousands of characters required to print the Chinese script meant, however, that nearly all books were printed from carved plates.

POLITICS & ECONOMY

1010* The **Thule Inuit culture** begins to spread from Alaska to Greenland through the Canadian Arctic

1010* **Tai peoples** begin to migrate southwards from the upper Mekong region into Mon and Khmer territory in Southeast Asia

1012 **Early ripening rice** from Vietnam boosts China's rice production and population by allowing two crops a year

1020* Newfoundland: The short-lived Norse settlement at **L'Anse aux Meadows** is abandoned

1021 Mahmud of Ghazni conquers the **Punjab**

1025 The southern Indian Chola dynasty raids the **Srivijaya** and **Pegu** kingdoms of the Malay peninsula

1031–90 The **Normans** conquer southern Italy and Sicily

1037–40 The **Seljuk Turks** invade the Ghaznavid emirate and occupy its western provinces

1038 The Tangut kingdom of **Xixia** is founded

1050* Towns and impressive ceremonial centres start growing in the **Mississippi basin**

1055 The Seljuks under Toghril Beg capture **Baghdad**

SCIENCE & TECHNOLOGY

1041–48 China: The first attempts are made to print with **movable type**

1048 The Persian astronomer, mathematician, alchemist, geographer and historian **Abu Rayhan Biruni** dies

1000 **1010** **1020** **1030** **1040** **1050**

RELIGION & PHILOSOPHY

1017 Egypt: The Persian mystic Hamza ibn Ali ibn Ahmed founds the **Druze faith**, a branch of Shi'a Islam

1054 The pope excommunicates the **patriarch of Constantinople**, causing a schism between the Roman and Greek churches

ART & ARCHITECTURE

1008 Iranian poet Firdawsi completes the **Shahnameh**, his epic legendary history of the Persian kings

1010* Japanese author Murasaki Shikibu writes the **Tale of Genji**

1056 Yingxian, China: The **Fogong temple pagoda**, the oldest surviving wooden pagoda in China, is constructed

1066 The **battle of Hastings**: William, duke of Normandy, conquers England

1071 The Seljuks defeat the Byzantines at **Manzikert** and subsequently overrun Anatolia

1076* **Ghana** is conquered by the Berber Almoravid empire

1086 *Domesday Book*, a detailed survey of English land ownership and property values, is compiled

1092 The death of the Seljuk sultan **Malik Shah** sparks a civil war and the break-up of the sultanate

1095–99 The **First Crusade**: Christian forces capture Jerusalem and establish principalities in Palestine and Syria

1090 The **magnetic compass** is first used on Chinese ships

1090 The **water-powered mechanical clock** is built for the Song court

1060 **1070** **1080** **1090** **1100** **1110**

1075–1122 The **Investiture Controversy**: the papacy and the Holy Roman emperors disagree over the right to appoint bishops

1088 The first European university is founded at **Bologna**

1098 French abbot Robert of Molesme founds the **Cistercian** monastic movement

1070–80 The **Bayeux Tapestry**, an embroidery depiction of the Norman conquest of England, is created

1080* Isfahan, Persia: The **Friday mosque** is constructed

1100–1206

SHOGUNS, CRUSADERS AND PHILOSOPHERS

IN 11TH- AND 12TH-CENTURY Japan, samurai warrior clans competed for control over weak emperors. In 1185, the Minamoto clan destroyed its main rival, the Taira, to emerge victorious. The clan's leader, Minamoto Yoritomo, established a *bakufu* (military government) at Kamakura in 1192. The emperor, now merely the nominal ruler of Japan, granted Yoritomo the title *shogun* (general), beginning a period of military rule that lasted until 1868. In northern China, the recently formed Jürchen Jin state conquered the Khitan Liao kingdom in 1125, before turning on the imperial Song dynasty and capturing their capital at Kaifeng. The end of this period saw the emergence of a new nomadic confederation on the Eurasian steppes: in 1204–6, the warlord Temujin united the Mongol tribes under his leadership and adopted the title Chinggis (Genghis) Khan ('universal ruler').

In the Middle East, the Christian crusader states were thrown on to the defensive when Zengi, emir of Seljuk Mosul, began to restore Muslim unity in the second quarter of the 12th century. Saladin, the ruling sultan of Egypt and Syria, recaptured Jerusalem in 1187 and reduced the crusader states to precarious enclaves on the Mediterranean coast. The crusades did nothing to improve relations between the Catholic West and the Byzantine empire, whose power was broken when in 1204 crusaders sacked Constantinople. At the end of this period, most of northern India came under

Muslim control after its conquest by Muhammad, sultan of Ghur in Afghanistan. After Muhammad's assassination in 1206, his Turkish slave-general Qutb-ud-Din seized power and founded a sultanate at Delhi.

The collapse of the Mesoamerican Toltec empire in 1168 created another longlasting power vacuum in Mexico. Around 1200 the Chimú state of the coastal lowlands in Peru emerged as the first regional power on the Pacific coast since the fall of the Tiwanaku and Wari empires over a century earlier. In North America, the end of this period saw the development of the Southeastern Ceremonial Complex among the semi-urbanized Mississippian cultures. The complex was characterized by the emergence of common cosmological motifs, and by the exchange of exotic materials and symbolic objects associated with rulership and war. At much the same time, Polynesians from Tahiti settled New Zealand, the last large uninhabited landmass except Antarctica.

In East Asia, Song China continued to demonstrate outstanding inventiveness during the 12th century, devising the earliest forms of cannon, and constructing ships with watertight bulkheads and even paddlewheels. By around 1200 China was also using water-powered machinery to produce textiles. The commercial economy was vast and included both local and longer-distance trade. Although merchants ran their own business affairs, the state kept strict political control and did not allow cities autonomy to govern themselves. The division of property equally among children meant that few families stayed wealthy over several generations.

The 12th century witnessed a strong resurgence of cultural life in Western Europe. One consequence of the Investiture Controversy between the pope and the Holy Roman emperor, which came to an end through the Concordat of Worms in 1122, was to draw scholars' attention to the contradictions and inconsistencies in scripture, and in both secular and church law. This led to renewed interest in the works of Classical Greek philosophers, especially Aristotle, and the application of their methods to studying theology and law. The majority of Aristotle's works were translated into Latin from surviving Arabic versions obtained in Muslim Spain, which still maintained a flourishing cultural life despite its political decline. Increased demand for education prompted the foundation of cathedral schools across Europe, some of which developed into universities. Western European architecture produced its first truly original style, Gothic, characterized by pointed arches and soaring vaults. The cultural developments of this period were not restricted to the church: secular literature flourished, as chivalric romances idealized the military aristocracy.

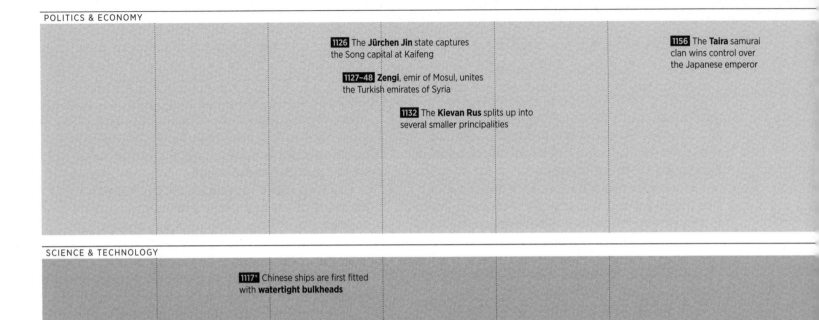

1126 The **Jürchen Jin** state captures the Song capital at Kaifeng

1127–48 **Zengi**, emir of Mosul, unites the Turkish emirates of Syria

1132 The **Kievan Rus** splits up into several smaller principalities

1156 The **Taira** samurai clan wins control over the Japanese emperor

SCIENCE & TECHNOLOGY

1117* Chinese ships are first fitted with **watertight bulkheads**

1100	1110	1120	1130	1140	1150

RELIGION & PHILOSOPHY

1122 The **Concordat of Worms** ends the Investiture Controversy between the papacy and the Holy Roman emperors

1140 Italian jurist Gratian's *Decretum* applies dialectic (logic) to the study of law

ART & ARCHITECTURE

1100* Cahokia, Illinois: **Monks Mound**, the largest pre-Columbian structure in North America, is completed

1113–50 Cambodia: The Khmer king Suryavaraman II begins construction of the **Angkor Wat** temples

1123 The Persian poet and scientist **Omar Khayyam** dies

1144 The abbey church of St Denis, near Paris, considered the **first building in the Gothic style**, is completed

1168 The **Toltec state** in Mexico collapses

1169–77 Saladin establishes himself as leader of Egypt and Syria, founding the **Ayyubid sultanate**

1175–1200 **Muhammad of Ghur** conquers northern India

1185 The **Minamoto** samurai clan defeats the Taira at the sea battle of Dan-no-ura

1187 **Saladin** defeats the crusaders at Hattin and recaptures Jerusalem

1192 Samurai leader **Minamoto Yoritomo** becomes the first shogun of Japan

1200* Polynesians from Tahiti settle **New Zealand**

1200* The **Chimú** expansion in the coastal lowlands of Peru begins

1204 The **Fourth Crusade** captures Constantinople

1204–6 Temujin unites the Mongol tribes and takes the title **Chinggis** (Genghis) **Khan**

1206 Muhammad of Ghur is murdered: **Qutb-ud-Din** seizes power and founds a sultanate at Delhi

1198 The Spanish Muslim philosopher and scientist **Ibn Rushd** (Averröes) dies

1200* **Water-powered textile machinery** is used in China for the first time

1160	1170	1180	1190	1200	1210

1170 The **University of Paris** is founded

1191 **Zen Buddhism** is introduced to Japan from China

1200* The **Southeastern Ceremonial Complex** develops among the Mississippian cultures

1193 The **Qubbat-ul-Islam mosque** is begun at Delhi

1200* Lalibela, Ethiopia: **Rock-cut churches** are built by the Ethiopian Orthodox church

1200* The temple mounds and plaza at **Moundville**, Alabama, are constructed

1ST–12TH CENTURIES

1207–1295

A NOMADIC WORLD

NOMADS DOMINATED the 13th century. The Mongol ruler Chinggis (Genghis) Khan sought success in war to consolidate the nomadic tribes he ruled, and in 1209 he began seventy years of conquests across Eurasia with raids on Xixia and the Uighurs (in present-day western China). By the time of his death in 1227, Chinggis Khan's empire stretched from Manchuria in the east to the Caspian Sea in the west. The speed, manoeuvrability and firepower of the Mongol armies' disciplined cavalry archers overwhelmed all opposition.

The Mongols systematically committed horrific atrocities, coercing many of their enemies to submit quickly and subsuming defeated forces into Mongol armies to fuel further conquests. Mongol attacks continued in East Asia, the Middle East and the Russian lands under Chinggis Khan's successors, his son Ögedei and his grandsons Güyük and Möngke. By 1259, the Mongols ruled the largest empire the world had ever seen, to be exceeded in area only by the future British empire.

In 1260, Khubilai Khan – another of Chinggis's grandsons – became Great Khan. His victory over the Chinese Song dynasty in 1279 was the last major Mongol conquest, but the nomads' campaigns had depopulated northern China, shifting the demographic and economic balance of the country to the south for the first time. Khubilai's later attempts to extend his rule to Japan and Southeast Asia ended in failure, and to the south and west, the sultanate of Delhi and the Mamluk sultanate of Egypt successfully repelled Mongol invasions. As the Mongol empire was too vast to be ruled by a single khan, subordinate khanates were created to govern the western conquests; after Khubilai's accession as Great Khan, the western khanates effectively became independent. Besides northern China, worst affected by the savage and destructive Mongol conquests was the Middle East: the nomads' sack of Baghdad in 1258 saw the destruction not only of the Abbasid caliphate but also of the city's great libraries, whose scholars were massacred.

However, the khans' rule eventually brought peace and security to a vast area of Eurasia, greatly increasing trade and cultural contacts between China and the West along the so-called 'Silk Roads'. By the end of the 13th century, the Mongols themselves were beginning to be assimilated by the peoples they had conquered. The Qipchaq khanate (Golden Horde) officially adopted the language of its mainly Turkish subjects; in the 14th century, along with the Mongol Ilkhans of Persia, it would adopt Islam, stoking the bitter hostility of its Christian Russian tributaries. Further east, Khubilai Khan adopted the Chinese dynastic name Yuan and the entire apparatus of Chinese imperial government. Traditional Mongol culture survived only on the Eurasian steppes, where the Mongols could continue their nomadic way of life.

In this period, West Africa came to be dominated by the Mali empire under its founding ruler Sunjata Keita.

Mali prospered by controlling the region's gold mines – the world's most important source of gold before the European colonization of the Americas. Southern Africa, meanwhile, witnessed the rise of its first major kingdom at Great Zimbabwe. In Mesoamerica, the Aztecs settled in the Valley of Mexico during the 13th century, adopting many aspects of the Toltec culture that had previously controlled the area.

The cultural revival of Western Europe continued in this period, with major technological developments including the invention of both the mechanical clock and the first reading glasses. One consequence of wider literacy was the rise of popular heretical movements challenging church authority on doctrine: these were suppressed by the Inquisition and the crusades. Crusaders enjoyed success against Europe's last remaining pagans in the Baltic, but were expelled from the Holy Land and the Byzantine empire.

1209 **Chinggis** (Genghis) **Khan** begins the Mongol conquest of Xixia and the Uighur khanates in modern-day western China

1210–30* Manco Qhapaq founds the **Inca** state at Cusco

1210–90* The **Aztecs** enter the Valley of Mexico

1211–36 **Iltutmish**, sultan of Delhi, consolidates Muslim power in northern India

1215 King John of England seals the **Magna Carta**, limiting the power of the monarchy

1220* The kingdom of **Great Zimbabwe** emerges in southern Africa

1227 **Chinggis Khan** dies: he is succeeded by his son Ögedei two years later

1230* **Mali** in western Africa becomes a great power under its founder Sunjata Keita

1241 The foundation of the **Qipchaq khanate** (Golden Horde) begins the break-up of the Mongol empire into separate khanates

1234 Korea: **Metal movable-type printing** is invented

1200	**1210**	**1220**	**1230**	**1240**	**1250**

1223–24 Crusaders besiege **Tartu**, the last pagan stronghold on the Estonian mainland

1232 The papacy sets up the **Inquisition** to fight heretical ideas

1200–75* The **Icelandic family sagas** are written

1200–1300 The **Great Enclosure** is built at Great Zimbabwe

1214 The monk **Esai** writes the first Japanese book about tea, *Kissa Yojoki*

1258 The Mongols sack **Baghdad** and execute the last Abbasid caliph

1260 **Khubilai Khan** becomes Great Khan of the Mongol empire

1260 Palestine: The Egyptian Mamluks defeat the Mongols at the battle of **'Ain Jalut**

1261 The Byzantine empire recaptures **Constantinople** from the crusaders

1268–79 Khubilai Khan conquers the Song empire, marking the start of the **Yuan dynasty**

1270 The **Solomonic dynasty** comes to power in Ethiopia

1287 Burma: The Mongols sack **Bagan**, and the city is permanently abandoned

1294 **Khubilai Khan** dies

1260 Early **hand guns** (hand cannons) are used by Mamluk armies

1270–1300* Europe: The **mechanical clock** is invented

1290* Italy: Wearable **reading glasses** are invented

1260 **1270** **1280** **1290** **1300**

1260–77* King **Mansa Uli** of Mali makes the *hajj* (pilgrimage) to Mecca

1274 The theologian **Thomas Aquinas**, the greatest exponent of scholasticism, dies

1292* Death of English philosopher **Roger Bacon**, an early advocate of empirical scientific methods

1295 The Ilkhan **Ghazan** converts to Islam

1258 Baghdad: The Mongols destroy the library of the **House of Wisdom**

1296–1405

FROM PLAGUE TO RENAISSANCE

IN CHINA, the power of the Mongol Yuan dynasty faded after Khubilai Khan's death in 1294. In 1351 the Red Turban peasant rebellion broke out, and in 1368 the rebel leader Zhu Yuanzhang expelled the Mongols and proclaimed himself the first emperor of the Ming dynasty. The Ming revived traditional Chinese imperial customs and restored the agricultural economy after a century of neglect under the Mongols. Experience of Mongol rule left a legacy of xenophobia in China, and the Ming dynasty was more inward looking than its predecessors.

Mongol rule in the Middle East ended earlier with the break-up of the Ilkhanate in 1335. The Qipchaq khanate ('Golden Horde') continued to dominate the Russian lands, but it had become effectively a Tatar (Turk) state. The last conqueror in the nomadic Mongol tradition was Timur (Tamerlane), who claimed descent from Chinggis (Genghis) Khan but was linguistically and culturally a Turk. Timur, emir of the Silk Road city Samarkand (reigned 1361–1405), reconquered the former Ilkhanate lands and almost destroyed the Central Asian Chagatai khanate. Timur's campaigns temporarily set back the growth of the Ottoman Turk sultanate, which had been founded in Anatolia at the turn of the 14th century. The Ottomans invaded Europe in 1354, making extensive conquests in the Balkans.

Further east, the Delhi sultanate under Muhammad ibn Tughluk began to extend Muslim power into central

India around 1330; much of the newly conquered territory, however, soon broke away under the Bahmani dynasty to form an independent Muslim-ruled state. The Muslim advance southwards was checked by the rise of the Vijayanagara kingdom, a bastion of Hinduism. In Southeast Asia, the kingdom of Siam – from which the modern kingdom of Thailand is directly descended – was founded in 1351. During this period, Indonesia came under the commercial domination of the maritime Majapahit kingdom, based on Java and the last major Hindu power of the region. In North America, prolonged drought destroyed the Ancestral Pueblo culture of the Southwest.

Arguably the most important event of this period was the Black Death, a pandemic of bubonic or pneumonic plague that broke out on the Eurasian steppes in 1347: it spread along trade routes to Europe, the Middle East, North Africa, India and China, before burning itself out around 1356. The total mortality can only be guessed at, but in Europe at least a third of the population is thought to have died, creating a serious labour shortage. The plague therefore led to wages and living standards increasing for most working people in Europe, but the income of the landowning aristocracy declined. Attempts by landowners to hold down wages and impose new burdens on tenants caused peasant revolts across the continent. All were violently suppressed, but with contrasting consequences in Eastern and Western Europe.

In the east, a previously largely free peasantry was forced into serfdom; on the other hand, in France serfs gained hereditary rights over their farms, and in England serfdom began to die out altogether. In China, the Black Death contributed to the peasant unrest that ended Mongol rule. Plague remained endemic for centuries, slowing population growth in many parts of Africa and Eurasia.

In Italy, the work of artists such as Giotto, and of the humanist poets Petrarch and Boccaccio, marked the beginning of the Renaissance, a movement that would transform the outlook of Western Europe over the following two centuries. Italian merchants' invention of double-entry bookkeeping around 1300 was a sign of increasingly complex economic development, while this period also witnessed the first use of gunpowder weapons in Europe. In Japan, the 14th century saw the development of classical Noh musical theatre, featuring masked characters and men playing female roles. In India, the Vijayanagara kingdom became a major centre of Hindu literature, art and architecture thanks to the generous patronage of its rulers: its capital's many hundreds of temples were built in a distinctive and eclectic style, incorporating features from a variety of earlier Hindu architectural models.

1299* The reign of Osman I, first ruler of the **Ottoman** sultanate in Anatolia, begins

1300* Italian merchants develop **double-entry bookkeeping**, the basis of modern accounting

1300* The **Ancestral Pueblo** culture of the American Southwest declines due to prolonged droughts

1330* Sultan Muhammad ibn Tughluk extends the power of the **Delhi sultanate** to central India

1335 The **Ilkhanate** breaks up into independent Mongol, Turkish and Persian states

1336 The kingdom of **Vijayanagara** is founded: it becomes the major Hindu power of southern India

1337 The **Hundred Years' War** breaks out between England and France

1340 The West African **Songhay** kingdom gains independence from Mali

1296* The oldest surviving **portolan chart** is drafted to improve coastal navigation

1330* **Cannon** is first used in Europe

1290	1300	1310	1320	1330	1340

1305 Pope **Clement V** moves the seat of the papacy from Rome to Avignon

1313 The Qipchaq (Golden Horde) khan Özbeg converts to Islam

1298 Venetian merchant **Marco Polo** dictates an account of his travels in China

1300–75 The Hohokam people of Arizona built multi-storey **great houses**

1305 Padua: the early Renaissance painter Giotto paints his masterpiece **frescoes of the Arena Chapel**

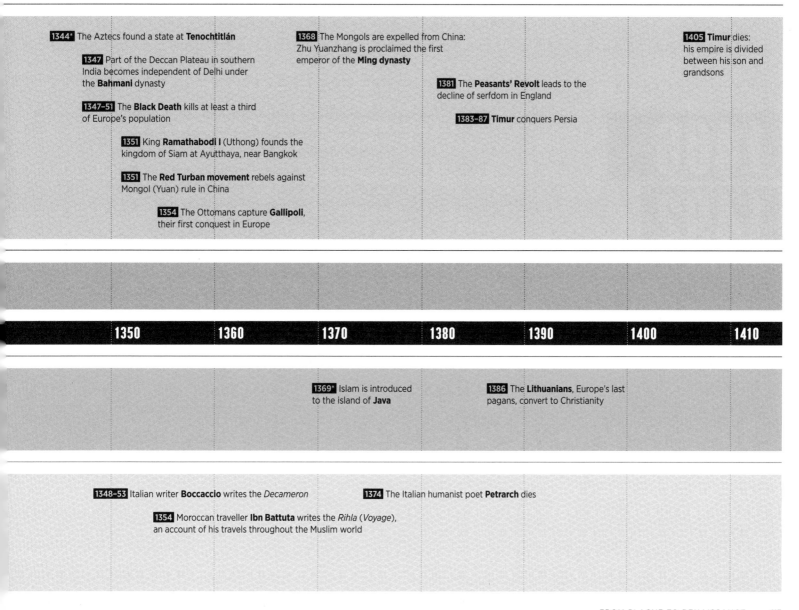

1344* The Aztecs found a state at **Tenochtitlán**

1347 Part of the Deccan Plateau in southern India becomes independent of Delhi under the **Bahmani** dynasty

1347–51 The **Black Death** kills at least a third of Europe's population

1351 King **Ramathabodi I** (Uthong) founds the kingdom of Siam at Ayutthaya, near Bangkok

1351 The **Red Turban movement** rebels against Mongol (Yuan) rule in China

1354 The Ottomans capture **Gallipoli**, their first conquest in Europe

1368 The Mongols are expelled from China: Zhu Yuanzhang is proclaimed the first emperor of the **Ming dynasty**

1381 The **Peasants' Revolt** leads to the decline of serfdom in England

1383–87 **Timur** conquers Persia

1405 **Timur** dies: his empire is divided between his son and grandsons

1350	1360	1370	1380	1390	1400	1410

1369* Islam is introduced to the island of **Java**

1386 The **Lithuanians**, Europe's last pagans, convert to Christianity

1348–53 Italian writer **Boccaccio** writes the *Decameron*

1374 The Italian humanist poet **Petrarch** dies

1354 Moroccan traveller **Ibn Battuta** writes the *Rihla* (*Voyage*), an account of his travels throughout the Muslim world

1406–1492

NEW WORLDS

IN 1492, EXPLORER Christopher Columbus discovered the Americas for the monarchs of Castile – and opened up a 'New World' to Europe. Columbus's landfall in the Caribbean was one of the major turning points of world history and began Europe's progress from relative isolation at the margins of the known world to a position of global dominance. The significance of Columbus's discovery, however, did not become evident for several decades.

Columbus's expedition across the Atlantic, and parallel Portuguese voyages along the West African coast, were the product of a European sense of vulnerability and exclusion. European consumers resented the cost of buying luxury goods, such as eastern spices and Chinese silks, through Muslim middlemen. Europeans were similarly alarmed by the resurgent Muslim power of the Ottoman Turk empire, which in 1453 conquered Constantinople, extinguishing the sad remnants of Byzantium.

Portugal hoped to trade directly with East Asia, and gain allies against Muslim states, by finding a sea route around Africa: Bartolomeu Dias successfully rounded the Cape of Good Hope in 1487–88. Columbus firmly believed that the lands he had discovered were part of East Asia, but other explorers who followed him across the Atlantic soon realized that he had actually discovered unsuspected continents. The Mesoamerican Aztec and Andean Inca empires, the greatest states that the Americas had so far seen, were equally unaware of the 'Old World'.

European expansion was made possible in the 15th century through advances in shipbuilding and navigation led by Portugal. Feudalism declined as rulers curtailed the independence of their aristocracies and created strong, centralized governments. This period also saw the cultural transformation of the Renaissance spread outside Italy: a major advance was Johannes Gutenberg's invention of the first movable-type printing press, with which he published the first commercially printed book, the *Gutenberg Bible*, in 1455. Printing increased the speed and reduced the costs of producing books, making them available to a much wider public, and by 1492 the technology had spread throughout Catholic Europe.

The Roman Catholic church reasserted its authority after a split in the late 14th century that had led to rival popes sitting at Rome and Avignon. In tandem with lay rulers' support for overseas exploration, the church also began to expand outside Europe: in Africa, the king of Kongo accepted forced conversion by the Portuguese missionaries in 1490. Granada, the last remaining Muslim enclave in Spain, was conquered by Castile in 1492 and the Spanish Inquisition supervised the conversion or expulsion of the Muslim and Jewish communities there. Following the fall of the Byzantine empire, Moscow assumed leadership of the Orthodox church. When Prince Ivan III began to use the title Tsar (Caesar) in 1472, he was consciously appropriating the Byzantine tradition, and he declared that Moscow had become the 'third Rome'. Despite Ottoman military success, Islam did not make great headway in either Greece or the Balkans, where the majority of the population stayed loyal to Orthodoxy. Islam continued to win converts in Africa and, especially, Indonesia.

Although the world's richest and most technologically advanced state in 1492, China – in contrast to European expansionism – had turned inwards. Earlier in the 15th century, the Ming emperors had launched a series of naval expeditions to Southeast Asia, India and East Africa to proclaim that China had re-established itself as a great power after the long years of Mongol occupation. But a resurgence of nomadic power forced the Ming to abandon their maritime ambitions and concentrate instead on fortifying their northern frontier by building, at vast expense, the Great Wall of China. Despite these external threats, intellectual life flourished under the Ming dynasty, with a huge effort sponsored by the state to edit and consolidate the canon of Chinese literature and learning in vast encyclopaedic works.

1405–33 Admiral **Zheng He** leads Chinese naval expeditions to Southeast Asia, the Middle East and East Africa

1407–28 China occupies the Vietnamese kingdom of **Dai Viet**

1421 **Beijing** becomes the capital of China's Ming dynasty

1428 Itzcóatl, king of Tenochtitlan, begins the expansion of the **Aztec empire**

1431 After the Thais sack **Angkor**, the Khmer capital is moved to Phnom Penh

1438 **Albert II** of Austria becomes the first Habsburg Holy Roman emperor

1441 Portugal begins the **slave trade** with West Africa

SCIENCE & TECHNOLOGY

1420* **Portolan navigational maps** are produced in Portugal

1433 Emir Ulugh Beg builds an **astronomical observatory** at Samarkand

1435 **Three-masted sailing ships** capable of oceanic voyages come into use

1436–55* Johannes Gutenberg develops the **movable-type printing press** in Europe

| 1400 | 1410 | 1420 | 1430 | 1440 |

RELIGION & PHILOSOPHY

1409 The **Yellow Hat school** of Tibetan Buddhism is founded

1417 The **Council of Constance** ends the Great Schism of the papacy

1431 **Joan of Arc** is burned by English forces at Rouen for heresy

ART & ARCHITECTURE

1406 The North African polymath **Ibn Khaldun**, author of works on historiography, social theory, government and economics, dies

1420–36 Italian architect Brunelleschi designs the dome of **Florence cathedral**

1430 Construction of the Inca sacred city of **Machu Picchu** begins

1450* **Great Zimbabwe** is supplanted by the Mutapa kingdom in southern Africa

1451 The **Afghan Lodi dynasty** wins control of the sultanate of Delhi

1453 The Ottoman Turks capture **Constantinople**, ending the Byzantine empire

1453 The **Hundred Years' War** ends with English defeat at Castillon

1464 **Songhay** supplants Mali as the major power in West Africa

1467–77 The **Onin War** leads to the rise of *daimyo* (warlords) and feudalism in Japan

1470 The Incas conquer the **Chimú empire**

1492 **Columbus**, sailing on behalf of Castile, crosses the Atlantic and reaches the Caribbean

1492 The fall of **Granada** completes the Catholic *Reconquista* (reconquest) of Spain

| 1450 | 1460 | 1470 | 1480 | 1490 |

1469 Guru Nanak, founder of the **Sikh religion**, is born

1478 The **Spanish Inquisition** is founded by Ferdinand of Aragon and Isabella of Castile

1490 King **Nzinga Nkuwu** of Kongo is converted to Christianity by Portuguese missionaries

1454 Construction of the **Topkapi Palace** in Constantinople begins

1455 The first commercially printed book, the *Gutenberg Bible*, is published at Mainz

1474 The Ming dynasty begins construction of the **Great Wall of China**

1493– 1532

EMPIRE AND DISSENT

TO PREVENT CONFLICT between the Iberian powers over the newly discovered lands of the Americas, in 1494 the papacy negotiated the treaty of Tordesillas, which divided the world into Portuguese and Spanish spheres of interest. As Portugal seized control of the lucrative East Indian spice trade from Muslim merchants and founded the first European colonies in India, it seemed that they had the better side of the deal.

But in 1519–21, Hernán Cortés and his tiny band of conquistadors discovered and conquered the Aztec empire of Mexico, and huge amounts of plundered gold and silver flooded into Spain. At the same time, epidemics of European diseases introduced by the conquistadors claimed vast numbers of native American lives and left the survivors demoralized. Similarly, in the 1520s the Inca empire reached its height under Wayna Qhapaq, but his unexpected death in a smallpox epidemic – which had spread south from a Spanish colony at Panama – threw the empire into civil war.

Spain's Habsburg ruler, Charles V (reigned 1516–56 and elected Holy Roman emperor in 1519), who also ruled Austria, Bohemia, the Netherlands and parts of Italy, became Europe's most powerful ruler. Charles's power, however, was threatened from within by the Protestant Reformation, and from outside by the Ottoman empire and France, which fought against encirclement by Habsburg lands. In 1526 the Ottomans crushed the Hungarians, and three years later they laid siege to the Austrian capital, Vienna. Although the siege failed, Hungary remained mostly under Ottoman rule.

Earlier in the 16th century, the Ottomans had conquered Syria, Palestine and Egypt, and had also captured northern Mesopotamia from Persia, recently re-established as a territorial state by the Safavid dynasty. To restore Persia after centuries of division and foreign rule, the Safavids worked to create a cohesive identity that would unite their subjects in loyalty to the state: by imposing Shi'a Islam as the state religion, they deliberately sowed dissension between the Persians and their rival Sunni Ottomans and Arabs. Safavid rulers were also generous patrons of the arts, promoting distinctive Persian decorative styles. Further east, in 1504 the Mughal leader Babur, a descendant of Timur and Chinggis Khan, established a state around Kabul (capital of modern-day Afghanistan); in 1526 he invaded India and captured Delhi, establishing the Mughal empire.

European political and cultural life in the 16th century was dominated by the Protestant Reformation, whose adherents rejected the spiritual authority of the papacy and founded a major new branch of Christianity alongside Roman Catholicism and Orthodoxy. The German monk Martin Luther instigated the Reformation in 1517 by attacking spiritual and financial abuses in the Catholic church. Although Luther was condemned as a heretic by the Catholic establishment, he found powerful protectors in the princes of northern Germany. Luther's theology justified the seizure of church lands, allowing the princes to enrich themselves at the church's expense; yet they also converted to Protestantism for political reasons, to assert their independence against their Habsburg overlord Charles V. In 1531, civil war divided the Holy Roman empire as the Protestant princes formed the Schmalkaldic League to defy Charles's attempt to enforce Catholic supremacy.

Earlier challenges to the authority of the papacy had failed because they had lacked support among the ruling classes, but conditions in the early 16th century were more favourable. The wealth that became the focus of reformers' complaints was very visible in Rome, thanks to the papacy's lavish patronage of artists such as Michelangelo and its ambitious plans for the re-construction of St Peter's basilica. Luther's ideas spread quickly and widely as print technology, now well established, meant that religious tracts could be produced cheaply and in large numbers. Nevertheless, the reform movement began to fragment almost immediately over disagreements about doctrine: the Swiss reformer Huldrych Zwingli, for example, advocated a more extreme form of Protestantism than Luther.

POLITICS & ECONOMY

1494 The **treaty of Tordesillas** divides the world between Portugal and Spain

1499 The **Swabian War**: the Swiss Confederacy becomes independent of the Holy Roman empire

1504 The **Mughals** under Babur conquer Kabul

1508 Portugal defeats the Indian Bijapur sultanate and establishes a colony at **Goa**

SCIENCE & TECHNOLOGY

1500* Hungary: The first **four-wheeled horse-drawn coaches** with steering and suspension are built

1500   **1510**

RELIGION & PHILOSOPHY

1497 Jews are expelled from **Portugal**

1501–24 Safavid shah **Ismail I** makes Shi'a Islam the state religion of Persia

ART & ARCHITECTURE

1501–4 **Michelangelo** creates his sculpture *David*

1508 **Sogi**, author of Japanese *renga* ('collaborative') poetry, dies

1503* **Leonardo da Vinci** paints the *Mona Lisa*

1514 The Ottomans defeat the **Safavids** at Chaldiran and conquer northern Mesopotamia

1516 The political union of Castile and Aragon creates the kingdom of **Spain**

1517 The Ottomans conquer **Egypt**

1517 Spain begins to regularly traffic African slaves to the **Caribbean**

1519 Charles, king of Spain, is elected Holy Roman emperor **Charles V**

1519–21 **Hernán** Córtes conquers the Aztec empire of Mexico for Spain

1520 **Suleiman the Magnificent** accedes to the Ottoman throne

1520–21 Portuguese merchants establish direct **maritime trade** between China and Europe

1521 The first Portuguese colonies are founded in **Brazil**

1523 Japanese *wako* **pirates** attack eastern China

1526 The Ottomans defeat the Hungarians at **Mohács**

1526 **Babur** defeats the Delhi sultanate at Panipat, conquering northern India

1529 The Ottoman siege of **Vienna** fails

1531 Protestant German princes form the **Schmalkaldic League** to defend their territories against the Catholic Holy Roman emperor Charles V

1520* The Swiss alchemist Paracelsus artificially produces **hydrogen gas** for the first time

1520

1530

1517 German monk **Martin Luther** writes his *Ninety-Five Theses* against abuses in the Catholic church, beginning the **Protestant Reformation**

1523 Swiss Protestant reformer **Huldrych Zwingli** persuades Zurich to abolish Catholic worship

1529 The Chinese neo-Confucian philosopher **Wang Yangming** dies

1513 Italian diplomat **Niccolò Machiavelli** writes *The Prince*, a treatise on statecraft considered amoral by contemporaries

1525* Beginning of the **Safavid school** of manuscript painting and illumination

1533–1598

COLONIZATION, REFORMATION AND COUNTER-REFORMATION

THE EUROPEAN IMPACT on the Americas was already considerable by 1600. Even areas that had not witnessed direct contact with Europeans were devastated by depopulation and social dislocation from European epidemic diseases. In 1531 the Spanish conquistador Francisco Pizarro invaded and conquered the Inca empire of South America, bringing Spain fabulous quantities of gold and control of the world's richest silver mines. Used to buy Asian luxuries, much of this silver made its way across the world to China and India, marking the opening of newly global economic relationships.

This period also saw the beginning of the Portuguese colonization of Brazil and the first, unsuccessful, attempts by England and France to colonize North America. Further south, the rapid decline of the native American population led Portugal and Spain to rely increasingly on the labour of slaves trafficked from Africa to staff their sugar plantations in Brazil and the Caribbean. In East Africa, meanwhile, Portuguese forces helped the Christian Ethiopian empire resist an invasion by its neighbour, the Islamic Adal sultanate under Ahmed Gran.

In the Middle East, the Ottoman empire consolidated its position as the leading Muslim power with further conquests in North Africa, Arabia, Mesopotamia and the Caucasus; its defeat, however, by the Spanish-led Holy League in 1571 at the naval battle of Lepanto showed Europeans that the empire was not invincible. Meanwhile, the Mughal empire's hold on northern India was shaken by the Suri rebellion of 1539–56, but under Akbar the Great (reigned 1556–1605) the empire recovered, conquering the Rajputs, Gujarat and the wealthy region of Bengal, to become one of the world's most powerful states.

Following a civil war in the late 15th century, Japan broke up into hundreds of autonomous feudal principalities as the authority of the shogunate collapsed. In the last two decades of the 16th century, a succession of able warlords reunified Japan: this process culminated in 1600 with the foundation of the Tokugawa shogunate, which ruled Japan until 1868. Across the East China Sea, the late Ming dynasty was a time of cultural brilliance but political weakness, as emperors struggled to contain successive economic crises, which were exacerbated by the huge expense of building the Great Wall.

In Western religion, the papacy responded to the Reformation by launching the Counter-Reformation to re-emphasize the tenets of the Catholic faith; it relied heavily on the intellectual Jesuit Order to educate Catholics in the faith and to counter Protestant arguments. Two major new Protestant movements emerged: the French reformer John Calvin's uncompromising version of Protestantism spread to Switzerland, France, the Netherlands and Scotland, while in England Anglicanism remained doctrinally closer to Catholicism than Lutheranism.

These dogmatic conflicts plunged Europe into a century of wars. The civil war that had plagued the Holy Roman empire for two decades finally ended in 1555 with the Peace of Augsburg, which allowed princes to decide the religion of their subjects. Charles V's failure to suppress Protestantism led to his abdication in 1556 and the division of the Habsburg dynasty into Spanish and Austrian branches: both remained strong supporters of Catholicism. Spain's attempt to eradicate Protestantism in the Netherlands provoked a long war of independence, while Philip II's attempt to invade England in 1588 (the 'Spanish Armada') and overthrow its Protestant queen Elizabeth I was defeated. France, too, suffered religious conflict, brought to a close by the Edict of Nantes in 1598, which granted toleration to Protestantism.

Despite these upheavals, there were important cultural developments in Europe in astronomy, architecture and cartography: Gerardus Mercator produced his famous world map in 1569. This period also saw the creation of magnificent Ottoman architecture, especially the mosques at Istanbul and Edirne built by Mimar Sinan for sultans Suleiman the Magnificent and Selim. The Sikh faith's most important monument, the Golden Temple at Amritsar, was similarly begun at this time.

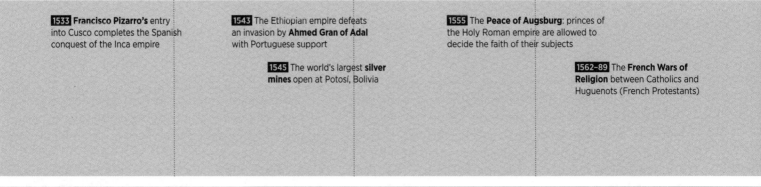

POLITICS & ECONOMY

1533 **Francisco Pizarro's** entry into Cusco completes the Spanish conquest of the Inca empire

1543 The Ethiopian empire defeats an invasion by **Ahmed Gran of Adal** with Portuguese support

1545 The world's largest **silver mines** open at Potosí, Bolivia

1555 The **Peace of Augsburg**: princes of the Holy Roman empire are allowed to decide the faith of their subjects

1562–89 The **French Wars of Religion** between Catholics and Huguenots (French Protestants)

SCIENCE & TECHNOLOGY

1542 Portuguese sailors introduce **firearms** to Japan

1530   1540   1550   1560

RELIGION & PHILOSOPHY

1534 Spanish priest **Ignatius Loyola** founds the Society of Jesus (the Jesuits)

1541 French theologian **John Calvin** introduces a strict form of Protestantism to Geneva

1545 The **Council of Trent** launches the Catholic Counter-Reformation

1548–51 The first Christian mission to **Japan** arrives in Kyoto

1554–58 *Popol Vuh* (Book of Counsel), an account of Maya gods and myths written in both Quiché Maya and European script, is compiled

1555 Portuguese Jesuits undertake a mission to **Ethiopia**

ART & ARCHITECTURE

1533 French writer **Michel de Montaigne**, who established the essay as a literary form, is born

1550–57 Istanbul: Mimar Sinan's **Suleimaniye mosque** is built

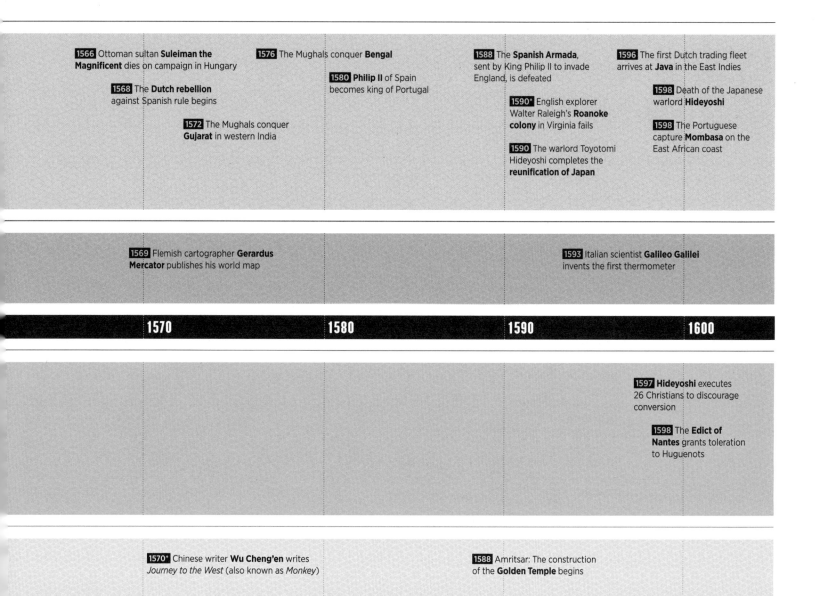

1566 Ottoman sultan **Suleiman the Magnificent** dies on campaign in Hungary

1568 The **Dutch rebellion** against Spanish rule begins

1572 The Mughals conquer **Gujarat** in western India

1576 The Mughals conquer **Bengal**

1580 **Philip II** of Spain becomes king of Portugal

1588 The **Spanish Armada**, sent by King Philip II to invade England, is defeated

1590* English explorer Walter Raleigh's **Roanoke colony** in Virginia fails

1590 The warlord Toyotomi Hideyoshi completes the **reunification of Japan**

1596 The first Dutch trading fleet arrives at **Java** in the East Indies

1598 Death of the Japanese warlord **Hideyoshi**

1598 The Portuguese capture **Mombasa** on the East African coast

1569 Flemish cartographer **Gerardus Mercator** publishes his world map

1593 Italian scientist **Galileo Galilei** invents the first thermometer

1570 1580 1590 1600

1597 **Hideyoshi** executes 26 Christians to discourage conversion

1598 The **Edict of Nantes** grants toleration to Huguenots

1570* Chinese writer **Wu Cheng'en** writes *Journey to the West* (also known as *Monkey*)

1588 Amritsar: The construction of the **Golden Temple** begins

1598

THE FIRST GLOBAL EMPIRE

The European maritime discoveries of the late 15th and early 16th centuries began a rapid transformation of the global economy. Western Europe became the hub of a global trading system while Spain built the first truly global empire.

KEY

- Hunter-gatherers
- Pastoral nomads
- Settled farming cultures and peoples
- Complex farming societies/chiefdoms
- Urbanized societies/kingdoms
- Empires
- Portuguese possessions
- Spanish possessions
- Uninhabited

IROQUOIS CONFEDERACY

VICEROYALTY OF NEW SPAIN

Cusco

VICEROYALTY OF NEW PERU

BRAZIL

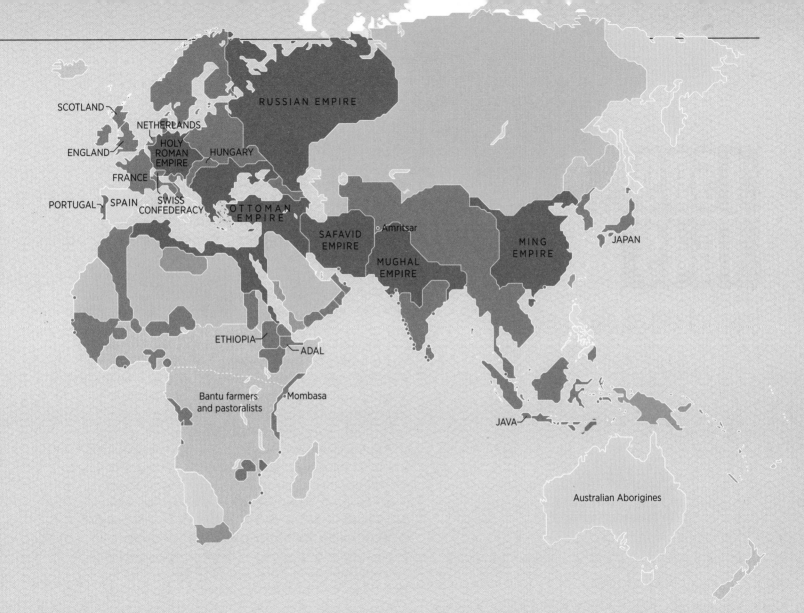

SCOTLAND

NETHERLANDS

ENGLAND

HOLY
ROMAN
EMPIRE

HUNGARY

RUSSIAN EMPIRE

FRANCE

PORTUGAL

SPAIN

SWISS
CONFEDERACY

OTTOMAN
EMPIRE

SAFAVID
EMPIRE

Amritsar

MING
EMPIRE

JAPAN

MUGHAL
EMPIRE

ETHIOPIA

ADAL

Bantu farmers
and pastoralists

Mombasa

JAVA

Australian Aborigines

1599–1649

CONFLICT AND COLONIZATION

POLITICALLY, THE FIRST half of the 17th century was marked by uprisings and conflict. In China, the costs of defending the Ming empire bore heavily on the peasantry. Widespread peasant rebellions broke out in 1628, and in 1641 rebel regimes began to seize power in the provinces. Exploiting this chaos, the Manchus invaded China in 1644, destroyed the rebel forces and seized power, installing their own Qing dynasty on the throne. From the outset, the Qing began to assimilate themselves to Chinese culture while retaining their own distinctive ethnicity.

In Europe, post-Reformation religious conflicts became entwined with a constitutional crisis in the Holy Roman empire's ruling Habsburg dynasty, precipitating the Thirty Years' War (1618–48). Although the war began as a Protestant revolt against the Catholic Habsburg emperor Ferdinand II, other powers could not ignore the troubles of the empire, and gradually most of Europe was drawn into the conflict.

The war entered its decisive phase when France declared war on the Habsburgs, leading to the effective destruction of the Holy Roman empire as a meaningful political entity (it was finally abolished by Napoleon in 1806). The main beneficiaries of the war were France, which became Europe's strongest power; the Netherlands, whose independence was finally recognized by Spain; and Sweden, which emerged as the great power of the Baltic. England, which avoided the Thirty Years' War, nonetheless suffered its own civil war, leading to the execution of its absolutist king, Charles I, by a victorious Parliament in 1649.

The first decades of the 17th century also saw France, the Netherlands and England join Spain and Portugal as colonial powers. Portugal's colonial interests were neglected after its dynastic union with Spain in 1580, giving the Dutch an opportunity to break the Portuguese monopoly on trade with the East Indies of Southeast Asia. England and France both founded colonies in North America and the Caribbean West Indies, and trading posts in West Africa and India.

European expansionism led to new confrontations across the world. During the 16th century, the Portuguese had introduced both firearms and Christianity to Japan. Firearms played a decisive role in the Japanese wars of reunification, but following the establishment of the Tokugawa shogunate in 1600, the shoguns abolished them. Foreign influences were increasingly kept at arm's length: the Portuguese were expelled for promoting Christianity and Japanese Christians were ruthlessly persecuted; Dutch traders were permitted to remain, but were confined to a single small island near Nagasaki; and the Japanese people themselves were banned from travelling abroad.

Japanese fears were rooted in religious difference: early 17th-century Europeans still held a primarily Christian worldview. God was seen as the ultimate source of political legitimacy and most monarchs claimed to rule by divine right. Religion was never far from the surface in the English Civil War: the Anglican establishment supported the king, while the more extreme Protestant Puritans supported Parliament. The desire to create a godly society was the main aim of the English Puritans who settled in New England in the 1620s.

The first half of the 17th century saw the development of the ornate Baroque architectural style in Italy, alongside some of the finest achievements of Islamic architecture in the Ottoman empire, the Safavid empire and Mughal India. The Italian scientist Galileo, one of the pioneers of using telescopes for astronomy, was prosecuted for heresy by the Roman Inquisition: he had advocated Copernicus's heliocentric universe, which conflicted with the biblical doctrine that the Earth did not move. Kepler's discovery of the laws of planetary motion, however, made the belief that the Earth lay at the centre of the universe increasingly untenable, while the works of the philosophers René Descartes and Francis Bacon show the beginnings of a rationalistic and scientific approach to understanding the world.

1600 Tokugawa Ieyasu founds the **Tokugawa shogunate**, which rules Japan until 1868

1603–18 **Shah Abbas**, Safavid emperor of Persia, seizes Mesopotamia from the Ottoman empire

1607 **Jamestown**, Virginia: Foundation of the first permanent English colony in the Americas

1615 **Nurhachi** becomes the ruler of the Jürchen (Manchu)

1618 Beginning of the **Thirty Years' War**: most of continental Europe is dragged into the conflict

1619 The **first African slaves** are trafficked to the English Virginia colony

1620 The **Pilgrim Fathers** arrive at Cape Cod

1626 The Dutch settle **New Amsterdam** (later New York) as part of the New Netherland colony

1609–19 German astronomer **Johannes Kepler** defines the laws of planetary motion

1609–10 Galileo discovers the **moons of Jupiter** using a telescope

1600   1610   1620

1601 **Matteo Ricci** leads a Jesuit mission to Beijing

1609 Tokugawa Ieyasu prohibits **Christianity** in Japan

1600* English playwright **William Shakespeare** writes his tragedy *Hamlet*

1606 Birth of **Rembrandt**, Dutch painter and printmaker

1611–30 Isfahan: Construction of the **Shah Mosque**, a major achievement of Safavid Persian architecture

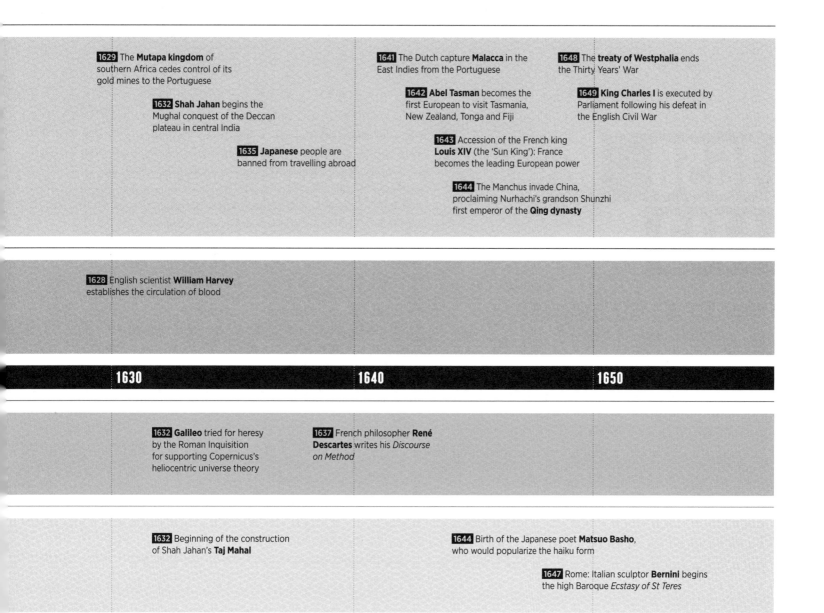

1629 The **Mutapa kingdom** of southern Africa cedes control of its gold mines to the Portuguese

1632 **Shah Jahan** begins the Mughal conquest of the Deccan plateau in central India

1635 **Japanese** people are banned from travelling abroad

1641 The Dutch capture **Malacca** in the East Indies from the Portuguese

1642 **Abel Tasman** becomes the first European to visit Tasmania, New Zealand, Tonga and Fiji

1643 Accession of the French king **Louis XIV** (the 'Sun King'): France becomes the leading European power

1644 The Manchus invade China, proclaiming Nurhachi's grandson Shunzhi first emperor of the **Qing dynasty**

1648 The **treaty of Westphalia** ends the Thirty Years' War

1649 **King Charles I** is executed by Parliament following his defeat in the English Civil War

1628 English scientist **William Harvey** establishes the circulation of blood

1630   **1640**   **1650**

1632 **Galileo** tried for heresy by the Roman Inquisition for supporting Copernicus's heliocentric universe theory

1637 French philosopher **René Descartes** writes his *Discourse on Method*

1632 Beginning of the construction of Shah Jahan's **Taj Mahal**

1644 Birth of the Japanese poet **Matsuo Basho**, who would popularize the haiku form

1647 Rome: Italian sculptor **Bernini** begins the high Baroque *Ecstasy of St Teres*

1650–1713

EXPANSION AND ENLIGHTENMENT

THE TWO GREATEST Muslim powers of the 17th century were both in decline by 1713. The Ottoman empire's final attempt to invade Christian Europe was crushingly defeated at Vienna in 1683. Hungary and Transylvania were lost to the Habsburgs in 1699 and the empire's North African provinces drifted into semi-independence in the first quarter of the 18th century. Under their emperor Aurangzeb (reigned 1658–1707), the Mughals came close to conquering all of India, but increasing religious intolerance provoked frequent Hindu and Sikh revolts. By the time of Aurangzeb's death, the Hindu Marathas had broken away and founded their own kingdom in western India. This marked a turning point in Mughal power, as the death of Aurangzeb led to a weakening in the dynasty's authority.

Further east, the establishment of strong centralized government under the Tokugawa shogunate ushered in a long period of peace, prosperity and stability in Japan. Kabuki theatre, poetry and printmaking flourished, and the Genroku era of 1688–1703 in particular came to be regarded as a cultural golden age. The educated and literate samurai class played an important role in policing and administering Tokugawa Japan; yet although samurai wrote extensively during the period on *bushido*, the samurai code of ethics, their actual military role declined.

The Chinese Qing dynasty's conquest of Mongolia in 1697 marked the beginning of the end of nomad peoples' domination of the Eurasian steppes, as they became inexorably squeezed between the Qing and the rapidly expanding Russian empire. Russia, previously sidelined from mainstream European developments, was rapidly modernizing under Tsar Peter the Great (reigned 1682–1725): his victory over Sweden in the Great Northern War demonstrated his success in turning Russia into a major power.

Western Europe was hardly immune to conflict in this period: two great wars were fought, both for dynastic advantage and to contain the power of Louis XIV's France. In the Nine Years' War, France defeated an alliance of the Netherlands, Austria, England and Spain, while the War of the Spanish Succession was caused by the extinction of the Habsburg line in Spain. The treaty of Utrecht, which ended the second of these in 1713, confirmed France's position as the leading continental European power, but it was forced to make important concessions to Austria and Great Britain (newly formed by the union of England and Scotland in 1707). Britain was now Europe's main financial and naval power, and had become a serious colonial rival to France in North America, the Caribbean and India. European colonial expansion further ushered in a new stage in the history of the Jewish diaspora: in 1654, the first Jewish community in the Americas was established at the Dutch colony of New Amsterdam (later to become New York).

Beyond the political sphere, late 17th-century Europe saw the beginning of the Enlightenment, an intellectual and artistic reaction against the religious wars that followed the Reformation. Enlightenment thinkers emphasized rationalism, empiricism and secularism, stressed the freedom of the individual, and openly questioned sources of political legitimacy and the nature of society. An important aspect of the Enlightenment was the spread of scientific societies and astronomical observatories, promoting the study of 'natural philosophy' (science).

The most important scientific figure of this period was Isaac Newton, whose laws of universal gravity and motion dominated physics until the early 20th century. Newton's invention of the reflecting telescope revealed the clearest views yet of the universe, while the development of the microscope expanded human knowledge in the other direction, revealing organisms too small for the naked eye to see. Another major technological development of the age was Thomas Savery's invention of the first commercially viable steam engine, which could be used to operate pumps in mines. However, belief in old superstitions, such as witchcraft, remained strong, as did religious intolerance. For example, in 1685 Louis XIV revoked the Edict of Nantes, which had in 1598 granted Protestants greater rights in Catholic France.

1659–74 The warrior **Shivaji** defeats the Bijapur kingdom, founding an independent Maratha state

1664 **New Netherland** captured by England: New Amsterdam renamed New York

1670 The English **Hudson's Bay Company** is founded to challenge the French monopoly over the Canadian fur trade

1680* **Plains Indians** begin to use horses for bison hunting

1682 Reign of the modernizing Russian tsar **Peter the Great** begins

1683 The **second Ottoman siege of Vienna** is defeated

SCIENCE & TECHNOLOGY

1668 Isaac Newton builds the first **reflecting telescope**

1674 Antonie van Leeuwenhoek observes bacteria and protozoa using a **microscope**

1650   **1660**   **1670**   **1680**

RELIGION & PHILOSOPHY

1651 **Thomas Hobbes** writes *Leviathan*, his treatise on the nature of society and legitimate government

1654 The first **Jewish settlement** in the Americas is founded at New Amsterdam

ART & ARCHITECTURE

1664–1710 Construction of Louis XIV's palace at **Versailles**

1673 Death, on stage, of the influential French comic and playwright **Molière**

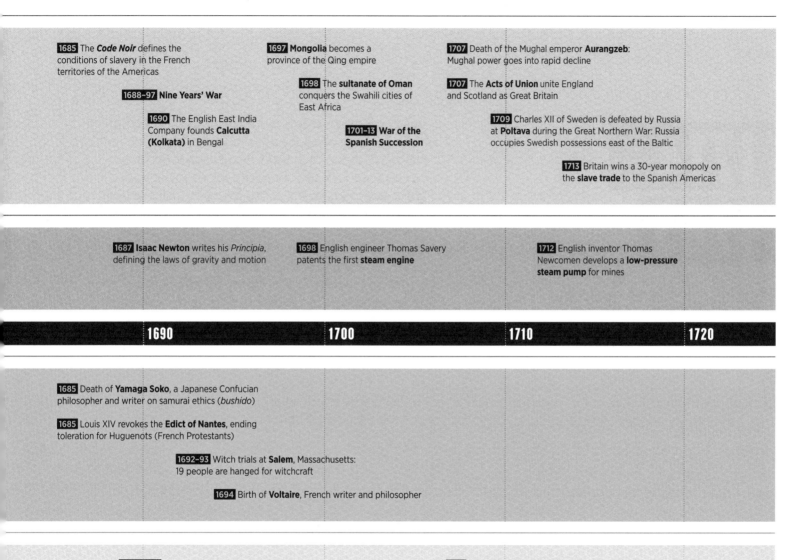

1685 The *Code Noir* defines the conditions of slavery in the French territories of the Americas

1688–97 Nine Years' War

1690 The English East India Company founds **Calcutta (Kolkata)** in Bengal

1697 **Mongolia** becomes a province of the Qing empire

1698 The **sultanate of Oman** conquers the Swahili cities of East Africa

1701–13 War of the Spanish Succession

1707 Death of the Mughal emperor **Aurangzeb**: Mughal power goes into rapid decline

1707 The **Acts of Union** unite England and Scotland as Great Britain

1709 Charles XII of Sweden is defeated by Russia at **Poltava** during the Great Northern War: Russia occupies Swedish possessions east of the Baltic

1713 Britain wins a 30-year monopoly on the **slave trade** to the Spanish Americas

1687 **Isaac Newton** writes his *Principia*, defining the laws of gravity and motion

1698 English engineer Thomas Savery patents the first **steam engine**

1712 English inventor Thomas Newcomen develops a **low-pressure steam pump** for mines

1690   **1700**   **1710**   **1720**

1685 Death of **Yamaga Soko**, a Japanese Confucian philosopher and writer on samurai ethics (*bushido*)

1685 Louis XIV revokes the **Edict of Nantes**, ending toleration for Huguenots (French Protestants)

1692–93 Witch trials at **Salem**, Massachusetts: 19 people are hanged for witchcraft

1694 Birth of **Voltaire**, French writer and philosopher

1688–1703 Kabuki theatre, poetry and printmaking flourish during the **Genroku era** in Japan

1707 Beijing: Beginning of the construction of the **Old Summer Palace**

1714– 1763

FROM INDUSTRY TO SLAVERY

THE COLONIAL RIVALRY between Britain and France came to a head in 1754 with the outbreak of the French and Indian War (1754–63) in North America over rival claims to the Ohio river valley. Britain enjoyed the advantages of naval dominance, greater financial resources and a colonial population of around 1.5 million, compared with France's colonial population of barely 60,000. By 1759 Britain had conquered French North America.

France and Britain also clashed in their colonies in the Caribbean and India. In 1756 the war became subsumed into the Seven Years' War, a European conflict that broke out when Austria, backed by France, Spain and Russia, attacked Prussia, which was supported by Britain. The end of the war in 1763 confirmed Prussia as a great European power, and ensured Britain's position as the leading colonial power and the dominant foreign power in India. British imperial expansion was aided by close attention to the science of navigation: the development of the marine chronometer in the mid-18th century allowed a ship's longitude to be calculated accurately for the first time.

The Qing empire of China, meanwhile, reached its peak during this period, conquering both Tibet and the Dzungar khanate, the last remaining Mongol state. The Safavid dynasty of Persia was overthrown in 1736 by Nader Shah, a brilliant general whose constant campaigning greatly enlarged the Persian empire but ruined its economy.

Following his assassination in 1747, Persian power went into rapid decline. Nader Shah's sack of Delhi in 1739 was the most dramatic sign of the Mughal empire's decline. Hindu Maratha attempts to dominate India in place of the Mughals was brought to a halt by the Afghans at Panipat in 1761, leaving the subcontinent divided among many rival powers.

In economic terms, the early 18th century saw the beginning in Britain of the Industrial Revolution – one of the major turning points in human history. It transformed the society and economy of Great Britain, followed by Europe and North America, and then the rest of the world. The mechanization of production, which was the central characteristic of the Industrial Revolution, enabled a huge increase in production and, eventually, began to deliver greatly improved living standards for ordinary working people. The revolution began with the gradual mechanization of the British textile industry, but even at the end of this period it was still mainly a cottage industry, reliant on manually operated machines.

Britain's industrial development was supported by the control of the Atlantic slave trade it had gained in the treaty of Utrecht. British manufactured goods had little appeal in India or China, but could be sold in West Africa for slaves, who in turn were exchanged in the Caribbean and North America for industrial raw materials such as sugar, cotton, dyes and tobacco. This became known as the 'slave trade triangle'. Alongside the demographic and cultural impact of West African peoples being sold into bondage, the slave trade also began to have a serious destabilizing impact on the internal politics of the region: stronger states, such as Dahomey and Asante, raided their weaker neighbours for captives.

In the Middle East, the Muslim scholar Muhammad ibn Abd al-Wahhab founded the Wahhabi (or Salafi) Islamic fundamentalist movement around 1740. In 1744 he allied with Muhammad ibn Saud, to whom he offered spiritual backing in return for the imposition of Wahhabism in the Saudi lands. In West Africa, the Muslim state of Futa Jalon used the doctrine of *jihad* to justify its conquests of non-Muslim neighbours. Another significant religious development in this period was the foundation of the mystical Hasidic branch of Judaism in what is now western Ukraine.

POLITICS & ECONOMY

1721 **Robert Walpole** becomes the first British prime minister

1724 The French and British economies are shaken by the collapse of the **Mississippi Company** and the **South Sea Company** (the 'South Sea bubble')

1724 **Dahomey**, in West Africa, flourishes as a partner of European slave traffickers

1725 **Futa Jalon** (in modern-day Guinea) becomes a *jihad* state under Ibrahim Sori and Karamoko Alfa

1733–35 The **War of the Polish Succession**: Poland falls under the dominion of Austria and Russia

1736 **Nader Shah** overthrows the Safavid dynasty in Persia

1739 Nader Shah sacks **Delhi**, removing the Mughal Peacock Throne to Persia

1740 Beginning of the reign of **Frederick II** ('the Great') of Prussia

SCIENCE & TECHNOLOGY

1727 Jaipur, India: The **Jantar Mantar** astronomical observatory is built

1735–62 John Harrison perfects the **marine chronometer**, greatly improving the accuracy of navigation

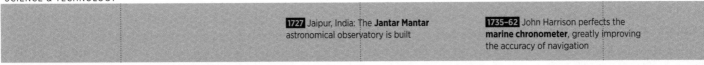

1720   1730   1740

RELIGION & PHILOSOPHY

1739 John Wesley founds the **Methodist** movement

1740* Israel ben Eliezer founds **Hasidic Judaism** in western Ukraine

1740* Muhammad ibn Abd al-Wahhab founds the **Wahhabi** Islamic fundamentalist movement

ART & ARCHITECTURE

1719 Daniel Defoe writes **Robinson Crusoe**, the first great English novel

1726 Compilation of the **Gujin Tushu Jicheng**, an 800,000-page Chinese encyclopaedia covering 10,000 subjects

1742 Dublin, Ireland: Handel's oratorio, **The Messiah**, is first performed

1744 Prince Muhammad ibn Saud founds the first **Saudi state** with Wahhabi support

1747 The assassination of **Nader Shah** leads to decades of political conflict in Persia

1747 Ahmed Shah Durrani founds the **Afghan** state

1750* *Derebeys* (valley lords) become semi-autonomous local rulers in Ottoman Anatolia

1754–63 The **French and Indian War**

1756–63 The **Seven Years' War** pits Austria, Spain, Russia and France against Prussia and Britain

1759 Britain conquers France's North American territories

1761 The Afghans defeat the Marathas at **Panipat**

1763 The **treaty of Paris**: France cedes Canada to Britain; Spain cedes Florida to Britain, but gains Louisiana from France

1751 American scientist and statesman **Benjamin Franklin** writes his *Experiments and Observations on Electricity*

1750　　　1760　　　1770

1762 Jean-Jacques Rousseau writes *The Social Contract*, his work on political legitimacy

1747 Qing emperor Qianlong rebuilds part of the **summer palace** in Beijing in Western style, using Jesuit architects

1750 Death of the German Baroque composer **Johann Sebastian Bach**

1756 Birth of the Austrian classical composer **Wolfgang Amadeus Mozart**

1764–1783

ROMANTICISM AND REVOLT

BRITAIN'S COLONIAL DOMINATION of North America proved short-lived. The British government generally left its American colonies to run their own affairs, without defining their exact status, rights or responsibilities. When the British government tried to recoup some of the costs of the Seven Years' War by taxing its American colonial subjects, the relationship between the two broke down: invoking the slogan 'no taxation without representation', in 1776 the Thirteen Colonies on the Atlantic coast declared independence as the United States of America.

When Britain failed to suppress the rebellion quickly, first France, then Spain and the Netherlands saw an opportunity to regain the territories they had lost in 1763, and joined the war on the side of the Americans. Following defeat at the siege of Yorktown, in 1783 Britain finally recognized American independence, but it had successfully defended the rest of its empire and made only minor territorial concessions to its European rivals.

In India, both Muslim and Hindu rulers struggled to fill the vacuum left by the decline of Mughal power. The British East India Company, which commanded its own army and navy, exploited these divisions to establish itself as a major territorial power on the Indian subcontinent, conquering Bengal, Bihar and the Northern Circars in the 1760s. Meanwhile, in 1770, during his explorations to accurately chart the Pacific, James Cook landed in Australia, claiming it for Britain and bringing an end to the Aborigines' isolation; this spelled the beginning of the end for their ancient Stone Age culture.

The Chinese Qing empire remained the world's richest and most populous state in this period. However, its expansion had ground to a halt after an attempt to conquer Burma ended with a face-saving tributary agreement in 1769. As the long-ruling emperor Qianlong (reigned 1736–95) aged, the government became increasingly corrupt and dysfunctional. High European demand for Chinese products sustained the economy, but around this time the East India Company began to redress the balance of trade by smuggling opium into China from its bases in Bengal.

China would not keep its industrial dominance for much longer. By the 1760s the Industrial Revolution was in full swing in Britain, as a succession of technological innovations, most famously the spinning jenny, made the mechanized mass production of textiles possible. In its earlier stages, the Industrial Revolution had depended on renewable power sources, such as watermills. James Watt's improvements to the design of steam engines transformed them into a viable source of power for large-scale industrial processes, while Britain's growing network of canals allowed coal and other bulk commodities to be transported efficiently around the country. By the end of this period, British industry was becoming rapidly dependent on fossil fuels. Abundant, cheap coal fuelled a rapid increase in iron production, for use not only in weapons and tools but also in construction. The Industrial Revolution also marked the advent of modern economics: in 1776 the Scottish economist Adam Smith published his groundbreaking work *The Wealth of Nations*.

This period saw continuing advances in European science, with important new discoveries in chemistry and astronomy: during this period hydrogen and oxygen were isolated for the first time, and in 1781 William Herschel discovered the planet Uranus. This growing sense that humans were mastering the physical and natural worlds was a major factor in the birth of the Romantic movement, a cultural rebellion against rationalism and materialism that exalted imagination, individualism and the love of wild nature. Romanticism began as a literary movement and was particularly influential in Germany: among its first great works were Goethe's novel *The Sorrows of Young Werther* (1774) and Schiller's play *The Robbers* (1781). Romanticism would grow to exercise a profound influence on European art and music, as well as on literature.

POLITICS & ECONOMY

1765–68 The British **East India Company** seizes control of Bengal, Bihar and the Northern Circars

1769–73 The **Great Bengal Famine**: Ten million people die

1769 **Burma** becomes a tributary of the Qing dynasty

1770–80 Peak of the transatlantic **slave trade**

1770 James Cook lands at Botany Bay and claims **Australia** for Britain

1772 **Edo** (modern-day Tokyo), capital of the Japanese shogunate, is destroyed by fire

1772 The **Tay Son** peasant rebellion breaks out in Tongking and Cochin China (both in modern-day Vietnam)

SCIENCE & TECHNOLOGY

1764* Britain: the invention of the **spinning jenny** advances the industrialization of textile manufacture

1766 British scientist Henry Cavendish discovers **hydrogen**

1769 Scottish inventor James Watt builds the first viable **condensing steam engine**

1760　　　　　1765　　　　　1770

RELIGION & PHILOSOPHY

ART & ARCHITECTURE

1765 Publication of the final text volumes of the *Encyclopédie*, the cornerstone of the French Enlightenment

1772 The Qing emperor **Qianlong** institutes a literary inquisition to purge 'evil' books: over 150,000 volumes are destroyed

1773 The **Boston Tea Party**: American colonists protest against British taxes

1774 **Louis XVI**, the last pre-revolutionary king of France, accedes to the throne

1776 The **United States of America** declare independence from Britain

1776 Scottish economist **Adam Smith** publishes *The Wealth of Nations*, laying the foundations of modern economics

1777 **Rio de Janeiro** becomes the capital of Brazil

1778–80 France, Spain and the Netherlands successively enter the **American War of Independence** against Britain

1780–81 Spain recaptures **Florida** from Britain

1781 Spain defeats an indigenous rebellion in Peru led by **Túpac Amaru II**

1782 Tay Son rebels massacre 10,000 Chinese settlers in **Hanoi**

1783 The **treaty of Paris**: Britain recognizes American independence

1781 American and French forces decisively defeat Britain at **Yorktown**

1774 British scientist Joseph Priestley and Swedish chemist Carl Scheele isolate **oxygen**

1781 Astronomer William Herschel discovers the planet **Uranus**

1775   1780   1785

1773 Pope Clement XIV dissolves the **Society of Jesus** (the Jesuits)

1776 **Thomas Paine**'s *Common Sense* calls for American independence

1781 **Immanuel Kant** writes his *Critique of Pure Reason*

1774 German author **Johann Wolfgang von Goethe** writes his epistolary novel *The Sorrows of Young Werther*

1779 Britain: The world's first **iron bridge** is built over the River Severn in Shropshire

1781 Friedrich Schiller's drama *The Robbers* marks the high point of the German Romantic **'Storm and Stress'** (*Sturm und Drang*) movement

13TH–18TH CENTURIES

1 *The Battle of Vienna 1683*, Franz Geffels, *c.* 1688, p. 134

2 *Portrait of Nader Shah*, Mughal School, *c.* 1740–50, p. 138

3 *The Lamentation of Christ*, Giotto di Bondone, *c.* 1304–6, p. 113

4 Chinggis Khan (*c.* 1162–1227) in combat, from the illuminated manuscript *Jami' al-tawarikh* (Universal History), Rashid-al-Din Hamadani, *c.* 1430, p. 102

5 *Portrait of Queen Elizabeth I* (Armada Portrait), George Gower, *c.* 1588, p. 125

6 *Allegory of the Dominions of Charles V* (detail showing Hernán Cortés), Peter Johann Nepomuk Geiger, 19th century, p. 120

7 *Galileo Galilei before the Holy Office in the Vatican*, Joseph-Nicolas Robert-Fleury, 1847, p. 131

8 Joan of Arc tied to the stake, from the illuminated manuscript *Les Vigiles de Charles VII* (The Vigils of King Charles VII), Martial d'Auvergne, 1475–1500, p. 118

1784–1812

ENLIGHTENED REVOLUTION?

FRANCE'S SUPPORT FOR the American Revolution left its economy ruined. Inflation, food shortages and high taxes, not to mention the successful example of the American colonists, led to the outbreak of revolution in 1789. Threats of Austrian and Prussian intervention came to a head in 1792: France declared war on Austria and repulsed invading Prussian armies at Valmy. Explicit Prussian support for the French monarchy provoked revolutionaries to declare a republic, and Louis XVI was executed in January 1793. French revolutionary fervour sparked over twenty years of near continuous conflict that affected almost all of Europe. Although Britain, secure in its control of the seas, supported a succession of coalitions against France, they were each defeated: by 1812, France dominated continental Europe.

French success was due in large part to the brilliant leadership of Napoleon Bonaparte, who seized power in 1799 and crowned himself emperor five years later. Napoleon overreached himself, however, when he invaded Russia in 1812 to enforce his 'Continental System', which sought to block Britain's trade with continental Europe. The invasion was a disaster: having stalled at Moscow, Napoleon's armies were decimated as they attempted to retreat through the harsh Russian winter. Napoleon found that his strongest supporters outside France were the Poles, who hoped he would restore their country's independence after it had been carved up between Prussia, Austria and Russia in 1795.

Independence rebellions also broke out elsewhere during this period, notably in the Spanish Americas after Napoleon occupied mainland Spain in 1808: Paraguay became the first independent Latin American state in 1811. To raise money for his wars, Napoleon sold Louisiana to the United States, which doubled in size as a result. Thanks to its naval power, Britain was able to pursue its colonial ambitions unhindered during the war years, occupying French and Dutch colonies and expanding its territories in India. Shortly before the war, Britain had established its first penal colony in Australia. Britain and the Ottoman empire expelled a French army from Egypt in 1798–1801, but the Ottoman government was unable to regain full control and the country became effectively independent.

Enlightenment thinkers were critical of Europe's absolute monarchies, often advocating instead principles of individual liberty, representative institutions and the separation of powers. These ideals became all the more potent after they were enshrined in the constitution of the United States in 1787. Compared with their American counterparts, French revolutionaries sought a much more fundamental transformation of society to accord with the Enlightenment notions of reason and secularism: Christianity was replaced with a 'Cult of Reason', and a revolutionary calendar was introduced to signal the start of a new era. As a result of the use of systematic mass terror against both counter-revolutionaries and ideological dissidents within the revolutionaries' own ranks, the French Revolution has often been seen as the prototype of 20th-century communist revolutions. Napoleon ended the revolution, but his *Code Napoléon* enshrined its principles of liberty and equality as the basis of the French system of civil law.

During the 18th century, a strong anti-slavery movement developed in Britain and the USA. In 1802 Denmark became the first European country to ban the slave trade, a move followed by Britain in 1807 (slavery itself was not abolished until 1833 8); it was, however, left unresolved by the US constitution. While many abolitionists had hoped slavery would gradually die out, Eli Whitney's invention of the cotton gin in 1793 enabled a great increase in American cotton production, revitalizing slavery in the southern states.

The French revolutionary principles of the 'rights of man' were not applied to African slaves, but they inspired a successful slave rebellion under Toussaint l'Ouverture in the French colony of Saint-Domingue, which became independent as Haiti. Women also failed to benefit from the supposed equality of the revolution: some of the earliest feminist literature began to appear in Britain and France. Important technological developments of this period included hot air balloon flights, steam locomotives and steamboats.

1787 The **constitution of the United States** is adopted by the Constitutional Convention in Philadelphia

1788 Britain founds a penal colony at **New South Wales** in Australia

1789 The storming of the Bastille begins the **French Revolution**

1789 **George Washington** is elected the first president of the United States

1791 Toussaint l'Ouverture leads a slave rebellion against the French government of **Saint-Domingue**

1792–1802 The **French Revolutionary Wars**: France defeats military interventions by Austria, Prussia and Britain

1793 King **Louis XVI** of France is executed

1796–1804 The **White Lotus** peasant rebellion devastates much of central China

1798 The **battle of the Nile**: Napoleon invades Egypt, but Nelson's Royal Navy destroys the French fleet

---

SCIENCE & TECHNOLOGY

1784 France: The Montgolfier brothers complete the first manned flight in a **hot air balloon**

1793 Eli Whitney invents the **cotton gin**, increasing American cotton production and revitalizing slavery in the southern states

1795 The **metric system** of measurement is adopted in France

1796 British physician Edward Jenner develops a vaccination for **smallpox**

1785   **1790**   **1795**

RELIGION & PHILOSOPHY

1792 **Mary Wollstonecraft** writes *A Vindication of the Rights of Women*, a key early work of feminist philosophy

1793–1801 The revolutionary government abolishes Christianity in **France**

ART & ARCHITECTURE

1799 **Napoleon Bonaparte** becomes dictator of France

1802 **Denmark** becomes the first European country to ban its citizens from participating in the slave trade

1803 The **Louisiana Purchase**: France sells Louisiana to the United States, doubling the latter's size

1803 British forces capture the Mughal capital at **Delhi**

1803–11 The Wahhabi Saudis occupy **Mecca**

1804 **Napoleon** crowns himself emperor of the French

1805 The **battle of Trafalgar**: Nelson's victory over France and Spain confirms British naval supremacy

1805 The **battle of Austerlitz**: Napoleon's armies rout Russian and Austrian forces

1806 Britain occupies the **Dutch Cape Colony**

1806 Napoleon abolishes the **Holy Roman empire** and recognizes Germany as the Confederation of the Rhine

1807 **Britain** abolishes the slave trade

1811 **Paraguay** gains independence after overthrowing its Spanish colonial administration

1812 Napoleon's invasion of **Russia** ends in a calamitous retreat

1812 The **USA** declares war on Britain and invades Canada

1804 British engineer Richard Trevithick builds the first **steam locomotive**

1807 American inventor Robert Fulton launches the first commercially viable **steamboat** on the Hudson River

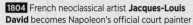

1800   **1805**   **1810**

1804 The ***Code Napoléon*** enshrines liberty and equality as the basis of French civil law, and is subsequently adopted by many European countries

1799 The **Rosetta Stone**, later the key to deciphering ancient Egyptian hieroglyphs, is discovered

1800 German composer **Ludwig van Beethoven** writes the first of his nine symphonies

1804 French neoclassical artist **Jacques-Louis David** becomes Napoleon's official court painter

1812

THE AGE OF EUROPEAN DOMINANCE

In the 17th and 18th centuries, England (later Great Britain), the Netherlands and France all built their own global empires. By 1815, Great Britain had emerged as the pre-eminent global power but, along the way, it lost its most prosperous American colonies, which became the independent United States.

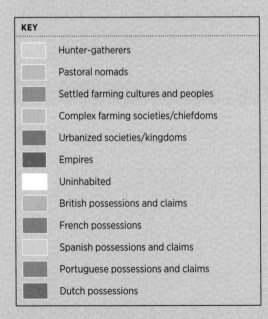

KEY

- Hunter-gatherers
- Pastoral nomads
- Settled farming cultures and peoples
- Complex farming societies/chiefdoms
- Urbanized societies/kingdoms
- Empires
- Uninhabited
- British possessions and claims
- French possessions
- Spanish possessions and claims
- Portuguese possessions and claims
- Dutch possessions

RUSSIAN EMPIRE

Rupert's Land

UPPER AND LOWER CANADA

UNITED STATES OF AMERICA

HAITI

PARAGUAY

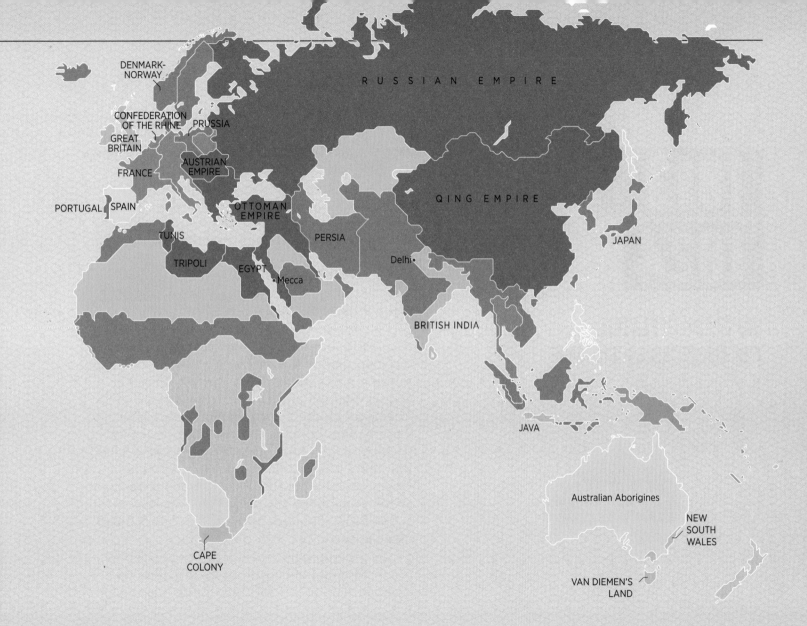

DENMARK-
NORWAY

CONFEDERATION
OF THE RHINE   PRUSSIA

GREAT
BRITAIN

FRANCE

AUSTRIAN
EMPIRE

PORTUGAL   SPAIN

OTTOMAN
EMPIRE

TUNIS

TRIPOLI   EGYPT

•Mecca

RUSSIAN   EMPIRE

QING EMPIRE

PERSIA

Delhi•

JAPAN

BRITISH INDIA

JAVA

Australian Aborigines

CAPE
COLONY

NEW
SOUTH
WALES

VAN DIEMEN'S
LAND

1813–1824

NAPOLEON DEFEATED, THE AMERICAS ASCENDANT

THE CATASTROPHIC FAILURE of Napoleon's Russian campaign was the turning point in his military success. In 1813 a coalition of Prussia, Austria, Russia, Britain and Sweden allied against an increasingly war-weary France. As the allies closed in on Paris in spring 1814, Napoleon abdicated and went into exile on the Italian island of Elba. Although he returned to power in 1815, France's defeat to Britain and Prussia at Waterloo the same year was final: he was exiled again, this time for life, to the remote British island of St Helena in the South Atlantic.

The Congress of Vienna in 1814–15, which was called to resolve the shape of post-Napoleonic Europe, reinstated conservative monarchies and tried to establish a stable balance of power between the continent's nations. The German states were organized into a loose German Confederation under Prussian and Austrian leadership. While the former Austrian Netherlands were united with the kingdom of the Netherlands, Austria was compensated with Venice, Milan and other north Italian city-states. Sweden, which had lost Finland to Russia during the conflicts of the previous decade, was compensated with Norway – at the expense of Denmark, which had consistently backed the losing side.

The Ottoman empire continued its slow decline in this period: following a rebellion, it was forced to grant local autonomy to the Serbs in 1817. Subsequently, when the

Greeks rose up against Ottoman rule in 1821, their cause was taken up by wealthy Western Europeans and Americans influenced by the Romantic movement and their classical education: such figures as the poet Lord Byron saw the Greek struggle as an extension of the ancient Greek wars against Persia. Egypt – one of the Ottomans' nominal dependencies – expanded, conquering Sudan and restoring Ottoman rule in Arabia. Meanwhile, western Africa was destabilized by the rise of the Masina jihadi state, and southern Africa was disrupted by the rise of the Zulu kingdom under Shaka, whose savage campaigns forced entire peoples to flee in the Mfecane ('crushing').

Napoleon's defeat allowed Spain to send troops to suppress the independence movements gaining ground in its South American colonies. However, vast distances, difficult conditions, and charismatic and skilful rebel leaders ultimately defeated the Spanish forces: by 1824, all that was left of the Spanish empire in America were Cuba and Puerto Rico. Inspired by the American Revolution, the leading rebel leader Simón Bolívar hoped to create a United States of Latin America, but differing regional interests were too strong to be overcome. The new states were divided by race and conflicting sectional interests, and frequently fell under the control of military dictatorships. Brazil declared independence from Portugal in 1822, but remained a monarchy under a Portuguese prince.

Elsewhere, Britain continued its empire-building in India and Southeast Asia.

The United States benefited from the decline of Spanish power, gaining Florida in 1819. However, the USA feared that other European powers might use the break-up of the Spanish empire to establish their own influence or control over the newly independent states of Latin America. This led to the proclamation in 1823 of the Monroe Doctrine, opposing further European colonialism in the Americas. This policy could not be effectively enforced at the time (it was mainly British opposition that deterred other European powers from intervening in Latin America), but as American power grew later in the 19th century it became a major principle of US foreign policy.

Another sign of American assertiveness was its declaration of war against Britain in 1812 because of border tensions with Canada and Britain's interference in neutral shipping. Although peace was agreed in 1814, slow transatlantic communications meant that fighting continued into 1815. Only minor concessions were made on either side, but the agreement that future disputes would be settled by arbitration allowed the USA and Canada to expand westwards without coming into violent conflict. Success in repelling American invaders during the war also fostered a new sense of Canadian national identity.

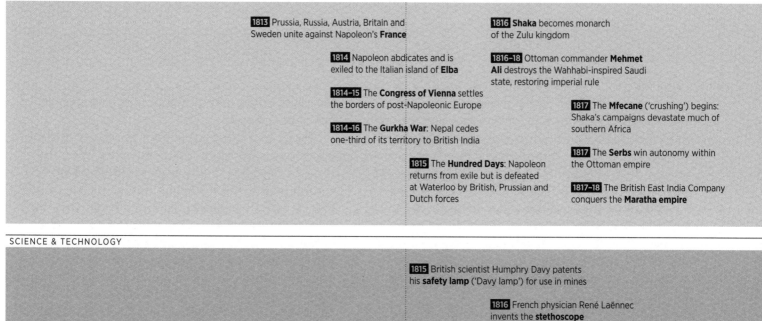

1813 Prussia, Russia, Austria, Britain and Sweden unite against Napoleon's **France**

1814 Napoleon abdicates and is exiled to the Italian island of **Elba**

1814–15 The **Congress of Vienna** settles the borders of post-Napoleonic Europe

1814–16 The **Gurkha War**: Nepal cedes one-third of its territory to British India

1815 The **Hundred Days**: Napoleon returns from exile but is defeated at Waterloo by British, Prussian and Dutch forces

1816 **Shaka** becomes monarch of the Zulu kingdom

1816–18 Ottoman commander **Mehmet Ali** destroys the Wahhabi-inspired Saudi state, restoring imperial rule

1817 The **Mfecane** ('crushing') begins: Shaka's campaigns devastate much of southern Africa

1817 The **Serbs** win autonomy within the Ottoman empire

1817–18 The British East India Company conquers the **Maratha empire**

SCIENCE & TECHNOLOGY

1815 British scientist Humphry Davy patents his **safety lamp** ('Davy lamp') for use in mines

1816 French physician René Laënnec invents the **stethoscope**

1810

1815

RELIGION & PHILOSOPHY

1811 Philadelphia: The first African-American Protestant church in the United States, the **African Methodist Episcopal Church**, is founded

ART & ARCHITECTURE

1813 British author **Jane Austen**'s second novel, *Pride and Prejudice*, is published

1814 American lawyer and poet Francis Scott Key writes **'The Star-Spangled Banner'**, later to become the US national anthem

1815–23 The **Brighton Pavilion**, an Indo-Saracenic summer palace designed by John Nash, is constructed

1818 The **US–Canada border** is agreed along the 49th parallel

1819 Simón Bolívar's victory over Spanish royalists at Boyacá secures the independence of **Colombia**

1819 The **Adams–Onis Treaty**: Spain cedes Florida to the USA

1819 Stanford Raffles founds **Singapore** as a British free-trade port

1820 The **Missouri Compromise** divides the United States into southern 'slave states' and northern 'free states'

1820 Russian explorer Fabian von Bellingshausen makes the first confirmed sigting of the **Antarctic continent**

1821 **Mexico** gains independence from Spain

1822 The **Greeks** win control of the Peloponnese and declare independence from the Ottoman empire

1822 **Liberia** in West Africa is founded as a state for freed African-American slaves

1822 **Brazil** gains independence from Portugal

1823 The USA proclaims the **Monroe Doctrine** against European intervention in the Americas

1824 Antonio José de Sucre's victory at Ayacucho secures the independence of **Peru** and **Bolivia**, ending Spanish rule in South America

1820 Danish physicist Hans Ørsted discovers **electromagnetism**

1820

1825

1823 The **Bible** is translated into Chinese

1824 British Romantic poet **Lord Byron** dies while fighting for the Greeks against the Ottomans at Missolonghi

1825–1848

NATIONALISM AND INDUSTRIALIZATION

THE SECOND QUARTER of the 19th century marked the growth and spread of nationalism in the West: the ideal that each nation should have its own state and that every member of a nation should live in the same state. For most of history people had owed their political allegiance to a dynastic or city-state, or to a feudal overlord. The implications of nationalism in a world dominated by multi-ethnic dynastic states were profound and not confined to politics. Nationalism demanded a cultural expression, too, in art, literature and music.

Nationalism developed from the Enlightenment ideas of popular sovereignty and natural rights, which shifted the balance of state power away from the ruler and in favour of the people. Nationalism first became a major political force in the American and French revolutions: their success inspired nationalist movements among many other European peoples. The Congress of Vienna (1814–15) had made few concessions to increasing nationalist sentiments, but their influence steadily grew throughout Europe. In 1831 Giuseppe Mazzini founded a movement for the unification of Italy; in 1832 the Greeks achieved statehood; and in 1839 Belgium became independent of the Netherlands.

In 1848 suppressed nationalist and republican feelings burst out in a wave of revolution and protest across Europe: nationalists installed democratic governments in Hungary, Bohemia, Moravia and Croatia; the Poles rose against

Prussia and Russia; anti-Austrian uprisings broke out across northern Italy; and a parliament met in Frankfurt aiming to unite Germany. The most successful challenge to established authority took place in France, where a republican revolution overthrew the restored monarchy. The *Communist Manifesto*, published in 1848 by Karl Marx and Friedrich Engels, looked beyond nationalism to class struggles and international communism, building on the work of such earlier philosophers as Hegel.

On a global scale, European powers consolidated and expanded their colonial possessions. By 1846 Britain had won control of almost the entire Indian subcontinent, begun the conquest of Burma and annexed New Zealand. Britain's victory in the First Opium War (1839–42) forced the Qing to open Chinese ports to foreign trade and led to Britain gaining the island of Hong Kong. A British invasion of Afghanistan in 1839–42 ended in disaster, however, and in southern Africa the Boers of Cape Colony escaped British rule by migrating into the interior to found their own republics. Other European nations also pursued their own imperial ambitions: between 1830 and 1848, France began the conquest of Algeria and annexed Tahiti and other Polynesian islands, while the Dutch began to tighten their control of the East Indies.

In North America, Texas joined the USA in 1845 after a successful rebellion by American settlers against Mexican rule in 1836; this precipitated the Mexican–American War (1846–48), during which the USA gained vast territories, including California. Further north, in the Oregon Treaty of 1846 Britain and the United States agreed to extend the US–Canadian border along the 49th parallel to the Pacific. At the same time, the arrival of large numbers of Catholic Irish immigrants, fleeing the horrors of the Great Famine in Ireland, was the first challenge to the 'Anglo-Saxon' Protestant dominance of the USA.

Economically, Britain was the world's leading industrial and mercantile nation during this period, accounting in 1830 for around 45 per cent of international trade. But by 1848 other European countries and the USA were industrializing quickly and experiencing rapid urban growth. The development of railways in Britain revolutionized transport, providing for the first time fast, comfortable overland travel, as well as economically viable long-distance land transport for bulky raw materials like coal and iron ore. However, in the long term railways turned out to be of greater advantage to large continental countries like the USA and Russia than to a compact island like Britain.

POLITICS & ECONOMY

1830 **Indian Removal Act**: Native Americans are forcibly removed from southern states to Oklahoma

1830 **The French July Revolution** sees Louis Philippe oust his cousin, King Charles X

1830–48 France conquers **Algeria**

1835–36 **The Great Trek**: Boers leave Cape Colony to escape British rule

1834 Creation of the **Zollverein** (customs union) under Prussian leadership

1831 **Giuseppe Mazzini** founds the Young Italy movement to create a unified Italian Republic

SCIENCE & TECHNOLOGY

1825 **The Stockton–Darlington railway**, the world's first passenger railway, opens in Britain

1831 British scientist **Michael Faraday** builds the first electric motor and generator

1825   1830   1835

RELIGION & PHILOSOPHY

1828 Ram Mahon Roy founds the reformist Hindu **Brahmo Samaj movement** in Bengal

1831 Death of the German philosopher **Hegel**

1836 Transcendentalist American philosopher **Ralph Waldo Emerson** writes the essay 'Nature'

ART & ARCHITECTURE

1828 Death of the Spanish romantic painter **Francisco Goya**

1830–48 Construction of the **Alabaster Mosque** of Muhammad Ali, Cairo

1830 **Eugene Delacroix** commemorates the July Revolution in Liberty Leading the People

1831* **Katsushika Hokusai** paints the collection of woodblock prints *Thirty-six views of Mount Fuji*

1832 Death of the German writer **Goethe** and completion of his play *Faust*

1839 **Belgium** gains independence from the Netherlands

1839–42 Britain defeats China in the **First Opium War**, forcing the Qing to open Chinese ports to foreign trade

1839–42 British invasion of **Afghanistan** is disastrously defeated

1840 The **treaty of Waitangi**: The Maoris of New Zealand accept British sovereignty

1843–48 **Maori rising** against British rule

1845 **Texas** joins the USA nine years after gaining independence from Mexico

1845–49 The **Great Famine in Ireland** prompts mass emigration, especially to the USA

1846 **Kashmir** becomes a British protectorate

1846 The **Oregon Treaty**: Britain and the USA divide Oregon country along the 49th parallel

1848 The **Year of Revolutions**: Liberal and nationalist revolutions break out in Europe

1837 British scientist Charles Wheatstone patents the **electric telegraph**

1844 In the United States, Samuel Morse and Alfred Vail develop **Morse code** for their telegraph system

1846 German astronomer Johann Galle discovers the planet **Neptune**

1840

1845

1848 Publication of the *Communist Manifesto*, written by Karl Marx and Friedrich Engels

1841 **Edgar Allan Poe** writes the first modern detective story, *The Murders in the Rue Morgue*

1849– 1861

CIVIL WAR AND SOCIAL CHANGE

THE UNITED STATES' westward expansion raised the possibility that new states where slavery was legal could be admitted to the union, sharply polarizing opinions on the issue. The debate came to a head following the election in 1860 of Abraham Lincoln as president, largely on the votes of the northern 'free states' (where slavery had been abolished). Lincoln's refusal to extend slavery to any new states led eleven southern slave states to secede from the union; in 1861 they formed the Confederate States of America. In April 1861, a Confederate attack on the Union garrison at Fort Sumter in South Carolina led to the outbreak of civil war.

In 1853, the Japanese Tokugawa shogunate was forced to end its policy of maintaining Japan as a closed society by the arrival of a squadron of US warships under Commodore Matthew Perry. The next year Japan opened two ports to foreign ships, and further trade concessions followed in 1858. In China, the Qing dynasty faced a succession of uprisings, most seriously the radical egalitarian religious and political Taiping (Heavenly Kingdom) rebellion, which broke out in 1850. The Qing finally suppressed the rebellion in 1864, but at the cost of around 20 million lives – and the dynasty's authority was shredded.

In the midst of the ongoing rebellion, Britain and France fought together against China in the Second Opium War (1856–60), gaining more favourable trading terms with the Qing, and Russia annexed the Amur region of Manchuria in northern China. However, Russia's ambitions to seize the ailing Ottoman empire's Danubian Principalities – in modern-day Romania – were thwarted by Britain and France in the Crimean War (1854–56). France began to create a Southeast Asian empire with the occupation of Saigon in Vietnam in 1859. By contrast, King Mongkut of Siam successfully staved off European intervention by taking the initiative to open his country to foreign trade. In East Africa, the Ethiopian emperor Tewodros II brought an end to the decentralized 'age of princes' and began to create a united government under his authority.

Despite the failure of the 1848 revolutions, nationalism continued its rise in Europe. The movement for Italian national unification, often called the *Risorgimento* (resurgence), began in earnest in 1859, when Piedmont–Sardinia expelled the Austrian empire from Italy with French support. The following year, a small revolutionary army led by Giuseppe Garibaldi invaded and conquered the Kingdom of the Two Sicilies; Garibaldi handed his conquest over to King Victor Emmanuel II of Piedmont–Sardinia, who was proclaimed king of Italy in 1861.

The British colonization of Australia expanded rapidly after Napoleon's defeat, spurred on by a gold rush in New South Wales: by 1859, free settlers far outnumbered convicts. Yet the Aboriginal population declined sharply, mainly due to epidemics of diseases introduced by the European colonists, but also due to deliberate genocide, especially in Tasmania. Britain had formally annexed New Zealand in 1840, but the British settlers' desire for land caused many conflicts with the indigenous Maori. Similarly, the commercialism and cultural insensitivity of the British East India Company created growing resentment of British rule in India: in 1857, the company's Indian troops rebelled and seized Delhi. The uprising was defeated in 1858, destroying hopes of preserving traditional Indian society free of Western influence.

The most important scientific development of this period was the publication of Charles Darwin's *On the Origin of Species* in 1859, in which he presented his theory of evolution by natural selection. Although the implications of his theory outraged the religious establishment, it quickly gained acceptance in the scientific community, revolutionizing the study of biology. Meanwhile, the laying of the first transatlantic telegraph cable in 1858 brought the age of instantaneous global communication a step nearer.

POLITICS & ECONOMY

1850 Beginning of the **Taiping (Heavenly Kingdom)** rebellion in central China: The resulting conflict claims 20 million lives

1851 A gold rush in **New South Wales** brings a flood of non-convict settlers to Australia

1851 London: The first world trade fair, the **Great Exhibition**, is held

1852–54 Britain recognizes the independence of the Boer republics of **Transvaal** and the **Orange Free State** in southern Africa

1853 American Commodore Matthew Perry's naval expedition to **Edo Bay** begins the opening of Japan to foreign trade

1854–56 The **Crimean War**: Britain and France halt Russian expansion in the Black Sea region

1855 Accession of **Tewodros II** of Ethiopia: His reign marks a revival of Ethiopian power

1855 King Mongkut opens **Siam** to British trade

SCIENCE & TECHNOLOGY

 1850   **1855**

RELIGION & PHILOSOPHY

1855 Death of the Danish philosopher **Søren Kierkegaard**, acknowledged as an early existentialist

ART & ARCHITECTURE

1851 London: Joseph Paxton designs the **Crystal Palace** to house the Great Exhibition

1851 **Herman Melville** writes his novel *Moby Dick*

1855 Washington, DC: Construction begins on Thomas Walter's design for the dome of the **US Capitol**

1856–60 Britain and France defeat China in the **Second Opium War**

1857 The **First War of Indian Independence** (Indian Mutiny): Indian troops rebel and capture Delhi

1858–60 Russia annexes the Amur region of **Manchuria** from Qing China

1859 French and Spanish forces occupy **Saigon** in Vietnam

1859 Anti-slavery activist John Brown conducts his **raid on Harper's Ferry** in Virginia

1859 The **Battle of Magenta**: Piedmont–Sardinia expels the Austrian empire from northern Italy

1860 The **Taranaki Wars** begin between British settlers and indigenous Maori over land ownership in New Zealand

1860 **Giuseppe Garibaldi** invades Sicily, granting the Kingdom of the Two Sicilies to Piedmont–Sardinia

1860 **Abraham Lincoln** is elected president of the United States

1861 **Victor Emmanuel II** of Piedmont–Sardinia is proclaimed king of a united Italy

1861 Serfs in Russia are liberated under Tsar **Alexander II**

1861 Feb: The secessionist **Confederate States of America** are proclaimed

1861 Apr: The Confederate bombardment of Fort Sumter begins the **American Civil War**

1856 Measurements taken by the Survey of India show **Mount Everest** to be the world's highest mountain

1858 The first **transatlantic telegraph cable** is laid from Ireland to Newfoundland

1859 **Charles Darwin** publishes *On the Origin of Species*, outlining his theory of evolution

1859 Pennsylvania the world's first **oil well** is drilled

1860

1859 British philosopher **John Stuart Mill** writes his key work on utilitarianism, *On Liberty*

1856 **Gustave Flaubert**'s landmark work of realist fiction, *Madame Bovary*, is published

1862–1871

NEW BORDERS, NEW LANDS

THE CONFEDERACY INITIALLY gained the upper hand in the American Civil War, but by 1863 the Union's superior resources were beginning to tell. Following the Union's decisive victory at Gettysburg in July 1863, the Confederacy was slowly ground down, and it finally surrendered in April 1865. The important part played by railways, ironclad warships and the industrialized production of armaments has led to it being seen as the first modern war.

An immediate consequence of the Union victory was the abolition of slavery across the United States. However, the post-war reconstruction programme's aim of introducing multiracial democracy in the former slave states produced a violent backlash, and by the early 1870s white supremacy had been restored. In 1867 the continental USA achieved its present extent with the purchase of Alaska from Russia. The same year, the British North American colonies (except Newfoundland) were federated and granted self-government as the Dominion of Canada. Further south, the failure of a French-sponsored Habsburg empire in Mexico (1864–67) ended European imperialist ambitions in the Americas. Among the independent states of Latin America, border disputes led to war between the Triple Alliance (Brazil, Uruguay and Argentina) and Paraguay: the worst war in South American history, it cost Paraguay 70 per cent of its population.

Nationalism continued to rearrange the political map of Europe with the unification of Germany in 1871. The creation of the *Zollverein* (customs union) under Prussian leadership in 1834 had begun to integrate the economies of the German states, and Prussia subsequently consolidated its dominance with wars against Denmark (1864) and Austria (1866). When Bismarck manoeuvred France into declaring war in 1870, reviving memories of Napoleon's occupation of Germany, the smaller German states allied with Prussia. The Prussian king Wilhelm I was proclaimed German emperor (Kaiser) following France's defeat, which cost it its eastern provinces of Alsace and Lorraine. During the war, Italy also annexed Rome, completing the process of national unification begun under Garibaldi.

In Japan, young samurai warriors organized attacks on foreigners and foreign shipping to resist the increasing Western influence on Japan that followed Perry's missions of 1853–54. After British, American, French and Dutch naval forces retaliated by bombarding Japanese ports, popular discontent became focused on the feudal shogunate. A brief civil war in 1867–68 saw the shogunate overthrown, and the emperor was restored to power. The emperor took up residence in Edo, the capital of the Tokugawa shoguns, which was renamed Tokyo. This development was labelled the Meiji (enlightened rule) Restoration, and began a period of rapid modernization in the country.

In North Africa, the opening of the Suez Canal in 1869 linked the Mediterranean directly with the Red Sea and created a much shorter route between Europe and India than sailing around the Cape of Good Hope. This saved not only time, but also fuel for the steamships that were becoming ever more important for commercial and naval use by the 1870s. As India was its most important colonial possession, control of the canal immediately became a key strategic issue for Britain, which purchased it in 1875. Steamships could hold a course independent of the wind direction, but they were much less self-sufficient than sailing ships – as a result, small oceanic islands assumed new strategic importance as coaling stations. It was not just at sea that the world was getting smaller: in 1869, the first transcontinental railway was completed in the USA.

In 1866, Gregor Mendel founded the science of genetics, but published his results in an obscure journal: it was many years before they became widely known. The mid-19th century also saw the birth in Britain of what would become the world's most popular spectator sport, association football (or soccer). It was just one of many sports that spread globally through the influence of the British empire.

1862 The conservative **Otto von Bismarck** becomes minister-president of Prussia

1863 1–3 Jul: Decisive Union victory over the Confederacy in the American Civil War at **Gettysburg**

1864 Austria and Prussia defeat **Denmark**, ending its occupation of Schleswig-Holstein

1864 British, American, French and Dutch naval forces bombard the southern Japanese city of **Shimonoseki**, to retaliate against attempts to expel foreigners from Japan

1864–67 Reign of the short-lived Habsburg emperor of Mexico **Maximilian I**

1864–70 Paraguay loses up to 70% of its population in its war against the **Triple Alliance** (Brazil, Uruguay and Argentina)

1865 Apr: Abraham Lincoln is assassinated; shortly afterwards, the Confederacy surrenders, ending the **American Civil War**

1865 Dec: The **Thirteenth Amendment** to the US constitution abolishes slavery

1866 **Prussia** asserts its leadership over Germany after defeating Austria in the Seven Weeks' War

1863 London: The world's first **underground railway** opens

1866 **Gregor Mendel** establishes the principles of heredity, marking the beginning of genetics

1865

1863 Bahá'u'lláh founds the **Bahá'í faith** in Iraq

1863 The English **Football Association** is founded, beginning the modern sport of association football (soccer)

1864–69 **Leo Tolstoy** writes his epic novel *War and Peace*

1867 The colonies of British North America (except Newfoundland) federate and are granted self-government as the Dominion of **Canada**

1867 The USA buys **Alaska** from Russia for $7.2 million (around $115 million today)

1867 The transportation of convicts to **Australia** ends

1868 The **Meiji Restoration**: rebel samurai overthrow the Tokugawa shogunate and restore the emperor to power, beginning the modernization of Japan

1868 Britain invades **Ethiopia**: its emperor Tewodros II commits suicide

1870 Italy annexes **Rome**, completing national unification

1870–71 The **Franco-Prussian War**: France is defeated and Napoleon III abdicates

1871 King **Wilhelm I** of Prussia is proclaimed emperor of Germany at Versailles

1867 British scientist Joseph Lister introduces **antiseptic surgery**

1869 Russian chemist **Dmitri Mendeleev** formulates the periodic table of elements

1870

1867 The first volume of Karl Marx's critique of capitalism, ***Das Kapital*** (*Capital*), is published

1870 The **First Vatican Council** proclaims the dogma of papal infallibility

1871 **Shinto** is established as the state religion of Japan

1867–68 British writer **Charles Dickens** tours the USA to give readings from his works

1869 The **Suez Canal** opens, linking the Mediterranean to the Red Sea

1869 United States: The **Pacific Railroad**, the first transcontinental railway, is completed

1871 Cairo: **Giuseppe Verdi**'s opera *Aida*, set in ancient Egypt, premieres

1872–1900

THE AGE OF EMPIRES

BY 1900, EUROPEAN global dominance was at its peak, with approximately half the world's landmass directly controlled by European colonial empires. While the Americas were largely independent of European control, the general population of the USA and the ruling elite of Latin America were mainly of European descent. In 1890, the end of Native American resistance, alongside the federal government's declaration that the western frontier no longer existed, marked the final consolidation of the continental USA. American expansion, however, continued westwards: in 1898, the Pacific islands of Hawaii were annexed as a territory of the United States.

The European takeover of Africa in this period was astonishingly rapid. Except in Algeria and the Cape, European power was still confined to coastal enclaves in 1872, but in 1884 the European powers agreed to partition Africa among themselves at the Congress of Berlin: within the next fifteen years they brought almost the entire continent under their control. Germany, Italy and Belgium became colonial powers as a result of this carve-up. Such rapid colonization was made possible by the Europeans' vastly superior military technology and by earlier advances in medicine that improved their life expectancy in tropical Africa. In 1876 Queen Victoria was proclaimed empress of India, but by the end of this period the British empire was struggling to conquer the South African Boer republics, which were newly equipped with modern German weapons.

The remaining non-European powers reacted to this new European dominance in different ways: Japan adopted European science and technology wholesale; the nationalist Young Turk movement campaigned to turn the crumbling Ottoman empire into a secular state; and Ethiopia bought modern weapons, defeating an attempted conquest by Italy. The Qing dynasty's failures to modernize China effectively or to defend the empire culminated in a humiliating eight-power invasion after Boxer rebels attacked foreign missionaries and diplomats in the summer of 1900.

European global dominance was as evident in science and technology as it was in the political sphere. Even global time was calculated in reference to a meridian that ran through London. Major inventions of the period included cinema, the internal combustion engine, the automobile, the submarine, the telephone and the electric light. In medicine, meanwhile, Sigmund Freud pioneered psychoanalysis. Most technological and scientific breakthroughs in this period were made in Germany and the USA – a clear sign that Britain had lost the industrial dominance that had sustained its global power during the previous century.

In sharp contrast to such dazzling scientific progress, the period saw a strong resurgence in Central and Eastern Europe of violent popular anti-Semitism. Jewish communities reacted by founding the Zionist movement to establish a homeland in Palestine, where, thanks to the relatively tolerant Ottoman authorities, the first modern Jewish settlements were founded in the 1880s. On the other side of the world, in 1893 New Zealand became the first country to grant all women the right to vote.

During this period, the first skyscrapers heralded the advent of architectural modernism in the USA. European neoclassical and neo-Gothic styles of architecture, however, remained dominant and were vigorously exported to colonial territories, often with little regard to their suitability for the local climate or architectural context. European building styles were similarly adopted in Japan as part of its modernization programme.

Japan's adoption of European culture was selective and did not undermine Japan's own cultural identity. Nevertheless, it did result in major social change as the introduction of modern military technology made the old samurai military aristocracy obsolete. Yet despite a samurai rebellion in 1877 being easily crushed by the new government army and its modern weapons, their traditional values and culture remained influential in Japanese society.

1876 Queen Victoria is proclaimed **empress of India**

1877 Japanese government forces defeat the **Satsuma samurai rebellion**

1881 The **First Boer War** ends in British defeat

1882 Germany, Austria–Hungary and Italy form the **Triple Alliance**

1884 **Africa** is partitioned between European powers at the Congress of Berlin

1876 German inventor Nikolaus Otto patents the **four-stroke internal combustion engine**

1876 Scottish-born inventor **Alexander Graham Bell** patents the **telephone**

1879 American inventor Thomas Edison invents the **electric lamp**

1885 German engineer Karl Benz patents the first practical **automobile**

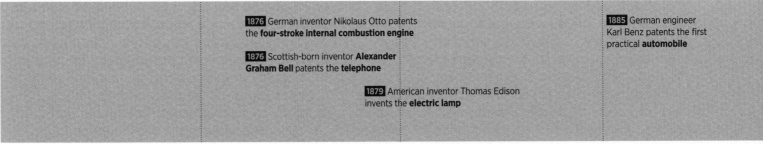

1870   **1875**   **1880**   **1885**

1875 Dayananda Saraswati founds the **Arya Samaj** Hindu reform movement

1882 Beginning of the **First Aliyah**: migration of Jewish populations to Palestine

1885 German philosopher **Friedrich Nietzsche** writes *Thus Spoke Zarathustra*

1874 **Richard Wagner** completes his opera cycle *The Ring of the Nibelung*

1882 Chicago: Completion of the first **skyscraper**, the ten-storey Home Insurance Building

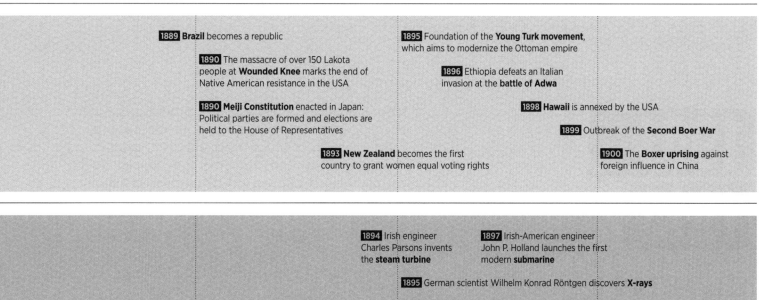

1889 Brazil becomes a republic

1890 The massacre of over 150 Lakota people at **Wounded Knee** marks the end of Native American resistance in the USA

1890 **Meiji Constitution** enacted in Japan: Political parties are formed and elections are held to the House of Representatives

1893 **New Zealand** becomes the first country to grant women equal voting rights

1895 Foundation of the **Young Turk movement**, which aims to modernize the Ottoman empire

1896 Ethiopia defeats an Italian invasion at the **battle of Adwa**

1898 **Hawaii** is annexed by the USA

1899 Outbreak of the **Second Boer War**

1900 The **Boxer uprising** against foreign influence in China

1894 Irish engineer Charles Parsons invents the **steam turbine**

1897 Irish-American engineer John P. Holland launches the first modern **submarine**

1895 German scientist Wilhelm Konrad Röntgen discovers **X-rays**

1895 Austrian scientist Sigmund Freud founds **psychoanalysis**

1895 Swiss scientist Svante Arrhenius makes the first quantified prediction of **climate change** caused by burning fossil fuels

1890   1895   1900

1897 Basel, Switzerland: The first **Zionist Congress** is held

1887 Calcutta (Kolkata): Construction of the Gothic—Saracenic style **Victoria Terminus** railway station

1889 Paris: Construction of the **Eiffel Tower**

1895 Paris: The Lumière brothers open the first **public cinema**

1901– 1913

THE PATH TO WAR

BRITAIN ENTERED THE 20th century as the leading colonial, financial and naval power. Its empire continued to expand, with the conquest of the Boer republics in Africa and the annexation of Malaya; but it also evolved, as Australia, New Zealand and South Africa became self-governing dominions in this period. Britain's pre-eminence, however, was challenged by the rising power of Germany and the USA. Britain saw the USA as a potential ally as well as a rival, but feared Germany's militaristic ambitions. When Germany began to construct a large naval fleet, the British responded with the revolutionary battleship HMS *Dreadnought*, triggering an international arms race. Britain also agreed 'ententes' ('understandings') with its colonial rivals France and Russia, which also felt threatened by Germany.

In East Asia, the balance of power shifted dramatically after Japan humiliated Russia in a war over spheres of influence in Manchuria in 1904–5. Russia's defeat created discontent with the tsarist regime and led to the introduction of an elected national assembly (*duma*) with limited powers. In China, the discredited Qing dynasty was overthrown by Sun Yat-sen's Tongmenghui revolutionary alliance following popular uprisings in 1911, and the country was declared a republic. From the outset, the new government struggled to assert its authority: the new president, Yuan Shikai, eventually banned his rivals, leading Sun Yat-sen to lead an unsuccessful rebellion against him in 1913. Tibet and Mongolia both successfully declared independence.

Tensions between the European powers grew steadily through 1913 and 1914, and boiled over following the assassination of the Austrian archduke Franz Ferdinand in Sarajevo by a Serbian nationalist on 28 June 1914. Austria–Hungary blamed Serbia for the assassination and declared war a month later after being assured of unconditional German support. To protect Serbia, Russia mobilized for war in response; its refusal to demobilize led Germany to declare war on Russia and its ally France. To avoid a long war on two fronts, Germany planned to defeat France quickly, outflanking its defences by invading through Belgium, and then transfer troops east to confront Russia.

Britain's ententes with France and Russia were not binding military alliances. Nevertheless, Germany's declaration of war against Belgium drew Britain into the war, as it had guaranteed Belgian independence. The German plan failed: slowed by Belgian and British resistance, its armies were stopped by the French short of Paris, thus committing Germany to the two-front war it had wished to avoid.

The First World War broke out at a time of unprecedented economic prosperity and technological progress in Europe and North America. European powers were brought into closer contact with their colonial possessions by radio, which freed long-distance communications from dependence on expensive telegraph cables. The Wright brothers' first powered aeroplane flight in 1903 began the development of the aircraft industry, and Henry Ford's mass-produced and relatively inexpensive Model T car heralded the beginning of an era when everyday personal mobility was no longer the privilege of the wealthy.

The development of the Haber–Bosch nitrogen fixation process, meanwhile, led to the invention of artificial fertilizers. These made possible an enormous increase in agricultural productivity, without which a rapidly increasing human population could not have been supported. Albert Einstein's *Theory of Relativity* and Niels Bohr's work on atomic structure revolutionized physics and provided new ways of understanding the universe.

The greatest engineering achievement in the early years of the 20th century was the construction of the Panama Canal, which linked the Caribbean directly with the Pacific Ocean. The canal was of great strategic benefit to the USA, as it made it possible to transfer warships between the Atlantic and Pacific without navigating around South America. The completion of the Trans-Siberian railway made it possible to travel by train across the entirety of the Eurasian continent. Huge passenger liners, powered by steam turbines, reduced transatlantic crossings to only five days.

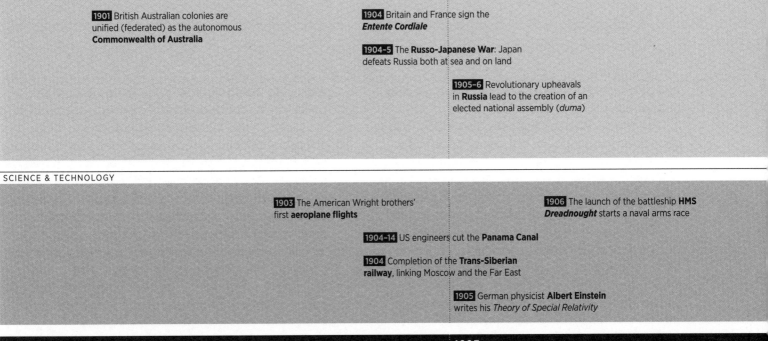

POLITICS & ECONOMY

1901 British Australian colonies are unified (federated) as the autonomous **Commonwealth of Australia**

1904 Britain and France sign the *Entente Cordiale*

1904–5 The **Russo-Japanese War**: Japan defeats Russia both at sea and on land

1905–6 Revolutionary upheavals in **Russia** lead to the creation of an elected national assembly (*duma*)

SCIENCE & TECHNOLOGY

1903 The American Wright brothers' first **aeroplane flights**

1906 The launch of the battleship **HMS** *Dreadnought* starts a naval arms race

1904–14 US engineers cut the **Panama Canal**

1904 Completion of the **Trans-Siberian railway**, linking Moscow and the Far East

1905 German physicist **Albert Einstein** writes his *Theory of Special Relativity*

1900

1905

RELIGION & PHILOSOPHY

1903 Russia: Kishinev (Chisinau) **anti-Jewish pogroms**

1906 Foundation of the **All-India Muslim League**

ART & ARCHITECTURE

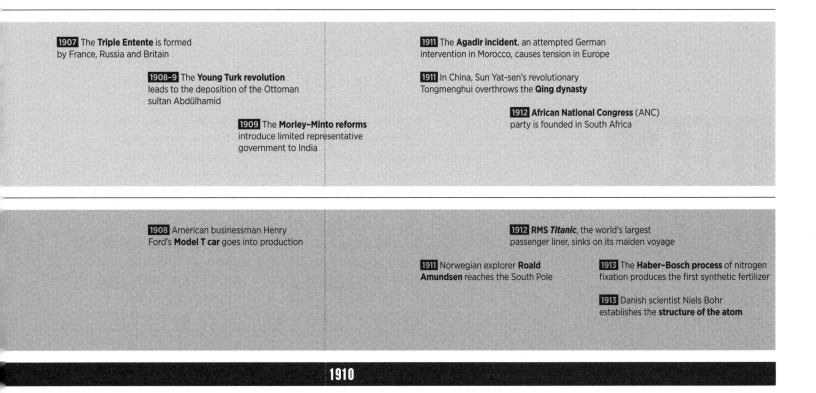

1907 The **Triple Entente** is formed by France, Russia and Britain

1908-9 The **Young Turk revolution** leads to the deposition of the Ottoman sultan Abdülhamid

1909 The **Morley–Minto reforms** introduce limited representative government to India

1911 The **Agadir incident**, an attempted German intervention in Morocco, causes tension in Europe

1911 In China, Sun Yat-sen's revolutionary Tongmenghui overthrows the **Qing dynasty**

1912 **African National Congress** (ANC) party is founded in South Africa

1908 American businessman Henry Ford's **Model T car** goes into production

1911 Norwegian explorer **Roald Amundsen** reaches the South Pole

1912 RMS *Titanic*, the world's largest passenger liner, sinks on its maiden voyage

1913 The **Haber–Bosch process** of nitrogen fixation produces the first synthetic fertilizer

1913 Danish scientist Niels Bohr establishes the **structure of the atom**

1910

1907 **Pablo Picasso** completes the proto-Cubist painting *Les Demoiselles d'Avignon*

1911-13 Japanese author **Mori Ogai** writes his novel *The Wild Geese*

1911-13 New York: Cass Gilbert designs the neo-Gothic **Woolworth Building**

1913 French author **Marcel Proust** begins his seven-volume *Remembrance of Things Past*

1913 Bengali author **Rabindranath Tagore** becomes the first Asian Nobel laureate

1914–1917

CONFLICT AND REVOLUTION

ONCE THE INITIAL German offensive of the First World War had been halted, the conflict on the Western Front quickly stagnated as each side dug a continuous line of trenches stretching from the Swiss border to the North Sea. In this war of attrition, offensives achieved tiny gains for enormous casualties. The battle of the Somme in 1916, for example, cost the lives of 146,000 British and French soldiers, but achieved an Allied advance of only 6 miles (10 km) in four months. The death toll among the defending Germans was almost as high.

The Allies benefited from superior manpower and command of the sea, allowing them to import food and war materials from their colonies and the USA; conversely Germany, cut off by a British naval blockade, was already suffering food and other shortages by early 1915. Germany turned to submarine warfare to weaken Britain's supply lines, but attacks on neutral shipping alienated the USA, leading it to join the Allies in April 1917. Previously, Japan, Italy, Portugal and Romania had joined the Allies, while the Central Powers included the Ottoman empire and Bulgaria. Because of the Allied naval blockade, Germany was unable to defend its colonies, most of which were quickly occupied by the Allies. After seizing Germany's possessions in China, Japan forced concessions from the weak Chinese government.

Russia's economy was the least developed of any of the major combatants. Although Tsar Nicholas II hoped the conflict might unite his people, incompetent handling of the war effort and food shortages discredited his government. Faced with strikes and mutinies, Nicholas abdicated in March 1917. The provisional government that subsequently took power continued the war, but in November it too was overthrown by Lenin's Communist Bolshevik party, which promised peace. The Bolsheviks signed an armistice with Germany in December of the same year, ending Russia's active participation in the war while peace terms were negotiated.

As the first large-scale industrial conflict, the First World War led to national economies being mobilized to produce munitions to an unprecedented degree. At the outbreak of war, few generals fully understood the potential of the new military technology developed in the late 19th and early 20th centuries. Machine guns, barbed wire, quick-firing breech-loading artillery and high-explosive shells gave a clear advantage to the defensive side. Cavalry, for centuries the offensive elite of most armies, was especially vulnerable to these new weapons and its obsolescence quickly became apparent. New technology was used to attempt to break the strategic stalemate: tanks, lighter machine guns and heavier artillery were developed; poison gas was deployed and countered with gas masks; and flamethrowers were used against bunkers.

The war also stimulated the new aircraft industry: in 1914 no power possessed purpose-built combat aircraft, yet within two years all were producing specialized fighter and bomber aircraft. Airships were used for naval reconnaissance and bombing raids. Though casualties were light, German airship raids on London demonstrated that civilian populations living far from combat zones were highly vulnerable to aerial attack. The First World War also saw the first genocide of the 20th century, perpetrated against the Armenians by the Ottoman government in retaliation for their support of Russia.

The shocking scale of the war provoked a powerful cultural response in art and literature that emphasized not martial glory but the human suffering and destruction of war. An important factor in this was mass participation in the conflict – the conscript armies of the First World War were made up mainly of civilians, not professional soldiers, and many of them needed ways to express their horror at what they experienced. At home, women took over many traditionally male industrial occupations to replace men who had been conscripted into the armed forces, galvanizing women's suffrage movements in the West.

`1914` 28 Jun: Austrian archduke **Franz Ferdinand** is assassinated by a Serbian nationalist in Sarajevo

`1914` 28 Jul: **Austria–Hungary** declares war on Serbia

`1914` 1–5 Aug: Outbreak of the **First World War**

`1914` 5–10 Aug: French forces halt the German advance on Paris at the **first battle of the Marne**

`1914` 26–30 Aug: The Germans repel the Russian invasion of East Prussia at the **Battle of Tannenberg**

`1914` 29 Oct: The **Ottoman empire** declares war on Britain, France and Russia

`1915` Formation of the **Home Rule League** in India

`1915` Jan: The **Australian and New Zealand Army Corps** (ANZAC) is formed in Egypt

`1915` 23 May: **Italy** declares war on **Austria–Hungary**

`1915–16` Around 600,000 **Armenians** die in a genocide orchestrated by the Ottoman government

`1915–16` The Allied **Gallipoli** campaign against the Ottomans ends in defeat

SCIENCE & TECHNOLOGY

`1915` **Albert Einstein** completes his general theory of relativity

`1915` Apr: The **Fokker Eindecker**, the first effective fighter aircraft, goes into service with German forces

1914

1915

RELIGION & PHILOSOPHY

`1914` **Halbmondlager** ('Half-moon camp'): German prisoner of war camp set up to house Muslim prisoners fighting on Allied side and attempt to convince them, using jihad ideology, to turn against their colonizers, UK and France. (1915 mosque built in this POW camp was the first mosque built in Germany)

ART & ARCHITECTURE

`1914` Production of Alfred Leete's iconic British army recruitment poster **Your Country Needs You**

`1916` Jan: Britain introduces **conscription**

`1916` 21 Feb–18 Dec: Costly German offensive against French forces at **Verdun**

`1916` 24–29 Apr: The **Easter Rising** in Dublin against British rule in Ireland

`1916` 31 May–1 Jun: The **battle of Jutland** in the North Sea between the British and German fleets

`1916` 1 Jul–19 Nov: Costly British offensive on the **Somme**

`1917` 16 Jan: The **Zimmermann Telegram** – Germany urges Mexico to invade the USA

`1917` 15 Mar: Faced with strikes and mutinies, **Tsar Nicholas II** of Russia abdicates; a provisional government is formed

`1917` 6 Apr: The **USA** enters the war against the **Central Powers**

`1917` 31 Jul–10 Nov: The **battle of Passchendaele** (the Third Battle of Ypres)

`1917` 7 Nov: The **Bolsheviks** under Lenin seize power in Russia

`1917` 3 Dec: Bolshevik **Russia** signs an armistice with Germany

`1917` Completion of the **Trans-Australian railway**

`1916` Feb: Britain begins production of the first **tanks**

`1916` Jun: The British **Sopwith Camel**, the most successful fighter aircraft of the war, goes into action

`1917` 2 Nov: The **Balfour Declaration** signals British support for a Jewish national homeland in Palestine

1916

1917

`1916` Zurich, Switzerland: Beginning of the avant-garde **Dada** movement, as a protest against the First World War

`1917` **Wilfred Owen** writes his highly influential war poem 'Anthem for Doomed Youth'

`1917` In the USA, the **first jazz record**, *Dixieland Jazz Band One-Step*, is released

`1917` Kuala Kangsar, Malaysia: Construction of Arthur Benison Hubback's Indo-Saracenic **Ubudiah Mosque**

1801–1917

1 *Napoleon I Bonaparte crossing the St Bernard Pass, May 1800*, Jacques-Louis David, 1801, p. 148

2 *Under the Wave off Kanagawa*, from the series *Thirty-six Views of Mount Fuji*, Katsushika Hokusai, *c.* 1830–32, p. 160

3 *The Battle of Adwa* (1 March 1896, during the First Italo-Ethiopian War), Ethiopian School, *c.* 1965–75, p. 173

4 *Opening of the Great Exhibition by Queen Victoria on 1st May 1851*, Henry Courtney Selous, 1851–52, p. 164

5 *The Battle of Gettysburg, Pa., July 3rd, 1863*, Currier & Ives, 1863, p. 166

6 *Great Battle at Lüshun Bay* (Battle of Port Arthur, 8–9 February 1904, Russo-Japanese war), Sadajiro Ariyama, 1904, p. 176

7 World War I, German soldiers in a trench throwing hand grenades. Press photograph, undated (*c.* 1915), colourized, p. 178

1918–1923

A FLAWED PEACE

RUSSIA PAID A high price for peace with Germany, losing control of swathes of Eastern Europe: Ukraine, Transcaucasia (broadly corresponding to modern-day Georgia, Armenia and Azerbaijan), Poland, the Baltic states and Finland were all relinquished in the treaty of Brest-Litovsk in March 1918. Russia's withdrawal from the war allowed Germany to transfer troops to the Western Front, launching a series of offensives to try to defeat the British and French armies before the USA could fully mobilize for war. The offensives failed and, by August 1918, the German armies were in steady retreat. Germany's Bulgarian and Ottoman allies agreed armistices in September and October respectively, and the Austro-Hungarian empire disintegrated as its constituent nationalities declared independence. Mutinies, strikes and protests over food shortages forced the German Kaiser (emperor) from power and Germany signed an armistice on 11 November 1918, bringing the First World War to an end. It had cost around 20 million lives.

Formal peace was agreed by the treaty of Versailles in 1919, which imposed heavy penalties on Germany for its role in starting the war. Germany lost its overseas colonial possessions and some of its home territory to Denmark, France and newly independent Poland. The Ottoman empire was reduced to present-day Turkey, which became a republic in 1923 under the leadership of Kemal Ataturk, who oversaw a radical programme of modernization and secularization.

Germany's defeat nullified the treaty of Brest-Litovsk, but Russia's Bolshevik government had to fight separatists and Polish forces to regain control of Ukraine. The outbreak of civil war in 1918 also forced the Bolsheviks to recognize the independence of the Baltic states and Finland, in order to concentrate on fighting their White counter-revolutionary opponents. With the Whites' defeat in October 1922, the Bolsheviks regained control over most of the former Russian empire, restructuring it as the Union of Soviet Socialist Republics (USSR), a group of nominally autonomous republics.

The mass slaughter of the First World War inspired strong pacifist sentiments. To prevent further conflict, the victors set up the League of Nations in 1920 to promote peace through collective security, disarmament and the international arbitration of disputes. The League oversaw the division of Germany's former colonies among the victors as mandates – a form of trusteeship granted with the intention that the territory would eventually become independent.

Britain and its colonies received the lion's share of the League's mandates, bringing the British empire to its greatest territorial extent. However, the First World War had also helped consolidate emerging national identities in Canada, Australia, New Zealand and South Africa, and strengthened nationalist resentment against British rule in Ireland. After a war lasting three years, most of the island of Ireland achieved autonomy as the Irish Free State in 1922. India had contributed greatly to Britain's war effort and expected to be rewarded with autonomous 'dominion' status, on a par with territories such as Canada and Australia. When this failed to happen, Indian support for national independence grew rapidly.

American president Woodrow Wilson was the major architect of the League of Nations, but he failed to overcome isolationist sentiment in the USA, which never joined. This, and the initial exclusion of both the Soviet Union and Germany, left the League lacking in credibility. The USA was the main beneficiary of the First World War: Britain and France had become deeply indebted to it during the war and American industry had profited by supplying munitions to the Allies. By the war's end, the USA had emerged as the world's dominant financial and industrial power. By the 1922 Washington Naval Treaty, Britain had accepted the USA as an equal naval power. In China, regional warlords backed by foreign governments fought for territory while revolutionary nationalism grew in the cities.

1918 3 Mar: Russia gives up Finland, Poland, the Baltic States, Ukraine and Transcaucasia in the **treaty of Brest-Litovsk**

1918 9 Nov: Kaiser **Wilhelm II** abdicates and Germany becomes a republic

1918 11 Nov: The Allies sign an **armistice** with Germany

1919 10 Apr: Mexican revolutionary leader **Emiliano Zapata** is assassinated by government forces

1919 13 Apr: The **Jallianwala Bagh** (Amritsar) **massacre**: British forces kill at least 379 people at an Indian independence rally

1919 18 Jun: The **treaty of Versailles** assigns 'war guilt' to Germany

1919 26 Nov: Outbreak of the **Irish War of Independence**

1920 Jan: Inauguration of the **League of Nations**

1920 16 Jan: The 18th Amendment of the US constitution bans the sale of alcohol, beginning the **Prohibition era**

1920 Dec: **Mohandas K. Gandhi** becomes leader of the Indian National Congress (INC)

SCIENCE & TECHNOLOGY

1918 UK: **ASDIC** (sonar) is developed for detecting enemy submarines

1918–1920 **Global flu pandemic** results in the death of 50–100 million people

1919 14–15 Jun: British aviators John Alcock and Arthur Brown make the first **non-stop transatlantic flight**, from Newfoundland to Ireland

1918

1919

1920

RELIGION & PHILOSOPHY

1918 21 Jan, Russia: The Bolshevik government confiscates all property held by the church to promote **atheism**

1920 31 Dec: The **Akali Dal** movement is founded to reform Sikhism

ART & ARCHITECTURE

1919 Weimar, Germany: Walter Gropius founds the **Bauhaus** school of contemporary arts and crafts

1921 5 May: Sun Yat-sen establishes a nationalist **Guomindang** government of China at Guangzhou

1922 6 Feb: The **Washington Naval Treaty** limits the size of the British, American, French, Japanese and Italian navies

1922 28 Feb: **Egypt** becomes independent under King Fuad I, but Britain retains control of the Suez Canal

1922 Oct: The Russian civil war ends with **Bolshevik** victory

1922 27–29 Oct: Benito Mussolini's **March on Rome** establishes the first fascist government

1922 6 Dec: Creation of the **Irish Free State**: most of the island of Ireland gains independence from Britain

1922 30 Dec: The **Union of Soviet Socialist Republics** (USSR) is established

1923 11 Jan: France occupies the **Ruhr** in western Germany, leading to hyperinflation of the German mark

1923 29 Oct: Establishment of the Republic of Turkey under **Kemal Ataturk**

1922 France: First vaccination for children against **tuberculosis**

1922 Canadian scientists Frederick Banting and Charles Best isolate **insulin** and use it to treat diabetic patients

1921   1922   1923

1921 Austrian philosopher **Ludwig Wittgenstein** seeks to define the relationship between language and reality in his *Tractatus Logico-Philosophicus*

1922 4 Nov: The **British Broadcasting Corporation** (BBC) begins transmitting

1922 26 Nov, Valley of the Kings, Egypt: Archaeologist Howard Carter discovers the richly furnished tomb of the Egyptian pharaoh **Tutankhamun**

1922 **T. S. Eliot** writes his modernist poem *The Waste Land*

1923 The founding figure of modern Chinese literature **Lu Xun** publishes his first collection of short stories *Na Han* (Call to Arms)

1924– 1938

DEPRESSION AND DICTATORSHIP

MOST EUROPEAN ECONOMIES struggled to recover from the First World War. In Central Europe, newly formed national borders broke up what had been a highly integrated free-trade area under the Austro-Hungarian empire. In Germany, the liberal, democratic Weimar Republic was burdened with the consequences of defeat, with high unemployment and hyperinflation undermining its economic credibility.

Such economic hardship, alongside the fear of Soviet communism, fostered the rise of right-wing dictatorships: many were inspired by the fascist dictator Benito Mussolini, who in 1922 had seized power in Italy. In Germany the Nazi party leader Adolf Hitler was appointed chancellor in 1933. Hitler repudiated the treaty of Versailles: the Nazi government rebuilt Germany's armed forces, reoccupied the demilitarized Rhineland, engineered union with Austria (*Anschluss*) and succeeded in gaining British and French agreement to the German annexation of the Sudetenland in Czechoslovakia. Elsewhere in Europe, the ideological battle between fascism and communism was fought out in the Spanish Civil War, which erupted in 1936 between left-wing republicans and conservative forces under Franco.

In China, the Guomindang party and its army under Jiang Jieshi launched the Northern Expedition against regional warlords in 1926, establishing a degree of stability after the political chaos of the previous decade. The communists in the south were defeated, but they retreated and re-established themselves in the north. Both Japan's annexation of the northern Chinese region of Manchuria in 1931 and the Italian conquest of Ethiopia in 1935–6 had demonstrated the impotence of the League of Nations at resolving conflict. The subsequent Japanese invasion of China in 1937, meanwhile, united the Guomindang government and the communists in resistance against the invaders: the communists spread their power widely behind Japanese lines and benefited from being seen as patriotic. Japan's invasion also led to tension with the USA, which increasingly saw it as a threat to its interests in the Pacific.

The American economy grew rapidly in the immediate post-war period, supported by rising wages and buoyant demand for consumer goods. American popular culture, epitomized by jazz music and Hollywood cinema, was exported worldwide, creating a self-confident, glamorous image of the USA, which was not tarnished even by the gangland crime waves that marked the Prohibition era. In October 1929, however, the overheated US stock market crashed. Millions of people from all walks of life were bankrupted, as the savings and borrowings they had poured into the stock market became worthless. The US economy began a sharp decline that continued unbroken until 1933: American GDP shrank by 30 per cent; unemployment exceeded 20 per cent. The USA's economic dominance ensured that the effects of the Great Depression were felt globally, and they were especially severe in Europe. In the United States, however, the election of Franklin D. Roosevelt as president marked a turning point: his reforming 'New Deal' policies of public works and social security programmes led to an economic recovery in the mid-1930s that eventually brought the country out of the Great Depression.

The USSR was faced with the double legacy of world war and civil war and by 1924 its productivity was still only two-thirds its pre-war level. Lenin's death the same year prompted a power struggle that ultimately revealed Josef Stalin as leader. Stalin's first Five-Year Plan increased Soviet industrial production, but through its widespread use of forced labour led to terrible human suffering. This was also the result of his ideologically driven collectivization of agriculture, which resulted in mass starvation in Ukraine and Central Asia.

The totalitarianism of the European dictatorships extended to all aspects of culture. Socialist realism became the official artistic doctrine of the USSR under Stalin to promote positive attitudes to the communist regime. The Nazis made skilful use of cinema for their propaganda while attacking the 'degenerate' modernist art of the Weimar period, burning 'un-German' books and banning performances of works by Jewish composers, as part of their wider attack on the German Jewish community.

POLITICS & ECONOMY

1924 21 Jan: **Lenin** dies; a power struggle breaks out for control of the Soviet government

1926–28 Guomindang general Jiang Jieshi's **Northern Expedition** superficially suppresses Chinese warlords

1928–33 The first **Five-Year Plan** in the USSR

1929 28-29 Oct: The **Wall Street Crash** precipitates the Great Depression and a global trading collapse

1929 Nov: Stalin announces the **collectivization of agriculture** in the USSR

1930 Oct–Nov: Getúlio Vargas leads a revolution in **Brazil**

1931 18 Sep: The **Mukden Incident** gives Japan the pretext to occupy Manchuria

SCIENCE & TECHNOLOGY

1925 Scottish scientist John Logie Baird demonstrates the first **television**

1926 American engineer Robert Goddard launches the first **liquid-fuelled rocket**

1928 Scottish biologist Alexander Fleming discovers the antibiotic **penicillin**

1925   **1930**

RELIGION & PHILOSOPHY

1925 **The Scopes Monkey Trial**: The state of Tennessee prosecutes John T. Scopes for teaching evolution

1928 Mar, Egypt: Hassan al-Banna founds his international Islamist party, the **Muslim Brotherhood**

ART & ARCHITECTURE

1927 Release of Austrian director **Fritz Lang**'s expressionist futuristic movie *Metropolis*

1930–31 New York, USA: American architect William F. Lamb designs the **Empire State Building**

1931 Rio de Janeiro, Brazil: French sculptor Paul Landowski creates his monumental Art Deco statue *Christ the Redeemer*

1932 Abd al-Aziz ibn Saud proclaims the kingdom of **Saudi Arabia**

1932-33 **Famines** in Ukraine and Central Asia

1933 30 Jan: **Adolf Hitler** becomes chancellor of Germany

1933 Mar–Jun: American president F. D. Roosevelt introduces the **New Deal** to lift the USA out of the Great Depression

1934 1 Dec: The assassination of Leningrad party secretary Sergei Kirov leads to Stalin's **Great Purge**

1935-36 **Mussolini** invades Ethiopia to create a new 'Roman empire'

1936-37 The **Indian National Congress** wins control of seven Indian provincial governments in elections

1936 17 Jul: Outbreak of the **Spanish Civil War** after an attempted fascist coup against the republican government

1937 Jul: Japan invades **China**; the communists form a united front with the Guomindang

1938 12 Mar: German **Anschluss** (union) with Austria

1938 29 Sep: The **Munich Agreement** – Britain and France acquiesce to the German annexation of the Sudetenland

1935 American chemist Wallace Carothers invents **nylon**

1938 German scientists Otto Hahn and Fritz Strassman discover **nuclear fission**, the basis of atomic energy

1935

1935 15 Sep: The **Nuremberg Laws** deprive German Jews of civil rights

1938 10 Nov: *Kristallnacht* – the Nazis orchestrate a pogrom against German Jews

1932 Stalin makes **socialist realism** the official artistic doctrine of the USSR

1933-37 San Francisco, USA: Construction of the **Golden Gate Bridge**

1937 Spanish artist **Pablo Picasso** paints *Guernica*, inspired by German bombing during the Spanish Civil War

1939–1942

A GLOBAL WAR

UNTIL 1939, HITLER'S territorial demands had concerned only areas with significant ethnic German populations, such as the Sudetenland. Britain and France had acquiesced, hoping that a united German state represented the limit of his ambitions. With the Nazi annexation of what remained of Czechoslovakia in March 1939, it was all too clear that this was not the case. When Germany invaded Poland in September 1939, Britain, France and their allies declared war, beginning the Second World War.

To ensure Germany would not be faced with a two-front war, Hitler had agreed with Stalin a week earlier to divide Poland between them as part of the Molotov–Ribbentrop pact. The USSR was also permitted to reoccupy the Baltic states. In 1940 Germany conquered Denmark, Norway, the Netherlands, Belgium and France in just three months. France was partitioned, with the Nazis occupying the north and the establishment of a collaborationist government in the south at Vichy.

Following France's surrender and the retreat of British forces from continental Europe, Hitler expected Britain to seek peace. However, the British government, led by Winston Churchill from 1940, resolved to continue the war. Hitler's hastily made plans to invade Britain were abandoned after the German *Luftwaffe* (air force) was defeated in the battle of Britain. The war widened to the Balkans and Africa after Italy joined Germany in June 1940, forming the Axis powers.

However, the poorly equipped Italians needed rescuing by the Germans in 1941 after defeats at the hands of both the Greeks, and the British in Libya and East Africa.

With Britain still undefeated, Hitler turned on the USSR, taking Stalin completely by surprise by invading in June 1941. The Germans advanced eastwards rapidly through the summer but were unprepared for the onset of the bitter Russian winter, and they were brought to a halt outside Moscow in December. Despite the speed of the German attack, the Soviet Union successfully removed much of its industrial capacity to safety beyond the Ural mountains. Officially still neutral, the USA under President Franklin D. Roosevelt gave Britain considerable material support through the Lend-Lease scheme begun in March 1941.

China received substantial American and Soviet aid and diplomatic support in its continuing war with Japan. Fearing the consequences of a threatened US oil embargo, the Japanese government under Emperor Hirohito planned to secure access to strategic raw materials by seizing European colonial territories in Southeast Asia. To prevent American interference, Japan launched a surprise attack on the US Pacific Fleet at its Hawaiian base of Pearl Harbor on 7 December 1941, bringing the United States into the Second World War.

For the next six months Japan enjoyed a spectacular run of victories, most importantly occupying the oil-rich Dutch East Indies. Having been bogged down over the winter, in spring 1942 the Germans regained the initiative in the USSR, advancing rapidly towards the oilfields of the Caucasus; in North Africa, meanwhile, a German–Italian offensive threatened British control of the Suez Canal. At the Wannsee Conference in January 1942, Germany's Nazi leaders had already begun to plan the war's greatest crime, the Holocaust.

By the end of 1942 the tide of war was turning in favour of the Allies. The British victory at the second battle of El Alamein in October drove the Germans and Italians out of Egypt. Days later Anglo-American forces invaded Vichy-held Morocco and Algeria. The German army's Soviet offensive was halted at Stalingrad in July amid bitter street fighting. By the end of the year, the Australians had forced a Japanese retreat in New Guinea and the Allies were conducting a war of attrition against Japanese positions in the Solomon Islands.

In an effort to bolster their military strategies, both the Allies and the Axis invested considerable resources in propaganda, using posters, the press and popular media such as cinema and radio. Large audiences in Nazi-dominated Europe listened to Britain's BBC illegally because of its reputation for truthfully reporting events.

1939 1 Apr: The surrender of republican forces ends the **Spanish Civil War**, beginning over three decades of dictatorship under Francisco Franco

1939 23 Aug: The **Molotov–Ribbentrop pact** secretly agrees the partition of Poland and the Soviet annexation of the Baltic states

1939 1–3 Sep: Germany invades Poland; Britain and France declare war, beginning the **Second World War**

1939 17 Sep: The USSR invades **Poland**

1940 10 May–25 Jun: Germany invades **the Netherlands**, **Belgium** and **France**

1940 23 Mar: In India, the Muslim League demands the creation of **Pakistan**, a separate state for Indian Muslims

1940 8 Aug–30 Sep: British victory in the **battle of Britain** ends the threat of German invasion

1939 27 Aug, Germany: First flight by a **jet-powered aircraft**

1940 Sep, USSR: the **T-34**, the war's most influential tank design, goes into production

1939

1940

1939 **John Steinbeck** writes *The Grapes of Wrath*, his great novel of Depression-era America

1941 Jan–Nov: British forces liberate **Ethiopia** from Italian occupation

1941 Mar: The **Lend-Lease Agreement** – the USA agrees to supply Britain with war materials

1941 22 Jun: The start of **Operation Barbarossa** – Germany invades the USSR

1941 5–31 Jul: **Ecuadorian–Peruvian War** – Peru occupies the Ecuadorian province of El Oro

1941 8 Sep: Beginning of the **siege of Leningrad** – one-third of the city's inhabitants perish

1941 7 Dec: The Japanese attack on **Pearl Harbor** brings the USA into the Second World War on the side of the Allies

1942 5 Feb: The **fall of Singapore** to Japan destroys British prestige in Southeast Asia

1942 Apr: The Allies begin an airlift of supplies to **China** from India

1942 4–16 Jun: The **Battle of Midway** – US naval victory over Japan turns the tide of the war in the Pacific

1942 Jul–Nov: The **Kokoda Track campaign** – Australia defeats Japanese forces in New Guinea

1942 14 Jul: The **Indian National Congress** demands immediate independence from Britain

1942 17 Jul: Beginning of the **battle of Stalingrad** – decisive victory by the Red Army over German forces

1942 23 Oct–4 Nov, Egypt: Britain decisively defeats German and Italian forces at the **second battle of El Alamein**

1942 8–16 Nov: **Operation Torch** – British and American forces invade Vichy-held Morocco and Algeria

1942 Jun, USA: The beginning of the **Manhattan Project** to develop the atomic bomb

1942 Oct, Germany: the first successful test flight of a **V-2 ballistic missile**

1941

1942

1942 20 Jan: The **Wannsee Conference** – Nazi leaders propose the 'final solution to the Jewish problem', beginning the Holocaust

1941 Jan: The BBC begins its **V campaign** of broadcasting to occupied Europe

1941 May: Initial release of Orson Welles's innovative film ***Citizen Kane***, often considered the best of all time

1941 Dec: **Dmitri Shostakovich** composes his *Symphony No. 7 'Leningrad'*, dedicated to the besieged city

1943–1945

A DEFEATED AXIS

FOLLOWING THEIR DEFEAT by the Soviet Union at Stalingrad in the winter of 1942–43, Nazi Germany managed to stabilize the Eastern Front. In an attempt to regain the initiative, German forces launched a new offensive in July 1943 at Kursk, in the southern USSR. The Soviet Red Army was prepared for the attack and defeated it in the largest tank conflicts of the war, before launching a massive counter-offensive that forced the Germans into a steady retreat. This was only the worst of many setbacks suffered by Germany in 1943: its ally Italy surrendered after an Allied invasion.

In June 1944, the D-Day landings by US, British and Canadian forces in Normandy opened a full second front in Europe and began the liberation of France. In the same month, the Red Army launched its summer offensive, Operation Bagration, costing Germany over 400,000 casualties and clearing its armies from Soviet soil. Finally, in 1945, the Allies invaded Germany from east and west. Hitler committed suicide when the Red Army entered Berlin in April and, on 7 May, Germany surrendered, bringing the war in Europe to an end.

In the Pacific theatre, the US 'island-hopping' campaign took American forces ever closer to Japan, often confronted by the suicidal resistance of *kamikaze* attacks. In 1944, the British and Indian armies repulsed a Japanese invasion of India and then moved to drive Japanese forces out of Burma. In June of the same year, US bombers began raiding

Japanese cities from China. Although a Japanese offensive to seize American airbases in China achieved substantial gains against the inefficient Guomindang army, the latter nevertheless tied down large numbers of Japanese troops. A full-scale Allied invasion of Japan proved unnecessary: Japan surrendered on 14 August 1945, shortly after the USA had dropped terrifyingly destructive new atomic bombs on the cities of Hiroshima and Nagasaki, and the USSR had invaded Manchuria. The war had cost some 60 million lives.

The key factor behind the Allied victory in the Second World War was that the USA, Britain and the USSR possessed a far greater combined industrial capacity, and were all far more effective at mobilizing their economies for war, than any of the Axis powers. Both sides made major technological advances during the war: Britain and Germany put the first operational jet fighter aircraft into use; Germany manufactured the first cruise and long-range ballistic missiles; and Allied codebreakers developed the first electronic computers. The development of atomic weapons by the USA, meanwhile, left it the world's unchallenged military superpower at the end of the war.

Allied planning for the post-war period included the foundation of the United Nations Organization (UNO) in June 1945 to promote international cooperation and prevent wars, as a more effective replacement for the League of Nations. The UNO followed the creation of both the International Monetary Fund (IMF) and World Bank in 1944 to promote international economic cooperation.

Summit meetings of the 'Big Three' Allied leaders – US president F. D. Roosevelt, British prime minister Winston Churchill and Soviet premier Josef Stalin – decided the borders of post-war Europe. The USSR retained the Baltic States and the Polish territory it had gained through the Molotov–Ribbentrop pact, and Poland was compensated with German territory. Germany and Austria were divided into US, Soviet, British and French occupation zones, and former Italian colonies in Africa were occupied by Britain and France. Japan was occupied by the USA and its former territory of Korea was divided into American and Soviet occupation zones. The Soviet forces that had driven Japan out of Manchuria remained in place to allow the Chinese Communist People's Liberation Army to move into the area.

`1943` 19 Apr–16 May: The **Warsaw Ghetto uprising** – 60,000 Jews are killed

`1943` 13 May: Axis forces in **North Africa** surrender

`1943` Jul: The Red Army defeats a German offensive at **Kursk** in the largest tank conflicts of the war

`1943` 25 Jul: Overthrow of **Mussolini** following the Allied invasion of Sicily

`1943` 27 Jul: The British bombing of **Hamburg** kills 42,600 people and leaves one million homeless

`1943` 3 Sep: **Italy** surrenders as the Allies land at Salerno, Taranto and in Calabria

`1943` 28 Nov–1 Dec: The **Tehran Conference** – Roosevelt, Churchill and Stalin meet to agree a strategy for the defeat of Germany

`1944–45` British and Indian offensive against Japanese forces in **Burma**

`1944` Mar–Jul: The Japanese invasion of **India** is defeated at Imphal and Kohima

`1944` Apr–Dec: **Japanese offensive** to capture US airbases in China

`1944` 6 Jun: **D-Day** – US, British and Canadian forces land in Normandy

SCIENCE & TECHNOLOGY

`1943` Dec: British engineer Tommy Flowers designs *Colossus*, the first **electronic computer**, for use in codebreaking

`1944` 25 Jul, Germany: the **Me 262** becomes the first jet fighter to see combat

1943

1944

RELIGION & PHILOSOPHY

ART & ARCHITECTURE

`1944` 15 Dec: American swing bandleader **Glenn Miller** disappears on a flight across the English Channel

1944 22 Jun–19 Aug: **Operation Bagration** – the Red Army clears German forces from Soviet territory

1944 Jul: Foundation of the **International Monetary Fund** (IMF) and the **World Bank**

1944 1 Aug–2 Oct: The **Warsaw Uprising** – German forces defeat Polish resistance fighters

1945 27 Jan: The Red Army liberates **Auschwitz concentration camp**, revealing the extent of the Holocaust

1945 4–11 Feb: Roosevelt, Churchill and Stalin discuss the post-war reorganization of Europe at the **Yalta Conference**

1945 19 Feb–26 Mar: The USA takes the Pacific island of **Iwo Jima** from Japanese forces

1945 22 Mar: The **Arab League** is founded in Cairo

1945 12 Apr: US president Franklin D. Roosevelt dies; he is succeeded by **Harry S. Truman**

1945 30 Apr: **Hitler** commits suicide as the Red Army enters Berlin

1945 7 May: **Germany** surrenders

1945 26 Jun: The Charter of the **United Nations** is signed at San Francisco

1945 17 Jul–2 Aug: The **Postdam Conference** – the USA, Britain and the USSR settle the post-war borders of Europe

1945 8 Aug: The USSR declares war on Japan, invading **Manchuria** and **Korea**

1945 6, 9 Aug: The USA drops **atomic bombs** on the Japanese cities of Hiroshima and Nagasaki

1945 10–15 Aug: **Korea** is divided between the USA and the USSR along the 38th parallel

1945 14 Aug: **Japan** surrenders, ending the Second World War

1945 16 Jul, USA: the first **atomic bomb** is exploded in the New Mexico desert

1945

1945 Dec: **Shinto directive** – US occupation orders the abolition of Shinto as the state religion of Japan

1945 Mar: Death in Bergen-Belsen concentration camp of **Anne Frank**, whose secret diary was published as the *Diary of a Young Girl*

1945 17 Aug: Publication of **George Orwell's** *Animal Farm*, an allegorical novel about the rise of Stalin

1938 ONWARDS

1. Hitler receiving the salute of the Columns during the annual Nuremberg Rally in Germany, September 1938, p. 188
2. US Pacific Fleet burning during the Japanese attack on Pearl Harbor, Hawaii, 7 December 1941, p. 193
3. Winston Churchill, Franklin D. Roosevelt and Joseph Stalin at the Yalta Conference, Crimea, February 1945, p. 199
4. Mao Zedong proclaiming the founding of the People's Republic of China in Tiananmen Square, Beijing, 1 October 1949, p. 203
5. The newly constructed Berlin Wall, August 1961, p. 211
6. The first manned moon landing, 20 July 1969, p. 213
7. Nelson Mandela outside Victor Verster Prison after his release, Cape Town, South Africa, 11 February 1990, p. 219
8. World Trade Center on fire during the 11 September attacks, New York City, USA, 11 September 2001, p. 221
9. US troops preparing to topple the statue of Saddam Hussein in Baghdad, Iraq, 9 April 2003, p. 225

1946–1953

THE COLD WAR

THE IMMEDIATE POST-WAR period saw the beginning of the Cold War – a political, ideological, economic and military confrontation that dominated global politics for four decades between the USA, the USSR and their respective allies. The Soviet Union and the USA avoided direct conflict, but the Cold War was often waged through proxy wars fought out across Latin America, Africa and Southeast Asia.

The Second World War ended with Soviet forces occupying most of Eastern Europe. Suspicious of his Western allies, Stalin was not prepared to give up the territory gained by the Red Army in the latter stages of the war. Communist dictatorships were imposed on Czechoslovakia, Poland, Hungary, Romania and Bulgaria, thus bringing down a so-called 'Iron Curtain' between east and west. Germany was also divided between West Germany, formed from the Western allies' zones of occupation, and Soviet-controlled East Germany. The USA responded with a policy of containing Soviet influence and giving financial aid to rebuild the economies of Western Europe through the Marshall Plan. The US-led North Atlantic Treaty Organization (NATO), founded in 1949, provided collective security against a possible Soviet invasion. Later the same year the USSR detonated an atomic bomb, thus achieving apparent military parity with the USA.

In the Chinese civil war, the USSR supported the communist People's Liberation Army (PLA) against Jiang

Jieshi's Guomindang government. In October 1949 the victorious communist leader Mao Zedong proclaimed the foundation of the People's Republic of China. The Guomindang fled to Taiwan with around 2 million refugees. Mao set about restoring the borders of the Qing empire by conquering previously independent Tibet in 1950; the USSR, however, refused to sanction the Chinese reoccupation of Mongolia, which remained a Soviet satellite state. When the Soviet-backed North Korean government invaded South Korea in 1950, the UN – whose meetings were being boycotted by the Soviet Union – authorized a US-led military intervention, beginning the Korean War. After communist China intervened on behalf of the north, the war ground to a stalemate in 1951. A ceasefire was finally agreed only in July 1953, five months after Stalin's death had provoked a power struggle in the Soviet Union.

The Second World War left the main European colonial powers severely weakened and facing a rising tide of nationalism across Asia and Africa. France, desperate to restore its prestige after the humiliation of German occupation during the war, committed to a long war against communist Viet Minh insurgents in Indochina, while attempting to bind its African colonies more tightly together in the French Union. The Netherlands fought to regain control of the East Indies from Indonesian nationalists, only to recognize Indonesia's independence in 1949.

Britain, bankrupted by the war, accepted that its position in India was untenable: unable to count on the loyalty of the Indian army and civil service, and facing escalating violence between Hindus and Muslims, it decided on a quick withdrawal. India was partitioned between Hindu-majority India and Muslim Pakistan, and both states became independent in 1947. Partition was marked by communal violence and mass population displacement as Hindus fled Pakistan and Muslims fled India. Less than three months after independence, India and Pakistan fought an inconclusive war over the northern territory of Kashmir. Ceylon (modern-day Sri Lanka) and Burma gained their independence from Britain in 1948, and in 1946 the USA granted its only significant colonial possession, the Philippines, independence.

Decolonization also proceeded rapidly in the Middle East: Lebanon had gained independence from France during the war and Syria followed in 1946; Britain recognized Jordan's independence the same year. Britain struggled to carry out a UN plan to partition Palestine into separate Jewish and Arab states. Unable to maintain control in the face of Jewish and Arab violence, Britain withdrew in 1948. Jewish settlers proclaimed the state of Israel, immediately defeating an attempt by the Arab League to expel them.

`1946` Mar: Outbreak of the **Chinese civil war** between the communists and the Guomindang

`1946` 17 Apr: **Syria** gains independence from France

`1946` 25 May: **Jordan** gains independence from Britain

`1946` 4 Jul: The **Philippines** gain independence from the USA

`1947` 5 Jun: The USA announces the **Marshall Plan** to rebuild the economies of Western Europe

`1947` 14–15 Aug: **India** and **Pakistan** gain independence from Britain

`1947` 29 Nov: The UN agrees a plan to partition **Palestine** into Jewish and Arab states

`1948–49` The **Berlin Airlift** breaks a Soviet blockade of West Berlin

`1948` 4 Jan: **Burma** gains independence from Britain

`1948` 30 Jan: **Gandhi** is assassinated by a Hindu nationalist

`1948` 4 Feb: **Ceylon** (present-day Sri Lanka) gains independence from Britain

`1948` 14 May: The proclamation of the State of Israel leads to the **First Arab-Israeli War**

`1949` 4 Apr: The treaty of Brussels founds the US-led **North Atlantic Treaty Organization** (NATO)

`1949` 1 Oct: The victorious communists under **Mao Zedong** proclaim the People's Republic of China

`1949` 27 Dec: **Indonesia** gains independence from the Netherlands under President Sukarno

SCIENCE & TECHNOLOGY

`1947` Mikhail Kalashnikov designs the **AK-47**, the world's most widely used assault rifle

`1949` 27 Jul, UK: the first flight of the **De Havilland Comet**, the first passenger jet

`1949` Sep: The USSR explodes its **first atomic bomb**

1946	1947	1948	1949

RELIGION & PHILOSOPHY

`1946` French philosopher **Jean-Paul Sartre** publishes his *Existentialism is a Humanism*, a defining work of existential philosophy

ART & ARCHITECTURE

`1945–52` Origin of modern Japanese **manga** comics and cartoon prints

`1947` American playwright **Tennessee Williams** writes his landmark drama *A Streetcar Named Desire*

`1949` Publication of French philosopher **Simone de Beauvoir**'s key work of feminist literature *The Second Sex*

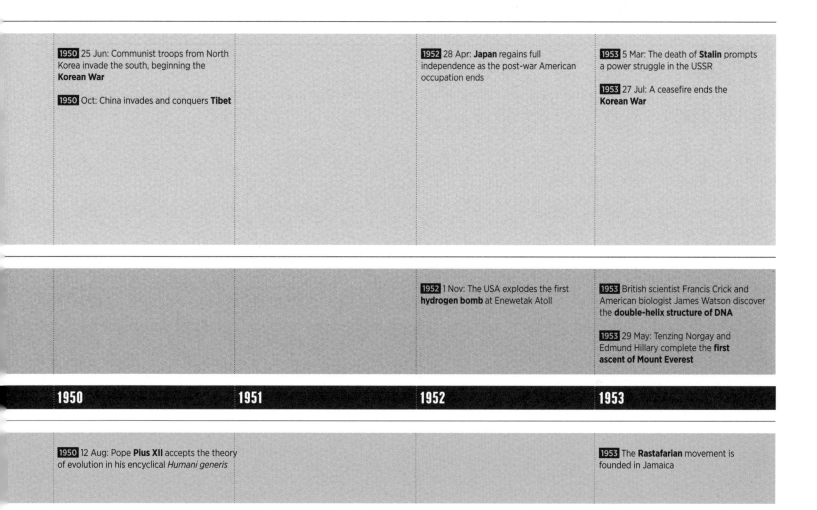

1950 25 Jun: Communist troops from North Korea invade the south, beginning the **Korean War**

1950 Oct: China invades and conquers **Tibet**

1952 28 Apr: **Japan** regains full independence as the post-war American occupation ends

1953 5 Mar: The death of **Stalin** prompts a power struggle in the USSR

1953 27 Jul: A ceasefire ends the **Korean War**

1952 1 Nov: The USA explodes the first **hydrogen bomb** at Enewetak Atoll

1953 British scientist Francis Crick and American biologist James Watson discover the **double-helix structure of DNA**

1953 29 May: Tenzing Norgay and Edmund Hillary complete the **first ascent of Mount Everest**

1950   1951   1952   1953

1950 12 Aug: Pope **Pius XII** accepts the theory of evolution in his encyclical *Humani generis*

1953 The **Rastafarian** movement is founded in Jamaica

1950 African-American singer and actor **Paul Robeson** has his passport cancelled because of his socialist and anti-racist views

1952 **John Cage** composes *4' 33''*, in which not a single note of music is played

1953 Jan: Premiere in Paris of Irish writer **Samuel Beckett**'s absurdist play *Waiting for Godot*

1954

THE COLD WAR

By 1900 Europe dominated the world. This world order collapsed rapidly following the two devastating world wars of the early 20th century and was replaced by the rivalry between two superpowers, the USA and the USSR. Though they avoided direct conflict, the Cold War was played out globally through diplomacy and proxy wars.

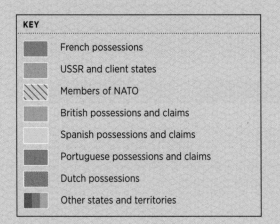

KEY

- French possessions
- USSR and client states
- Members of NATO
- British possessions and claims
- Spanish possessions and claims
- Portuguese possessions and claims
- Dutch possessions
- Other states and territories

CANADA

UNITED STATES OF AMERICA

JAMAICA

Easter Island
(CHILE)

CHILE

UNION OF SOVIET SOCIALIST REPUBLICS

WEST
GERMANY

EAST
GERMANY

NETHERLANDS

UNITED
KINGDOM

POLAND

CZECHOSLOVAKIA

FRANCE

HUNGARY

ROMANIA

BULGARIA

MONGOLIA

NORTH
KOREA

SOUTH
KOREA

JAPAN

TUNISIA

SYRIA

LEBANON

PEOPLE'S
REPUBLIC OF
CHINA

MOROCCO

ISRAEL
PALESTINE

IRAQ

WEST
PAKISTAN

JORDAN

ALGERIA

EAST
PAKISTAN

BURMA

REPUBLIC OF
CHINA

INDIA

FRENCH WEST AFRICA

FRENCH
EQUATORIAL
AFRICA

PHILIPPINES

FRENCH
INDO-
CHINA

CAMEROON

CEYLON

INDONESIA

AUSTRALIA

1954– 1962

WINDS OF CHANGE

THE DISINTEGRATION OF European colonial empires gathered pace after 1950 and by 1962 they were reduced mostly to small island territories. France's federation in Indochina was dissolved in 1954 after the decisive Viet Minh victory at Dien Bien Phu. France fought a destructive war to retain control of Algeria, which had a large ethnic French population, but conceded defeat in 1962. Britain began to grant its African colonies independence in this period, with the Gold Coast becoming independent Ghana in 1957. Portugal, Europe's oldest colonial power, showed no willingness to decolonize its empire, but wars of independence broke out in Angola and Mozambique in 1961; India seized Goa the same year. Nothing symbolized the decline of the European colonial powers so much as the failed intervention of Britain and France in Egypt after its president, Gamal Abdel Nasser, nationalized the Suez Canal in 1956.

In the aftermath of the Korean War, the USA increased its support for anti-communist regimes in Asia, such as the government of South Vietnam (which opposed the Communist Viet Minh in North Vietnam) and the Guomindang in Taiwan. The United States also gave uncritical support to repressive right-wing regimes in Latin America, but nevertheless failed to prevent a communist government winning power in Cuba under Fidel Castro. In 1962, the world seemed to be on the brink of a nuclear war when the USSR attempted to site armed nuclear missiles in Cuba, and the USA threatened military retaliation: the USSR eventually backed down. In 1955 the USSR had created an equivalent to NATO by enrolling its European satellite states in the Warsaw Pact; its first military action was the crushing of an anti-Soviet uprising in Hungary in 1956.

In the USA, the 1950s was a time of unparalleled affluence. American industry emerged from the Second World War completely undamaged by enemy bombing, and production was quickly turned from armaments to consumer goods. Car ownership became widespread and a television became the focus of every living room. Although American society remained conservative and racially segregated, established values were increasingly challenged by a rebellious youth culture: rock and roll music topped the record charts and new fashions moved away from the austerity of the war years.

Western European countries also experienced rising affluence in this period, as their economies recovered from the effects of war. Economic growth was sustained by 'mixed market' economics that combined free markets with varying degrees of government spending on infrastructure and welfare. In 1957, France, West Germany, Italy, the Netherlands, Belgium and Luxembourg began to integrate their economies as part of a single market area by founding the European Economic Community (EEC), the forerunner of today's European Union. The community's founders believed that economic integration would go hand-in-hand with political integration and peace in Europe.

The economies of communist Eastern Europe and the USSR grew more slowly, yet saw a limited easing of political repression after Stalin's death in 1953 and the rise to power of Nikita Khrushchev. The USSR's achievements in space challenged American technological leadership: the Soviet Union launched the first artificial satellite into orbit in 1957, and the first human into orbit four years later. Japan also recovered from the war and by 1960 had begun a period of rapid industrial expansion. However, Mao's disastrous Great Leap Forward campaign, which introduced the communalization of industry and agriculture, led to both a rapid slowdown in the Chinese economy and 'Three Bitter Years' of famine that killed around 36 million people.

While it is easy to focus on the headline-grabbing breakthroughs in nuclear and space technology, the most far-reaching scientific development of this period was the introduction of the oral contraceptive pill in 1960, which gave women effective control over their fertility. As a consequence, by 1962 many countries were witnessing a revolution in sexual behaviour and a substantial increase in women's participation in higher education and the labour market.

1954 13 Mar–7 May: Decisive Viet Minh victory over France at the siege of **Dien Bien Phu**

1954 The **Geneva Agreements** dissolve French Indochina: **Laos** and **Cambodia** gain independence and **Vietnam** is partitioned

1955 14 May: The **Warsaw Pact** is created as Soviet-bloc counter to NATO

1956 25 Feb: Soviet leader Nikita Khrushchev denounces Stalin in the **Secret Speech**

1956–59 The **Cuban Revolution**: Fidel Castro overthrows the US-supported Batista regime and forms a communist government

1956 23 Oct–10 Nov: Members of the Warsaw Pact crush an anti-Soviet uprising in **Hungary**

1956 29 Oct–6 Nov: Britain and France invade **Egypt** after President Gamal Abdel Nasser nationalizes the Suez Canal

1957 6 Mar: The Gold Coast becomes the first West African country to win independence as **Ghana** under Kwame Nkrumah (from Britain)

1957 25 Mar: The Treaty of Rome founds the **European Economic Community** (EEC)

SCIENCE & TECHNOLOGY

1954 Jan: USA: the first **nuclear submarine**, USS *Nautilus*, is launched

1957 4 Oct: The USSR launches the first **artificial satellite**, *Sputnik-1*

1954   1955   1956   1957

RELIGION & PHILOSOPHY

1955 India passes the Hindu Marriage Act and the Untouchability Act to modernize Hindu **marriage laws** and the **caste system**

ART & ARCHITECTURE

1955 Jul: Bill Haley's ***Rock Around the Clock*** is the first rock and roll recording to top the US charts

1958-61 Mao's **Great Leap Forward** attempts breakneck economic growth, but fails disastrously

1959-61 At least 30 million people die in the **Great Chinese Famine**

1960 The **Sino-Soviet split** – the USSR ends all development aid to China

1960* **Japan** enters a period of rapid industrial expansion

1960 10-14 Sep: The **Organization of Petroleum Exporting Countries** (OPEC) is founded at Baghdad

1961 **Wars of independence** begin in Portugal's African colonies

1961 May: US military advisers are sent to assist the government of South Vietnam against the communist North

1961 Aug: The **Berlin Wall** is built to prevent emigration from East to West Berlin

1961 18-19 Dec: India seizes **Goa** from Portugal

1962 **Australian Aborigines** are given the right to vote in national elections

1962 5 Jul: France recognizes **Algerian** independence

1962 Oct: The **Cuban Missile Crisis**: the USA launches a naval blockade after the USSR builds missile bases in Cuba

1960 Jun, USA: The first female **oral contraceptive** is approved for use

1961 21 Apr: Soviet astronaut **Yuri Gagarin** becomes the first human in space, orbiting the earth in *Vostok-1*

1958	1959	1960	1961	1962

1959 New York: Opening of the new Guggenheim Museum building, designed by American architect **Frank Lloyd Wright**

1961 British composer **Benjamin Britten** writes his *War Requiem*, a choral commemoration of the victims of war

1962 5 Aug: Death of the celebrated American film star **Marilyn Monroe**

1963–1975

POP, SPACE, REVOLT

IN 1965 the United States committed combat troops to the war between South Vietnam and the communist Viet Cong rebels, backed by North Vietnam. Against US material superiority, the communists resorted to guerrilla warfare, which spread into neighbouring Laos and Cambodia. American forces withdrew after a face-saving peace deal with North Vietnam in 1973, but the communist insurgency continued: Vietnam was eventually reunited under a communist government in 1975. The same year, communist governments were also established in Cambodia and Laos. In Latin America, the USA opposed even democratically elected communist leaders, engineering a military coup against the Marxist government of Chile in 1973.

The USSR had shown equal intolerance of ideological difference in its own back yard when it sent Warsaw Pact forces to occupy Czechoslovakia and crush the Prague Spring reform movement in 1968. A new element in the Cold War was the split between the USSR and Mao's People's Republic of China (PRC); this began with ideological differences in 1960, but by 1969 had escalated to armed clashes along the Sino-Soviet border. In 1971 the PRC took China's seat at the UN, replacing representatives of the Guomindang government in Taiwan, and the opening of trade and diplomatic relations with the United States in 1972 marked the beginning of a de facto Sino-US alliance against the USSR.

The independence in 1975 of Angola and Mozambique from Portugal heralded the end of European colonialism in Africa. Its last vestiges were the Spanish enclaves of Ceuta and Melilla in North Africa; the apartheid regime in South Africa; and in Rhodesia (modern-day Zimbabwe), a regime led by members of the white minority had declared independence from Britain rather than accept black majority rule. Newly independent African states – victims of the European colonial powers' arbitrary division of the continent – inherited a destabilizing legacy of suppressed ethnic tensions, which have often led to civil war and humanitarian crises. India and Pakistan fought two wars in this period, in 1965 and 1971, the latter ending with the creation of Bangladesh.

By 1975, the impact of the unresolved conflict between Israel and its Arab neighbours had spread far beyond the Middle East. In 1948–49, during its war of independence, Israel had occupied all of Palestine except for the small territories of Gaza and the West Bank, causing millions of Palestinian Arabs to become stateless refugees. In the Six Day War of 1967, Israel defeated an alliance of Egypt, Syria, Jordan and Iraq, occupying Gaza and the West Bank, as well as Egypt's Sinai Peninsula and Syria's Golan Heights. After Israel defeated an offensive led by Egypt and Syria in 1973, Arab oil-exporting countries imposed an oil embargo on the USA and Europe in retaliation for their support of Israel, causing a worldwide recession. Attacks on Israeli targets abroad by the Palestine Liberation Organization (PLO) made international terrorism an issue of global concern.

This period witnessed major cultural upheaval. In Western Europe and the USA, society became more liberal as affluent young people rebelled against traditional conservative and religious values. Opposition to racial segregation and the Vietnam War led to mass protest movements in the USA. In the West, pop culture flourished, particularly in music and art. In China, however, Mao's Cultural Revolution threw the country into turmoil as young Red Guards attacked 'bourgeois' culture, persecuting intellectuals and destroying antiquities and historical sites. In Cambodia, the Khmer Rouge under Pol Pot also targeted 'bourgeois' culture, aiming to eradicate it through a genocide that killed a quarter of the Cambodian population.

The most impressive technological achievement of this period was the American Apollo programme's successful manned landing on the Moon in 1969, although this owed more to Cold War rivalry than to the search for scientific knowledge. Back on Earth, the Boeing 747 'jumbo jet' airliner, which first flew in 1969, began the era of affordable long-distance air travel.

POLITICS & ECONOMY

1963 22 Nov: US president **John F. Kennedy** is assassinated in Dallas, Texas

1964 28 May: The **Palestinian Liberation Organization** (PLO) is found in Jerusalem

1965 8 Mar: The USA first dispatches combat troops to **South Vietnam**

1965 6 Aug: USA: the **Voting Rights Act** outlaws discriminatory voting practices

1965 11 Nov: White settlers in **Southern Rhodesia** declare unilateral independence from Britain

1967 5 –10 Jun: The **Six Day War** – Israel defeats a coalition of Arab states and occupies the West Bank, Gaza, Sinai and the Golan Heights

1968 Jan–Sep: US and South Vietnamese forces defeat the **Tet Offensive** launched by the Viet Cong and North Vietnam

1968 May: Student riots in **Paris** lead to a liberalization of French social values

1968 21 Aug: The **Prague Spring** liberalization movement in Czechoslovakia is ended by an invasion of Warsaw Pact members

SCIENCE & TECHNOLOGY

1964 Japan: *Shinkansen*, high-speed bullet trains, begin operating

1967 3 Dec, South Africa: The first **human heart transplant** is carried out

1963   1964   1965   1966   1967   1968

RELIGION & PHILOSOPHY

1966–69 Most Buddhist monasteries in **Tibet** are destroyed by Chinese Red Guards

1968 25 Jul: Pope Paul VI condemns artificial birth control in his encyclical *Humanae vitae*

ART & ARCHITECTURE

1963–64 **Beatlemania**: Wave of intense hysteria among fans of the UK pop group the Beatles

1965 British fashion designer Mary Quant creates the **miniskirt**

1966–69 The **Cultural Revolution** in China is marked by the persecution of intellectuals and the destruction of artistic treasures

1967 Colombian author **Gabriel García Márquez** publishes his magic realist novel *One Hundred Years of Solitude*

1967 The **Summer of Love**: Hippie counterculture rebellion in the USA, focused on San Francisco

1967–72 Construction of American architect Minoru Yamasaki's **World Trade Center** in New York

1969 Mar–Sep: Military clashes on the **Sino-Soviet border**

1971 3–16 Dec: The **Third India–Pakistan War** ends with East Pakistan gaining independence as Bangladesh

1973 15 Jan: The **Paris Peace Accords** end direct US intervention in Vietnam

1973 6–26 Oct: The **Yom Kippur War** – Israel defeats a surprise attack led by Egypt and Syria

1973–74 Arab members of OPEC impose an **oil embargo** on the USA and Europe

1974 25 Apr: The **Carnation Revolution** – the dictatorship in Portugal is overthrown

1974 9 Aug: US president Richard Nixon resigns after the **Watergate scandal**

1975 17 Apr: The communist **Khmer Rouge** take over Cambodia, killing approximately 25% of the population in forced labour camps

1975 25 Jun: **Mozambique** gains independence from Portugal

1975 11 Nov: **Angola** gains independence from Portugal, prompting the outbreak of civil war

1975 20 Nov: Death of Spanish fascist dictator **Francisco Franco**

1969 9 Feb, USA: First flight of the **Boeing 747** ('jumbo jet') airliner

1969 20 Jul, USA: The Apollo 11 mission completes the first **manned Moon landing**

1969   **1970**   **1971**   **1972**   **1973**   **1974**   **1975**

1971 Egypt: Completion of the **Aswan High Dam** to control Nile floods and generate electricity

1973 Completion of Danish architect Jørn Utzon's **Sydney Opera House**

1976–1991

A NEW DAWN?

THE LAST GREAT crisis of the Cold War began in 1979 when the USSR invaded Afghanistan to support its communist government against an Islamist *mujahideen* insurgency. Soviet forces never managed to win full control of the country and soon became bogged down in a guerrilla war with the *mujahideen*, who received aid – including anti-aircraft missiles – from the US Central Intelligence Agency (CIA). The USSR finally withdrew only in 1989, its prestige damaged, leaving Afghanistan to be fought over by rival warlords.

The Soviet economy stagnated in the 1970s and failed to keep pace with American scientific development, especially in military technology. In 1985 Mikhail Gorbachev became Soviet leader and recognized the need to revitalize the USSR: he therefore introduced the reforming policies of *glasnost* (openness) and *perestroika* (restructuring). The relaxation of state repression that followed encouraged popular demands for liberalization in the USSR's Warsaw Pact satellites. These movements culminated in the overthrow of communist governments in Eastern Europe, most dramatically with the fall of the Berlin Wall in 1989 and the reunification of Germany a year later. Disaffected Soviet generals, dismayed by the loss of Soviet influence in Eastern Europe, attempted a military coup to depose Gorbachev in August 1991. Although the coup failed, it precipitated the constituent republics of the USSR declaring independence and its formal dissolution in December the same year.

Events in Eastern Europe inspired a Chinese student-led democracy movement in 1989, but this was brutally crushed by the army. After Mao's death in 1976, a power struggle had broken out between the radical 'Gang of Four', led by Mao's widow Jiang Qing, and a reforming faction under Deng Xiaoping. After the military removed the 'Gang of Four', Deng gradually abandoned Marxist economic policies while maintaining a one-party state; thanks to healthy industrial growth and improving living standards, the Chinese Communist Party remained in power. In Latin America, meanwhile, the USA was successful in containing communism, supporting repressive right-wing dictatorships in Guatemala and El Salvador against left-wing peasant rebels.

In many Western countries, the economic recession caused by the Arab oil embargo of 1973 led to governments rejecting the post-war consensus of a mixed economy in favour of 'neo-liberal' *laissez-faire* economics that advocated tax cuts and market deregulation to stimulate economic growth. The Conservative government of Margaret Thatcher in the UK, and Ronald Reagan's administration in the United States, adopted such policies most enthusiastically.

Continuing instability across the Middle East contributed to the rise of Islamic fundamentalism as a major political and cultural force in this period. Its first major manifestation was the Shi'ite revolution in Iran, led by the Ayatollah Khomeini, which overthrew the repressive regime of the US-backed shah in 1979. Fears that revolutionary fervour might spread to Iraq led its dictator Saddam Hussein to wage a bloody, but ultimately indecisive, eight-year war against Iran. Deeply indebted by the war, Iraq invaded neighbouring Kuwait to seize its oilfields in 1990, but was expelled by a US-led coalition the following year.

Nonetheless, the Iranian revolution did inspire the foundation of the Shi'ite Hezbollah movement in Lebanon in 1982, which pioneered the use of suicide bombers in attacking Israeli and US targets. On the other side of the Islamic theological divide, the Sunni *mujahideen* fighting the Soviets in Afghanistan were inspired by the ideology of *jihad*; their example in turn encouraged the foundation of the Palestinian Hamas jihadi movement in 1987 and the Muslim separatist insurgency that broke out in Indian-administered Kashmir in 1989.

The introduction of affordable personal computers and the development of the World Wide Web were the most important technological developments of this period. Although their full potential was scarcely evident in 1991, they would come to revolutionize the way people worked, shopped, spent their leisure time and communicated.

1976 9 Sep: **Mao Zedong** dies; a coup removes the 'Gang of Four', led by Mao's widow Jiang Qing

1978 **Deng Xiaoping** introduces a 'socialist market economy' in China, beginning the abandonment of Marxist policies

1979 Jan–Feb: Ayatollah Khomeini leads an Islamic revolution in **Iran**

1979 16 Jul: Ba'ath party leader **Saddam Hussein** becomes dictator of Iraq

1979 27 Dec: The USSR invades **Afghanistan** in support of its Marxist government

1980 18 Apr: **Zimbabwe** (formerly Southern Rhodesia) gains independence from Britain under majority rule

1980 22 Sep: Beginning of the **Iran–Iraq War**

1983 25 Oct: The USA invades **Grenada** following an attempted Marxist coup

---

SCIENCE & TECHNOLOGY

1977 The Commodore PET and the Apple II, the first mass-produced **personal computers**, go on sale

1981 21 Apr, USA: First NASA **space shuttle** flight

1984 The **HIV virus**, the cause of AIDS, is identified in Paris

---

1976 **1977** **1978** **1979** **1980** **1981** **1982** **1983** **1984**

RELIGION & PHILOSOPHY

1978 19 Jul, Britain: The first baby conceived using **IVF** is born

1982 Lebanon: The Islamic fundamentalist movement **Hezbollah** (Party of God) is founded

1984 3–6 Jun: Indian forces expel Sikh separatists from the **Golden Temple** at Amritsar

---

ART & ARCHITECTURE

1977 Paris: Opening of the **Georges Pompidou Centre**, designed by Richard Rogers and Renzo Piano

1982 **Michael Jackson**'s *Thriller* becomes the bestselling album of all time

1984 Nigerian author **Wole Soyinka** becomes the first African writer to win the Nobel Prize in Literature

1985 11 Mar: **Mikhail Gorbachev** comes to power in the USSR and introduces the reforming policies of *glasnost* (openness) and *perestroika* (restructuring)

1988 8 Aug: The **8888 uprising** against military rule in Burma

1989 4 Jun: Chinese pro-democracy movement is violently suppressed in the **Tiananmen Square massacre**

1989 Nov: Collapse of the **Berlin Wall**

1990 11 Feb: **Nelson Mandela** is released from prison, beginning the dismantling of apartheid in South Africa

1990 25 Feb: The Marxist **Sandinistas** lose power in Nicaraguan elections

1990 2 Aug: Iraq occupies **Kuwait**

1990 3 Oct: **Germany** is reunified

1991 17 Jan–28 Feb: **Operation Desert Storm** – a US-led coalition liberates Kuwait

1991 19–21 Aug: A failed military coup against Gorbachev precipitates the collapse of the **USSR**

1991 21 Dec: The **USSR** is formally dissolved

1989 France/Switzerland: Tim Berners-Lee invents the **World Wide Web** at CERN

1985   **1986**   **1987**   **1988**   **1989**   **1990**   **1991**   **1992**

1989 Feb: Ayatollah Khomeini issues a *fatwa* calling for the murder of **Salman Rushdie**, author of *The Satanic Verses*

1991 British artist **Damien Hirst** completes his *The Physical Impossibility of Death in the Mind of Someone Living*, a shark preserved in formaldehyde

1992–2001

A WORLD IN FLUX

DESPITE THE OPTIMISM of pro-democracy movements in the late 1980s, the end of the Cold War created new problems of its own. Centralized state control lay at the heart of the highly integrated Soviet economy, leaving its newly independent republics with a difficult economic legacy in the wake of its collapse: only the Baltic republics of Estonia, Latvia and Lithuania successfully transitioned to democracy and free-market capitalism. In Russia itself, the economy almost collapsed, as super-rich 'oligarchs' acquired previously nationalized assets, while most people's living standards declined sharply in the face of rampant hyperinflation. Elsewhere in the now defunct Warsaw Pact, Czechoslovakia split peacefully into separate Czech and Slovak republics.

Soviet hegemony had also contained ethnic tensions in the Balkans and the Caucasus, but these now erupted in terrorism, war and ethnic cleansing. In Chechnya, Russia became entangled in a succession of bitter conflicts with Islamic separatists throughout the 1990s. In Yugoslavia, meanwhile, only an independent-minded communist government and fear of Soviet intervention had held this federation of over half a dozen ethnic and religious groups together. Following the Soviet Union's disintegration, Yugoslavia rapidly dissolved in a complex series of bloody civil wars that descended into racially motivated violence. Such crimes against humanity were not, however, limited to Europe: in Rwanda, the Hutu majority government perpetrated genocide against the Tutsi minority, leaving a million people dead.

The fall of the USSR had left the United States as the sole superpower, its economic, military, and ideological dominance apparently unchallenged. The USA had used its political might to oversee agreements between Israel and the Palestine Liberation Organization (PLO), the Oslo accords, which afforded recognition to a Palestinian state. In 1994, meanwhile, the United States invaded the Caribbean island of Haiti to restore democratic government after a military coup three years earlier. Yet any sense of American invulnerability was abruptly shattered on 11 September, 2001, when Islamist Al-Qaeda terrorists crashed hijacked aircraft into both New York's World Trade Center, and the Pentagon in Washington, DC. After the Soviet withdrawal from Afghanistan in 1989, most of the country had fallen under the control of the Islamic fundamentalist Taliban, who had allowed Islamist groups such as Al-Qaeda to establish terrorist training camps in their territory. In response, American forces invaded Afghanistan with their NATO allies one month after 9/11.

During this period, Britain became physically connected to continental Europe for the first time in 8000 years through the Channel Tunnel, completed in 1994 after two centuries of hypothetical suggestions. The same year, China began construction of the Three Gorges Dam, the world's largest hydroelectric power station, on the Yangtze river. The project reflected China's newfound confidence following Deng Xiaoping's reforms: its economy expanded rapidly in the first half of the 1990s, and in 1997 it gained control over the former British colony of Hong Kong.

This period also witnessed rapid technological evolutions, with 1996 seeing the birth of Dolly the Sheep – the first mammal to be cloned – and the release of the first MP3 audio player. In tandem with the United States' political dominance came the increasing influence of American culture in music, film and television. Modern art moved towards 'conceptual' forms under figures like Damien Hirst, who emphasized the idea behind a work over traditional notions of aesthetic value.

Perhaps most importantly in global terms, in this decade the threat of climate change became an issue of political as well as scientific concern. The effects of carbon dioxide released by burning fossil fuels were steadily realized, but competing demands for environmental protection and economic development meant that a number of initiatives sponsored by the UN to tackle the problem achieved little: neither the 1992 UN Framework Convention on Climate Change, nor the Kyoto Protocol agreed five years later, enjoyed lasting success.

POLITICS & ECONOMY

1992 1 Apr: After **Bosnia** declares independence from Yugoslavia, war breaks out between Serb, Croat and Muslim communities

1992 9 May: The **UN Framework Convention on Climate Change** is agreed

1993 1 Jan: **Czechoslovakia** splits into the Czech Republic and Slovakia

1993 24 May: **Eritrea** gains independence from Ethiopia

1993 20 Aug: The **Oslo I accord** – Israel and the Palestine Liberation Organization (PLO) agree to the formation of a Palestinian state

1993 1 Nov: The European Community becomes the **European Union** (EU)

1994 War breaks out between Russia and Muslim separatists in **Chechnya**

1994 1 Jan: The **North American Free Trade Area** (NAFTA) comes into effect

1994 Apr–May: Ethnic conflict in **Rwanda** results in the genocide of the Tutsi minority

1994 19 Sep: The United States invades **Haiti**, overthrowing the military regime

1995 Jul: The **Srebrenica massacre** – Bosnian Serbs murder 8,000 Muslims

1995 4 Nov: Israeli prime minister **Yitzhak Rabin** is assassinated by an opponent of the Oslo accords

1995 14 Dec: The **Dayton Agreement** – a US-brokered ceasefire ends the Bosnian war

1996 Sep: The Muslim fundamentalist **Taliban** seize power in Afghanistan

SCIENCE & TECHNOLOGY

1992 USA: **planets outside the Solar System** are first definitively detected

1994 China: Construction of the **Three Gorges Dam**, the world's largest hydroelectric plant, begins

1996 UK: **Dolly the sheep** is the first mammal to be cloned

1996 USA: Audio Highway's Listen Up, the first **MP3 audio player**, is released

1992 **1993** **1994** **1995** **1996**

RELIGION & PHILOSOPHY

1992 China: Li Hongzhi founds the **Falun Gong** cult

1992 6 Dec: Hindu fundamentalists destroy a 16th-century mosque at **Ayodhya**, allegedly built on the birthplace of the god Rama

ART & ARCHITECTURE

1994 May: The **Channel Tunnel** is completed, linking the UK and France

1997 1 Jul: The UK returns **Hong Kong** to Chinese rule

1998 6 Dec: **Hugo Chávez** is elected president of Venezuela, proclaiming a 'Bolivarian revolution'

1999 Mar: NATO conducts a bombing campaign against **Serbia** after Albanians are expelled from Kosovo

1999 May–Jul: The **Kargil War**: conflict breaks out between India and Pakistan in Kashmir

2001 1 Apr: The Netherlands become the first country to legalize **same-sex marriage**

2001 11 Sep: Islamist Al-Qaeda terrorists crash hijacked aircraft into the **World Trade Center** (New York) and the **Pentagon** (Washington, DC)

2001 7 Oct: The United States leads an invasion of **Afghanistan** to defeat the Taliban

1998 28 May: **Pakistan** detonates an atomic bomb for the first time

1997   **1998**   **1999**   **2000**   **2001**

2001 Afghanistan: The Taliban destroy the 6th-century monumental **Buddhas of Bamiyan**

1997 Bilbao, Spain: Canadian-American architect Frank Gehry's **Guggenheim Museum** opens

1998 Kuala Lumpur, Malaysia: Argentine-American architect César Pelli's **Petronas Towers** are completed

1997 26 Jun, UK: The first book in J. K. Rowling's *Harry Potter* series is published

2002–2010

RECESSION AND INVENTION

BY 2010 the United States was coming to terms with the reality of its relative decline in a newly multilateral world, as economic growth boomed spectacularly in Brazil, India, and, especially, China, which surpassed Japan in 2010 to become the world's second largest economy. Benefitting from a huge pool of cheap labour and a deliberately undervalued currency, China gained an enormous competitive advantage over other manufacturing economies, building huge trade surpluses and foreign currency reserves. China's success was aided by buoyant consumer demand in the USA – but American spending relied on easy credit and an unsustainable property bubble, as levels of private debt soared. In 2008, the bubble burst: the overheated US real estate market collapsed, precipitating a financial crisis in the American banking system that quickly spread to Europe and triggered the most serious economic downturn in the West since the Great Depression of the 1930s.

In contrast, the first half of this period was marked by growing optimism in Europe as members of the European Union (EU) took steps to further integrate their economies and expand the union's membership. In 2002, fourteen EU states introduced a common currency, the Euro. Eastern European countries, meanwhile, queued up to join NATO and the EU, seeing these organizations as the best guarantee of their independence and future prosperity in the face of Russia's increasing authoritarianism under its new president

Vladimir Putin. Gas exports to Europe and China increased the Russian government's income during this period, underpinning a more assertive foreign policy. Threats to Ukraine's gas supply discouraged it from pursuing pro-Western policies. After Georgia applied to join NATO, Russia invaded its northern regions of South Ossetia and Abkhazia to warn the US-led alliance not to expand into what it considered its own sphere of influence.

In Afghanistan, the United States and its allies drove the Taliban from power, but failed to eradicate the movement completely, and it quickly re-emerged as a potent terrorist organisation. The invasion of Iraq in 2003 was scarcely more successful. Although Saddam Hussein's regime was quickly overthrown, violence between Sunni and Shi'ite militia groups reduced the country to near anarchy. In Latin America, the establishment and survival of popular left-wing governments challenged the American hegemony asserted in the Monroe Doctrine two centuries earlier: after Hugo Chávez's election as president of Venezuela at the end of the 1990s, Evo Morales became the first elected Amerindian leader of Bolivia in 2005.

The 2000s witnessed the continuing search by engineers and architects for ever more ambitious designs. Airbus released its A380, the largest passenger aircraft ever built, with a capacity of over 800 people. In Dubai, the Burj Khalifa skyscraper became the world's tallest building in 2010, reflecting the ambitions of the Gulf states by exceeding the previous record holder by over 300 metres. New frontiers also opened up in scientific research: the Large Hadron Collider, the world's largest particle accelerator, was completed, while American scientists produced a complete map of the human genome for the first time.

The full impact of the microchip only became evident during this period, as computers and mobile telephones become affordable and accessible: by the end of the decade the first smartphone, Apple's iPhone, had been released. In tandem with this new technology came the advent of social media as websites such as YouTube and Facebook were launched. In the cultural sphere, American author Cormac McCarthy explored post-apocalyptic visions of society in his Pulitzer-winning novel *The Road*. In 2005, however, the continued limits on freedom of expression in parts of the world were underlined when Turkish author Orhan Pamuk was charged with 'insulting Turkishness' for statements he made about the Armenian genocide.

POLITICS & ECONOMY

2002 1 Jan: The **Euro**, the common European currency, is introduced in 14 EU countries

2003 20 Mar–30 Apr: The United States leads an invasion of **Iraq**, overthrowing Saddam Hussein

2004 1 May: Ten countries, mostly former Soviet satellites in Eastern Europe, join the **EU**

2005 22 Nov: **Angela Merkel** becomes the first female chancellor of Germany

2005 18 Dec: **Evo Morales** becomes the first elected Amerindian president of Bolivia

SCIENCE & TECHNOLOGY

2003 15 Oct: China completes its first successful **manned orbital space flight**

2003 USA: The Human Genome Project issues a complete map of the **human genome**

2005 14 Feb: The video-sharing website **YouTube** is founded

2005 27 Apr: The **Airbus A380**, the world's largest passenger aircraft, makes its first flight

2002 **2003** **2004** **2005**

RELIGION & PHILOSOPHY

2005 2 Apr: Pope **John Paul II** dies

2005 30 Sep: Cartoons of **Muhammad** are published in Denmark, causing riots in Muslim countries

ART & ARCHITECTURE

2005 Dec: Turkish novelist **Orhan Pamuk** is charged with 'insulting Turkishness' for writing about the Armenian genocide of 1915–16

`2006` 19 Sep: Thai prime minister **Thaksin Shinawatra** is deposed in a bloodless military coup

`2006` 30 Dec, Iraq: **Saddam Hussein** is executed for crimes against humanity

`2008` 7–16 Aug: Russia invades **Georgia** in support of separatists in South Ossetia and Abkhazia

`2008` 15 Sep: American bank **Lehman Brothers** goes bankrupt, precipitating an international financial crisis

`2008` Dec: Israel invades the **Gaza Strip** in response to Palestinian rocket attacks

`2009–10` Iran: Massive street protests follow the re-election of **Mahmoud Ahmadinejad** as president

`2009` 18 May: The **Sri Lankan civil war** comes to an end as government forces defeat the Tamil Tigers

`2010` Aug: **China** overtakes Japan to become the second largest economy in the world

`2010` 31 Aug: US forces end combat operations in **Iraq**

`2007` Jun, USA: Apple releases the **iPhone**, the first smartphone

`2008` Sep: France and Switzerland: the **Large Hadron Collider**, the world's largest particle accelerator, is completed at CERN

`2010` USA: The first **synthetic bacterial cell** is created

2006   **2007**   **2008**   **2009**   **2010**

`2006` UK: Evolutionary biologist **Richard Dawkins** denounces religious belief in *The God Delusion*

`2009` Nov: Voters in Switzerland ban the construction of **minarets** in a referendum, leading to criticism in the Islamic world

`2006` British artist **Anish Kapoor**'s sculpture *Cloud Gate* is installed in Chicago

`2006` American author **Cormac McCarthy** publishes his post-apocalyptic novel *The Road*

`2008` Beijing, China: The **Beijing National Stadium** (Bird's Nest), designed by Swiss architects Jacques Herzog and Pierre de Meuron, is completed

`2010` American architect Adrian Smith's **Burj Khalifa**, the tallest human structure ever built, opens in Dubai

2011– NOW

A WORLD FRAGMENTED

IN JANUARY 2011, a wave of popular protests erupted in Tunisia: the demonstrators, aggrieved by rising unemployment, corruption and a lack of political rights, eventually forced President Ben Ali from power. In October of the same year, a democratic constitution was introduced in the country, and the first freely elected government took power. The revolution's success inspired similar demands for democracy across the Arab world: this movement, known as the 'Arab Spring', destabilized the Middle East and its consequences reverberated across the world.

Yet in no other country was the success of the Tunisian revolution repeated. Although the Egyptian government was overthrown in February 2011, and democratic elections a year later brought the Islamist Muslim Brotherhood to power, the latter's moves to increase the role of Islam in the state resulted in its removal in 2013 by a military coup. Further west in Libya, NATO intervened in October 2011 to support rebels opposed to the dictator Muammar Gaddafi. While Gaddafi was deposed and killed, the rebels lacked unity and Libya slid into civil war in 2014.

In Syria, a complex civil war broke out in 2011 after protests against the authoritarian rule of Bashar al-Assad were violently supressed. Bruised by the failure of its earlier interventions in Afghanistan, Iraq and Libya, the West refused to involve itself in the conflict, even after the Syrian regime used chemical weapons against civilians. Russia saw an opportunity to reassert its influence in the Middle East by supporting Assad, turning the tide of the war against the rebels – but in 2018 it remained unresolved. Millions of Syrians, meanwhile, had fled to both neighbouring countries, and to the European Union (EU), creating a political crisis and contributing to the rise of populist anti-immigrant and Eurosceptic parties in many member states. Notably, fear of unregulated immigration was a major factor in the United Kingdom's vote to leave the EU in 2016.

Iraq after the fall of Saddam Hussein was a breeding ground for jihadi terrorist groups, the most prominent and brutal of which was so-called Islamic State in Iraq and Syria (IS), which aimed to recreate the medieval Islamic caliphate. Taking advantage of the surrounding chaos, IS seized control of a large part of northern Iraq and Syria from 2012 onwards. By the middle of 2018, however, the Iraqi army, supported by the United States, Iran and Kurdish militias had destroyed the IS 'caliphate'.

This period also saw Russia move to re-establish its role in Europe by intervening in Ukraine: it annexed the Crimea and supported a rebellion in the eastern Donbass region, effectively stymying Ukraine's hopes of joining NATO and the EU. China strengthened its position in Southeast Asia by illegally constructing artificial islands to support its claim to sovereignty over the South China Sea. Nonetheless, while remaining buoyant, China's economic growth slowed

considerably in this period: confounding many predictions, it failed to overtake the USA as the world's largest economy.

The liberalization of global trade that followed the end of the Cold War brought benefits to the developing world, as hundreds of millions of people were lifted out of poverty. By 2018, many of the world's fastest growing economies were in Africa, where countries were overcoming the raft of problems bequeathed to them after decolonization. Yet conversely, the industrial working classes of the USA and Europe found their jobs exported to countries where labour costs were lower. Combined with stagnant living standards and the slow recovery from the financial crisis of 2008, faith in established political parties and economic orthodoxies was increasingly undermined. In the 2016 American presidential election, these grievances led to the victory of Donald Trump, a businessman with no previous political experience, whose unconventional approach to politics marked a sea change from earlier administrations.

Beyond politics, the potential disruptive power of the Internet became fully apparent during this period, as social media became ever more ubiquitous. Already a platform for spreading conspiracy theories and 'fake news', in the hands of authoritarian regimes it also became a weapon to subvert democratic elections, steal intellectual property, and make damaging – and deniable – cyberwarfare attacks on commerce and infrastructure.

2011 14 Jan: Tunisian president **Zine El Abidine Ben Ali** is deposed after mass protests

2011 11 Feb: Egyptian president **Hosni Mubarak** is ousted following demonstrations against police violence

2011 Mar: The **Syrian Civil War** erupts between President Bashar al-Assad, supported by Russia, and rebel forces

2011 Sep: The **Occupy** movement protests against inequality and corporate greed

2011 20 Oct: **Muammar Gaddafi**, leader of Libya, is killed by NATO-backed opposition forces

2012 26 Feb, Florida: Travyon Martin, an African-American teenager, is shot dead, precipitating the **Black Lives Matter** movement

2012 17 Jul: **Mohammed Morsi**, the Islamist Muslim Brotherhood candidate, is elected president of Egypt

2012–17 So-called **Islamic State** (IS) purports to re-establish the caliphate over its territories in Syria and Iraq

2013 May: American computer scientist **Edward Snowden** leaks thousands of classified US intelligence documents

2013 3 Jul: Mohammed Morsi is deposed as president of Egypt in a military coup, and is succeeded by his defence minister **Abdel Fattah el-Sisi**

2014 Feb–Mar: Russia annexes **Crimea** from Ukraine

2014 May: The second **Libyan Civil War** breaks out; two provisional governments seek control over Libya

2012–13 Scientists at CERN discover the **Higgs boson**, key to our understanding of particle physics

2012 Aug, USA: the NASA rover *Curiosity* lands on Mars

2011   2012   2013   2014

2013 13 Mar: Jorge Mario Bergoglio is elected Pope **Francis**, the first Pope from outside Europe since the 8th century

2011 A print of *Rhein II*, by German photographer **Andreas Gursky**, becomes the most expensive photograph ever sold at $4.3 million

2012 Korean musician Psy's K-pop song *Gangnam Style* becomes the first video to reach 1 billion views on YouTube

2014 3 Nov: American architect David Childs's **One World Trade Center** opens in New York

2015 Jul: The United States restores diplomatic relations with **Cuba** for the first time since the 1950s

2016 23 Jun: The United Kingdom votes to leave the **European Union**

2016 8 Nov: American businessman **Donald Trump** is elected president of the United States

2017 10 Mar: **Park Geun-hye**, president of South Korea, is impeached following a corruption scandal

2017 27 Oct: **Catalonia** declares independence from Spain, but it is not recognized by any other state

2018 18 Mar: **Vladimir Putin** is re-elected president of Russia for a fourth term

2015 The social media website **Twitter** reaches 300 million active monthly users

2015–17 USA: increasingly powerful **quantum computers** are developed

2018 The **UK** and **Australia** are connected by a non-stop flight for the first time

2015   2016   2017   2018

2018 25 May, Ireland: A referendum overturns the constitutional ban on **abortion**

2016 American singer-songwriter **Bob Dylan** wins the Nobel Prize in Literature

2018 22 May: American author **Philip Roth** dies

21ST CENTURY
AN AGE OF UNCERTAINTY

The collapse of the USSR in 1991 left the USA as the sole superpower. However, little more than a decade later the USA's global dominance came to be challenged by the rising power of China and a resurgent Russia.

KEY

- European Union
- Members of NATO
- Other states and territories

UNITED STATES OF AMERICA

CUBA

BRAZIL

RUSSIA

UNITED
KINGDOM

IRELAND

GERMANY

European Union

UKRAINE

SPAIN

TUNISIA

SYRIA

IRAQ

AFGHANISTAN

PEOPLE'S
REPUBLIC OF
CHINA

NORTH
KOREA

SOUTH
KOREA

LIBYA

EGYPT

SUDAN

SOUTH
SUDAN

AUSTRALIA

A–Z OF PEOPLES, NATIONS AND CULTURES

This glossary provides information about the places and peoples mentioned in the main text and on the maps and timelines. Cross-references are given in bold. Major world regions and chronological periods are also defined.

Abbasid caliphate The second major Islamic dynasty in the Middle East, the Abbasids seized power from the **Umayyads** in AD 750. The last Abbasid caliph was executed by the **Mongols** in 1258.

Abkhazia Unrecognized modern state in the Caucasus; became de facto independent from **Georgia** in 1992–93.

Aborigines The native peoples of **Australia**. The ancestors of the Aborigines arrived c. 60,000 years ago from Southeast Asia in what was one of the earliest seaborne migrations in human history.

Adal Islamic state of northeast Africa, flourished 15th–16th centuries AD.

Afghanistan Landlocked, ethnically diverse Asian country. Because of its strategic position at the crossroads of South Asia, Central Asia and the Middle East, a long succession of empires have fought to control the region, including the **Persians**. The modern Afghan state was founded in 1747 by Ahmed Shah Durrani.

Akkadian empire Mesopotamian empire, widely considered the world's earliest imperial state, founded by Sargon the Great (r. 2334–2279 BC), flourished c. 2334–c. 2193 BC.

Alans Iranian-speaking nomad people of the Caspian steppes. First recorded by the **Romans**, they are claimed as ancestors by the modern Ossetians of the Caucasus.

Albania Predominantly Muslim southern European country, which became independent from the **Ottoman** empire in 1912. The Albanians are descended from the ancient Illyrian peoples.

Algeria Muslim, mainly Arabic-speaking, North African state, most of whose population is of **Berber** descent. The modern state originated as a French colonial territory, conquered in 1830–48. Algeria became independent from **France** in 1962.

Almoravids Berber dynasty that supported Islamic reform and created an empire in North and West Africa, and **Spain** (1056–1147).

Ancestral Pueblo Early farming culture of the southwestern deserts of North America; flourished from c. AD 700 to c. 1300 when it collapsed, it is thought, due to prolonged drought.

Anglo-Saxons Early Germanic peoples, comprising the Angles, Saxons and Jutes, from northern **Germany** and **Denmark**, who migrated to Britain in the 5th century AD.

Angola Southern African country. Formerly a Portuguese colonial territory acquired between 1575 and the 1891, it became independent in 1975.

Arabs A major Semitic people, originally from the Arabian peninsula, who became widespread across the Middle East and North Africa as a result of the Islamic conquests of the 7th century AD. The earliest record of the Arabs dates to 853 BC.

Aragon Christian Spanish kingdom founded in 1035. Aragon was united to **Castile** in 1469 by a dynastic marriage, leading to the creation of the kingdom of **Spain** in 1516.

Aramaeans A group of Semitic peoples of **Syria** first recorded in the 16th century BC. The Aramaeans disappeared as a distinct people around the 6th century BC.

Argentina Latin American republic. Argentina declared independence from **Spain** in 1816 as the United Provinces of Rio de la Plata. After **Bolivia** and **Uruguay** seceded from the United Provinces in 1825–28, the remaining provinces reorganized themselves as the Argentine Confederation: Argentina was constituted as a unitary state in 1853.

Armenia Kingdom of the Transcaucasus region that emerged from the break-up of the empire of Alexander the Great. Converted to Christianity *c.* AD 300, frequently under foreign rule since 428. Modern Armenia became independent of the **USSR** in 1991.

Asante Sub-group of the Akan peoples of the Guinea coast of West Africa. United by Osei Tutu *c.* 1701, the Asante formed a powerful kingdom, which was eventually conquered by the British in 1901.

Assyria Major power of northern Mesopotamia from *c.* 1800 BC until its conquest by the Babylonians and **Medes** in 612 BC. The Assyrians spoke Akkadian, a Semitic language also spoken by the Babylonians.

Athens Major city state and leading cultural centre of **Greece**'s Classical Age (480–356 BC). Athens lost its independence in 338 BC, when it was conquered by Philip of **Macedon**. It became the capital of the modern Greek state in 1832.

Australia The modern country of Australia was formed when Britain united its Australian colonies to form the self-governing Commonwealth of Australia in 1901; it became fully independent in 1931.

Austria European state that originated as a duchy of the **Holy Roman empire** in 1156. Under the Habsburg emperors (1438–1918) Austria became the major Central European power; following the fall of the Habsburgs, Austria was reduced to a minor state. United to **Germany** 1938–45 by the *Anschluss*.

Austro-Asiatics Group of peoples native to Southeast Asia and eastern India, including the **Vietnamese**, **Khmer** and **Mon** peoples.

Austro-Hungarian empire State created by the introduction of the Dual Monarchy, a union of the crowns of the Austrian empire and **Hungary** in 1867. Officially known as Austria–Hungary because Hungarians refused to accept the implied unity of the Austro-Hungarian title. The Dual Monarchy collapsed in 1918 after Austria–Hungary's defeat in the First World War.

Austronesians A widespread group of peoples of Australasia, Southeast Asia and Madagascar, thought to have originated on Taiwan or mainland China in prehistoric times, including the **Malays**, **Chams**, **Polynesians** and Malagasy.

Avars A nomad people consisting of Turkic and other tribes who emerged from the break-up of the Rouran (or Juan-juan) nomad confederacy in the 6th century AD and migrated to Europe. Decisively defeated by the **Franks** in 796, the Avar khanate had disintegrated by *c.* 810.

Axum (Aksum) Early Ethiopian trading kingdom with links to southwestern Arabia, flourished *c.* 1 BC–AD 975.

Ayyubids Sunni Muslim dynasty, founded by Saladin in 1174, that ruled **Egypt**, **Syria** and northern **Iraq** until 1250.

Aztecs Peoples originally from northwest **Mexico**, who migrated into the central Valley of Mexico around the 13th century AD. Between 1428 and 1519 they were the dominant power of **Mesoamerica**.

Babylon Major Mesopotamian city state, founded mid-3rd millennium BC; conquered by the **Persians** in 539 BC and abandoned *c.* 140 BC.

Bactria Greek kingdom of Central Asia, **Afghanistan** and, from *c.* 180 BC, northern **India**; it became independent of the **Seleucid empire** *c.* 255 BC. The kingdom was destroyed by the **Kushans** in the 2nd century BC.

Bagan (Pagan) The earliest **Burmese** kingdom, named after its capital city Bagan, a major Buddhist centre. Flourished from the mid-9th century AD until its destruction by the **Mongols** in 1287.

Baluchistan Mountainous region, now mostly in **Pakistan**, named for the majority ethnic group, the Balochi.

Bangladesh South Asian state, formerly East **Pakistan**. Bangladesh became independent in 1971 following a war of independence, aided by an Indian invasion.

Basketmaker cultures Preceding the **Ancestral Pueblo** culture in southwestern North America, Basketmaker cultures (*c.* 1200 BC– *c.* AD 700) were transitional between hunting and gathering, and maize farming, which was adopted around the end of the 1st millennium BC.

Belgium European kingdom, originally the southern half of the **Spanish Netherlands**. Transferred to Austrian control in 1713, the territory was formally annexed by **France** in 1795, and then united with the **Netherlands** in 1815. Belgium became independent in 1839.

Bell Beaker cultures Widespread late **Neolithic/** early **Bronze Age** cultures of Western Europe, named for the distinctive shape of their pottery drinking vessels. Flourished *c.* 2500–1800 BC.

Bengal Historic region of South Asia, now divided between India and **Bangladesh**.

Berbers (Amazigh) Pre-Arab inhabitants of North Africa with scattered communities in **Morocco**, **Algeria**, **Tunisia**, **Libya**, **Egypt**, **Mauretania**, Niger and **Mali**. The Berbers of Mediterranean North Africa were often called Moors by Europeans after the Mauri, an ancient Berber people.

Bijapur Muslim sultanate of southwest **India**, founded in 1527 following the fall of the Bahmani sultanate; conquered by the **Mughals** in 1686.

Boers (Afrikaners) White South Africans of Dutch ancestry.

Bohemia Region of Central Europe and early medieval **Slav** kingdom absorbed into the **Holy Roman empire** in the 10th century AD, now part of the **Czech Republic**.

Bolivia South American republic, which became independent from **Spain** in 1824–25; its present-day borders were settled in 1938.

Bosnia–Herzegovina Balkan state with a mixed Bosniak, **Serb** and Croat population. The country's declaration of independence from **Yugoslavia** in 1991 was followed by a civil war (1992–95) that left it divided into two autonomous entities, the Bosniak-Croat-dominated Federation of Bosnia and Herzegovina, and the Serb-dominated Republika Srpska.

Brandenburg–Prussia German principality created by the union of the electorate of Brandenburg and the duchy of **Prussia** in 1618; it became the kingdom of **Prussia** in 1701.

Brazil South American republic. Brazil was claimed by **Portugal** in 1500 and colonization began in 1534. Brazil declared independence from Portugal in 1822.

Bronze Age Technological division of human prehistory defined by the use of bronze tools and weapons, but not iron. The term was first applied to European prehistory in the 19th century and subsequently applied to the rest of Eurasia and North Africa. The term is not applied to Sub-Saharan Africa, where bronze and iron technology were adopted at the same time. Bronze tools and weapons never became widely used in the pre-Columbian Americas.

Bulgaria East European republic, became independent of the **Ottoman** empire in 1878 and attained its modern borders in 1913. The Bulgarians are **Slav** in language and culture.

Burgundians Early Germanic people who invaded the **Roman empire** in AD 406–7.

Burgundy Kingdom founded by the **Burgundians** in AD 443; conquered by the Franks in 532–34. 2. Frankish kingdom created in AD 887, absorbed by the **Holy Roman empire** in 1033.

Burma Southeast Asian republic, known as Myanmar since 1989. The first Burmese state was founded at **Bagan** in the 9th century AD. Conquered piecemeal by the British in the 19th century, Burma regained its independence in 1948.

Buwayhid emirates (Buyid) **Persia**n Shi'ite confederation that dominated an area approximating to present-day **Iran** and **Iraq** from *c.* AD 934 until its overthrow by the **Seljuk** Turks in 1055.

Byzantine empire Modern name given to the largely Greek-speaking eastern Roman empire following the fall of the western Roman empire in the 5th century AD. The Byzantine empire ended with the conquest of its capital, Constantinople, by the **Ottomans** in 1453.

Cambodia Southeast Asian kingdom of the **Khmer** people, its development began with the kingdom Chenla (*c.* AD 550–802). French colony 1863–1953. Cambodia became a republic in 1970, but the monarchy was restored in 1993.

Canaanites Middle Eastern Semitic-speaking peoples of the Levant 5th–2nd millennia BC; best known for devising the first alphabetic writing system.

Canada North American country. The name Canada was first applied to the area of **New France** north of the Great Lakes. Following the British conquest of New France, Canada became part of the colony of Quebec, later divided into Upper and Lower Canada and then reunited as the Province of Canada in 1841. Modern Canada was created by the confederation of the Province of Canada with the colonies of Nova Scotia and New Brunswick in 1867. Canada became independent of Britain in 1931.

Cape Colony Dutch colony at the Cape of Good Hope, founded 1652. Annexed by Britain in 1806, it became a province of **South Africa** in 1910.

Carolingian empire Founded by the Frankish ruler Charlemagne (*r.* AD 768–814). The name of the empire is derived from Charlemagne's name in Latin, *Karolus Magnus* (Charles the Great). The empire was partitioned between his grandsons in 843 and finally broke up in 889. Both **Germany** and **France** trace their origins to the break-up of the empire.

Carthage North African city state near modern Tunis. Founded by **Phoenician** settlers in, according to tradition, 814 BC, Carthage became a major mercantile power with a loose-knit empire in the western Mediterranean. In the 3rd century Carthage came into conflict with the **Romans**, who conquered and destroyed the city in 146 BC.

Castile Christian Spanish kingdom. The union of the crowns of Castile and **Aragon**, which resulted from the marriage of Ferdinand of Aragon to Isabella of Castile in 1469, led to the creation of the kingdom of **Spain** in 1516.

Celts Major group of peoples who dominated Western and Central Europe during the European **Iron Age** of the 1st millennium BC.

Ceylon See **Sri Lanka**.

Chagatai khanate Mongol khanate in Central Asia created for Chagatai, second son of Chinggis Khan, in 1225. Its western territories were conquered by Timur the Lame in the later 14th century. The khanate survived in an increasingly decentralized form until it was overthrown by the **Uzbeks** and **Oirats** in 1678.

Chaldaeans Semitic nomad people of northern Arabia who settled in Mesopotamia between 1000 and 900 BC, founding dynasties in many cities, including **Babylon**.

Chalukyas Powerful dynasty that dominated central and southern **India** from the mid-6th century AD until 753 when they were overthrown by the **Rashtrakuta** dynasty. The dynasty revived in the mid-10th century, but declined again during the 12th century.

Champa Kingdom of the **Chams** in Southeast Asia, an important mercantile and naval power; founded c. AD 192, conquered by **Dai Viet** in 1611 after centuries of decline.

Chams An **Austronesian** people indigenous to the area that is now **Vietnam** and **Cambodia**.

Chavín culture The first regionally important culture and art style of **Peru**, named after the ritual complex at Chavín; flourished c. 850–300 BC.

Chile South American republic; became independent from **Spain** in 1818.

Chimú (Chimor) South American peoples and kingdom of **Peru**, founded c. AD 900, expanded to control the coastal lowlands c. 1200. Conquered by the **Incas** in 1470.

China, People's Republic of Chinese communist state proclaimed in 1949 by Mao Zedong. Since 1979 Marxist economics have been gradually abandoned but the Communist Party has maintained its monopoly on power. The People's Republic was admitted to China's seat at the United Nations in 1975, formerly held by the **Republic of China**.

China, Republic of Chinese republic founded in 1911 following the fall of the **Qing** dynasty. Since the Communist victory in the Chinese civil war in 1949 the Republic of China has consisted of Taiwan and two small offshore islands.

Chinchorro tradition South American fishing culture of northern **Chile**, 7th century–late 1st century BC.

Chola Hindu Tamil dynasty of southern **India** (3rd century BC–AD 1279), which was the major maritime power of the Indian Ocean from c. 850 to 1126.

Cimmerians The earliest of the **Iranian** horse-mounted nomad people of the western Eurasian steppes, absorbed by the **Scythians** in the 6th century BC.

Colombia South American republic that became independent from **Spain** as Gran Colombia in 1819.

Confederate States of America Eleven southern slave-owning states, which seceded from the USA 1861–65: Alabama, Arkansas, North Carolina, South Carolina, Florida, Georgia, **Louisiana**, Mississippi, Texas, Tennessee and **Virginia**.

Confederation of the Rhine A French-dominated confederation of 16 German states formed by Napoleon after the abolition of the **Holy Roman empire** in 1806. The confederation was dissolved in 1813.

Croatia Historic region of the Balkans, named after the **Croats**, and former Yugoslav republic, independent 1991.

Croats Slav people of the Balkans in Eastern Europe, emerged 7th–8th centuries AD.

Crusader states Christian states in **Palestine** and **Syria** founded after the First Crusade (1095–99): the Kingdom of Jerusalem (1099–1291), County of Tripoli (1109–1289), Principality of Antioch (1098–1268), County of Edessa (1098–1150).

Cuba Caribbean republic. Claimed for **Spain** by Columbus in 1492. Spain relinquished sovereignty after its defeat in the Spanish–American War of 1898 and Cuba became formally independent in 1902.

Cyprus Mediterranean island state. Became a crusader kingdom in 1191; control passed to **Venice** in 1473 (formal annexation in 1489); conquered by the **Ottoman** Turks in 1570; ceded to Britain in 1878; independent in 1960; divided into Greek and Turkish states since 1974.

Czechoslovakia Central European state of the Czech and Slovak peoples. It became independent on the collapse of the **Austro-Hungarian empire** in 1918; partially integrated into Germany 1939–45; divided into separate Czech and Slovak republics in 1993.

Czech Republic Central European country comprising the historic regions of **Bohemia** and Moravia created on the dissolution of **Czechoslovakia** in 1993.

Dahomey West African kingdom that prospered in the 18th century as a major participant in the transatlantic slave trade. Conquered by **France** 1892–94; independent in 1960. Known as **Benin** since 1975.

Dai Viet Vietnamese state that emerged following the fall of the Chinese Tang dynasty empire in 907; formally constituted as a kingdom in 939. Divided into **Tongking** and Cochin China after 1620; reunited and renamed **Vietnam** in 1802.

Delhi, sultanate of Major Islamic power of northern India under several Turkic and Afghan dynasties. Founded 1206, conquered by the **Mughals** in 1526.

Denmark Scandinavian kingdom, emerged in the 9th–10th centuries AD.

Dong Son culture Late **Bronze Age**/early **Iron Age** culture of northern **Vietnam** *c*. 700–200 BC.

Dutch East Indies The Dutch East Indian empire. The Dutch East India Company founded a base at Bantam in Java in 1603 and over the next 300 years extended their control over most of the East Indian archipelago. The Dutch East Indies declared independence as **Indonesia** in 1945, which was recognized by the Dutch in 1949.

Dvaravati Indianized kingdom of Southeast Asia, probably inhabited by the **Mons**, founded in the 6th century AD; gradually absorbed by the **Khmer empire** between the 10th and 12th centuries.

Dzungar khanate Oirat Mongol state, the last great independent nomad power of the Eurasian steppes, which developed in the 17th century AD; conquered by the Manchu **Qing** empire in 1759.

East Germany (German Democratic Republic) Communist state created in the Soviet occupation zone of **Germany** in 1949; united with **West Germany** in 1990.

Easter Island Island in the South Pacific Ocean first settled by **Polynesians** *c*. AD 700, annexed by **Chile** in 1888. The island is famous for the giant *moai* (carved stone heads) erected by its inhabitants *c*. 1250–1500.

Ecuador South American republic. Ecuador became independent from **Spain** in 1822, becoming part of Gran Colombia, from which it seceded in 1830.

Egypt Egypt was home to the world's earliest territorial kingdom, founded *c*. 3000 BC. The history of the modern Egyptian state conventionally begins in 1882 with the establishment of a British protectorate over Egypt, intended to secure control over the Suez Canal. Nationalist agitation led Britain to grant Egyptian independence in 1922, although it maintained a military presence until 1954.

El Paraiso culture Fishing, gathering and farming culture of coastal **Peru** *c*. 1800–850 BC, named for a large U-shaped ceremonial site.

El Salvador Central American republic which became independent in 1841 following the break-up of the **Federal Republic of Central America**.

England Kingdom of the English, created AD 927; united with **Scotland** to form the Kingdom of Great Britain in 1707.

Ephthalites (White Huns or, in India, Hunas) Central Asian nomad confederation of the 5th–6th centuries AD; founded a kingdom in **Afghanistan** and northwest India *c*. 475, which broke up in the later 6th century. Their exact relationship to the **Huns** of Europe is uncertain.

Eritrea Country in the Horn of Africa. Eritrea was annexed by **Italy** in 1890 and occupied by the British in 1941. In 1951 Eritrea was federated with **Ethiopia**. Discontent with Ethiopian rule led Eritrea to declare independence in 1991, recognized internationally in 1993.

Estonia Baltic republic. Estonia became independent of the Russian empire in 1918. It was occupied by Soviet forces in 1939, becoming a republic of the **USSR**. Estonia regained its independence in 1991.

Ethiopia Christian East African kingdom (republic since 1974), successor to **Axum**; emerged around the late 10th–early 12th centuries AD. Ethiopia successfully resisted European colonization in the 19th century, but was conquered by **Italy** in 1935; liberated by British forces in 1941.

Etruscans Major people of pre-Roman Italy, in the 6th century BC they formed a loose league of city states that was conquered by the **Romans** in the 4th century BC.

Faroe Islands North Atlantic archipelago first settled permanently by **Norse** *c*. AD 825; currently an autonomous province of **Denmark**.

Fatimid caliphate Shi'ite **Berber** state, AD 909–1171, founded in **Tunisia**. At its height in the late 10th century, the caliphate controlled all of North Africa. The capital was moved to Cairo in 969.

Federal Republic of Central America Latin American state formed in 1823 by former provinces of the Spanish American empire.

The union broke up in civil wars between 1838 and 1841 into the independent countries of Costa Rica, **El Salvador**, **Guatemala**, Honduras and **Nicaragua**.

Fiji Pacific archipelago first settled by the Austronesian **Lapita culture** *c.* 1500 BC and, a millennium later, by **Melanesians**. British colony 1874–1970.

Five Dynasties A succession of five short-lived dynasties, which ruled various parts of the Yellow river region of China between the fall of the **Tang** dynasty in AD 907 and the accession in 960 of the **Song** dynasty, which reunified China in 979.

France Western European country, named for the **Franks**, which emerged from the break-up of the Frankish **Carolingian empire** in AD 889.

Franks Early German tribal confederation, originating in the 3rd century AD. Following the fall of the western Roman empire they won control of Gaul (the region comprising modern **France**, **Belgium** and part of western **Germany**) forming a powerful kingdom under the Merovingian dynasty (511–751). Under the Carolingian dynasty the Frankish kingdom (an empire from 800) dominated Western Europe. The modern nations of France and Germany emerged from the break-up of this empire in 889.

French Indochina French Southeast Asian colony comprising the countries of **Laos**, **Vietnam** and **Cambodia**, which **France** conquered between 1859 and 1900.

French Polynesia French Pacific territory comprising the Society Islands (including **Tahiti**), Bass Islands, Gambier Islands, **Marquesas Islands** and the Tuamotu Archipelago. French rule established between 1842 and 1889.

Funan Indianized Southeast Asian kingdom founded 1st century AD; at its peak in the 3rd century; absorbed by Chenla in the 6th century.

Futa Jalon (Fouta Djallon) West African kingdom of the Fulani people founded in the 17th century AD; from 1725 a Muslim jihadi state; conquered by **France** 1896.

Georgia Christian kingdom of the Caucasus region, founded in AD 978. It was divided between the **Ottoman** and **Safavid** empires in 1555. Recovered independence in the 18th century, but was annexed by **Russia** in 1801. Constituted a republic of the **USSR** in 1936, Georgia became independent in 1991.

Germans Group of peoples originating in **Bronze Age** Europe.

Germany 1. Medieval European kingdom that developed from the break-up of the **Carolingian empire** in the 9th century AD and became the dominant part of the **Holy Roman empire**. 2. Modern European nation state created in 1871 under Prussian leadership. Between 1949 and 1990 Germany was divided into two states, **West Germany** and **East Germany**.

Ghana 1. Early West African trading kingdom in present-day **Mali** and Mauritania, flourished 7th–11th centuries AD; conquered by the **Almoravids** in 1076. 2. The former British West African colonial territory of **Gold Coast**, which became independent in 1957.

Ghaznavid emirate State founded by Mahmud of Ghazni (*r.* 997–1030), which controlled **Afghanistan**, **Iran**, the Indus valley and parts of Central Asia. The emirate survived until 1151.

Goa Indian city-port captured by the Portuguese in 1510, annexed by **India** in 1961.

Gold Coast British West African colony. British presence on the Gold Coast was established with the acquisition of Cape Coast Castle in 1664. The Gold Coast colony was formally created in 1821 and became independent as **Ghana** in 1957.

Golden Horde (Ulus of Jochi) Mongol khanate of the western Eurasian steppes founded in 1241 by Chinggis Khan's grandson Batu. Although Mongol-led, the Horde was made up mainly of Turkic **Tatars**. The khanate broke up in 1502 after a century of decline.

Goths Early German people first recorded in the 3rd century AD. In the 5th century they became divided into two groups: the **Visigoths**, who founded a kingdom in Aquitaine and **Spain** (417–711), and the **Ostrogoths**, who founded a kingdom in **Italy** (493–562).

Granada, emirate of The last Muslim state in **Spain**, founded in 1228, conquered by **Castile** and **Aragon** in 1482–92.

Great Britain See **United Kingdom**.

Great khanate Mongol empire, founded by Chinggis Khan in 1206, which survived until 1370. From 1260 to 1368 the Great Khans also used the Chinese dynastic title Yuan.

Great Zimbabwe Southern African city and kingdom, probably of the Shona people; flourished 13th to mid-15th centuries AD.

Greece European country. In ancient times Greece was divided into hundreds of city states. In the 4th century BC, Greece was conquered by **Macedon** and subsequently came under the control of the **Roman**, **Byzantine** and **Ottoman** empires. The modern Greek state declared independence from the **Ottoman** empire in 1822, officially recognized in 1832.

Greenland The world's largest island. Greenland was first inhabited by ancestral **Inuit** peoples over 4,000 years ago. In AD 986 a **Norse** colony was founded in southwest Greenland. Since 2009 Greenland has been an autonomous country of the kingdom of **Denmark**.

Grenada Caribbean island nation. Claimed, but not colonized, by **England** in 1609 and sold to **France** in 1650. Captured by the British in 1762, briefly reoccupied by France 1779–83; independent in 1974.

Guatemala Central American republic that became independent of the **Federal Republic of Central America** in 1838.

Guinea West African republic. Colonized by **France** in the 1890s, it became independent in 1958.

Gujarat Historic region of South Asia, now divided between **India** and **Pakistan**; an independent Muslim sultanate 1411–1572.

Guptas Major Hindu dynasty of **Magadha** that dominated northern **India** c. AD 320–c. 550.

Gurjara–Pratiharas Hindu dynasty of northern India (6th–11th centuries AD); at their peak c. 836–910 they were a major barrier to the expansion of Muslim control in **India**.

Haiti Caribbean state comprising western Hispaniola. Formerly the French colony of **Saint-Domingue**, it became independent in 1804 following a slave rebellion.

Han The second dynasty of imperial China 206 BC–AD 220, which has given its name to the ethnic Chinese. Conventionally divided into Western Han (206 BC–AD 9) and Eastern Han (AD 25–220) separated by the short-lived Xin dynasty.

Hebrews Semitic-speaking people of the Levant, probably of **Canaanite** origin, whose religious beliefs formed the basis of Judaism. Their kingdom, founded c. 1020 BC, split into the rival kingdoms of **Israel** and **Judah** c. 928 BC.

Hittites people of Anatolia, first recorded 19th century BC. A major imperial power from c. 1600 until c. 1200 BC when most of their territory was conquered by the **Phrygians**. The Hittites finally disappeared in the early 1st millennium BC.

Hohokam culture Early farming culture of southwest North America, ancestral to the modern Pima and Papago nations; at its peak c. AD 500–c. 1375.

Holy Roman empire German-dominated European empire, founded when the German king Otto I was crowned Roman emperor in AD 962. Conflicts with the papacy in the 11th–12th centuries undermined the authority of the emperors and the empire gradually developed into a loose confederation of autonomous principalities. The title of Holy Roman emperor, held by the Austrian Habsburg dynasty from the mid-15th century, continued to be prestigious, however. The empire was abolished by Napoleon in 1806.

Hong Kong Island off southern China ceded to Britain in 1842 following the First Opium War. Adjacent territories on the mainland were added in 1860 following the Second Opium War. Returned to Chinese sovereignty in 1997.

Hungary Central European state founded in AD 1000. In 1541 most of Hungary came under **Ottoman** control. The remainder was annexed by the Austrian Habsburg emperors. By 1718, the Habsburgs had driven the Ottomans out of Hungary. Following a Hungarian revolt, Hungary became an equal partner with Austria in the **Austro-Hungarian empire** in 1867. Hungary became independent on the collapse of the empire in 1918.

Huns Confederation of pastoral nomad peoples from Central Asia who migrated to Eastern Europe in the late 4th century AD. The Huns broke up after the death of their greatest leader, Attila, in 453 and disappeared in the 6th century.

Hurrians People of northern Mesopotamia and Anatolia, known mid-3rd millennium–early 1st millennium BC. Their most important kingdoms were **Mitanni** and Urartu.

Iberia, kingdom of Early Georgian kingdom of the Caucasus region, emerged in the 4th century BC. Frequently tributary to Rome or Persia, Iberia came under **Arab** rule in AD 653.

Iceland North Atlantic country, it became autonomous under the Danish crown in 1918 and became an independent republic in 1944.

Idrisids Muslim dynasty of **Arab** origin that ruled **Morocco** AD 780–985.

Ilkhanate Mongol khanate of **Persia** and **Iraq**, founded by Chinggis Khan's grandson Hülegü in 1256. The khanate broke up in 1335.

Incas A people of the Peruvian Andes, present by at least c. AD 1200, who take their name from the title of their ruler, the Inca. In the late 15th and early 16th centuries they controlled the largest empire known to have existed in the pre-Columbian Americas. They were conquered by the Spanish in 1531–35.

India Republic comprising the greater part of the Indian subcontinent. The modern state of India became independent in 1947 following the partition of the British Indian empire into the Hindu-majority state of India and the Muslim state of **Pakistan**.

Indonesia Country of Southeast Asia and Australasia. Indonesia was founded when the **Dutch East Indies** declared independence in 1945 (recognized in 1949). In 1962 Indonesia annexed Dutch New Guinea, achieving its present-day borders.

Inuit (Eskimo) Hunting peoples of the North American Arctic, **Greenland** and far northeastern Siberia, from where their ancestors migrated to North America c. 5400–4800 BC.

Iran Major Middle Eastern country with a largely Shi'ite Muslim population. The modern Iranian state was founded by the **Safavid** dynasty, which ruled 1501–1736. Iran was known internationally as Persia until 1935.

Iraq Middle Eastern country, created as a British League of Nations mandated territory in 1920 from territory formerly ruled by the **Ottoman** empire: it became independent in 1932.

Ireland European country comprising most of the island of Ireland. The modern state of Ireland was founded in 1922 with the creation of the Irish Free State, a self-governing dominion of the British empire. It became fully independent as Ireland (or Éire) in 1937, although the British monarch remained legally head of state. This final link with Britain was broken by the adoption of a republican constitution in 1949.

Iron Age Technological division of human prehistory in which iron tools and weapons came into widespread use. It is a largely Eurasian concept, but is also applied to sub-Saharan Africa. The dating of the Iron Age is variable because iron technology was adopted at different times in different parts of the world. Iron technology was not adopted in the Americas before the arrival of Europeans.

Israel 1. Biblical Hebrew kingdom founded c. 928 BC, conquered by Assyria in 721 BC. 2. Modern Jewish state founded in Palestine in 1948.

Italy 1. Medieval kingdom comprising the northern half of present-day Italy which emerged from the final break-up of the Frankish **Carolingian empire** in AD 889. It became part of the **Holy Roman empire** in the mid-10th century. 2. French puppet state in northern Italy created by Napoleon in 1805; dissolved 1814. 3. The modern state of Italy was created in 1861 following the annexation of the kingdom of the **Two Sicilies** by the kingdom of Piedmont–Sardinia.

Jamaica Caribbean nation. Jamaica became a Spanish colony around 1524; it was captured by **England** in 1655; independent in 1962.

Japan Island nation in East Asia. The first Japanese kingdom emerged c. AD 300 and by c. 600 it had developed centralized institutions and an imperial constitution based on Chinese models. After 1192 the emperors were sidelined by powerful military governors called shoguns who ruled in their name. The origins of the modern Japanese state date to the overthrow of the shogunate in 1868 and the restoration of imperial government.

Jin 1. Chinese dynasty, ruled AD 265–420, divided into Western Jin (265–316) and Eastern Jin (317–420). Western Jin briefly unified China in 280 after a period of division. Eastern Jin controlled only south China. 2. **Jürchen** dynasty which ruled northern China from 1125 until 1234 when their state was destroyed by the **Mongols**.

Jomon Hunter-fisher-gatherer culture of Japan 10,000–300 BC, probably representing the ancestors of the modern Ainu people.

Jordan (officially the Hashemite kingdom of Jordan) Middle Eastern country, known as Transjordan before its independence from Britain in 1946.

Judah Biblical Hebrew kingdom founded c. 928 BC, conquered by **Babylon** in 586 BC.

Jürchen A Tungusic people of Manchuria who adopted the name Manchu in the 17th century AD.

Kannauj Historic region of northern **India**. Under King Harsha (r. AD 606–47) it was the centre of an empire that controlled most of northern India.

Kashmir Strategically important region in the northwest corner of South Asia, frequently disputed by neighbouring great powers. Currently divided between **India** and **Pakistan**.

Khitans East Asian nomadic Mongol people 4th–13th centuries AD.

Khmer empire Indianized state AD 802–1431, the direct precursor of **Cambodia**. At its peak in the 11th–13th centuries, the empire was the major power of Southeast Asia. The removal of the capital from Angkor to the region of Phnom Penh conventionally marks the end of the empire.

Kiev, principality of Early Russian state founded by the Scandinavian **Rus** c. AD 882, but with a largely **Slav** population. By 1000 the state had become Slav in language and culture, and Orthodox Christian in religion. From the mid-11th century Kiev began to break up into separate principalities.

Koguryo Early Korean kingdom founded, according to tradition, in 37 BC (but possibly over a century later); destroyed by the Chinese **Tang** empire in AD 668.

Kongo Central African kingdom of the Bakongo people, founded in the 15th century AD. From the

17th century onwards Kongo gradually lost its territory to the Portuguese, becoming part of **Angola** in the 19th century.

Korea East Asian country unified by, and named for, the Koryo dynasty (founded AD 918) in 936. Korea was annexed by **Japan** in 1910. Following Japan's defeat in 1945, Korea was divided along the 38th parallel, with the **USA** administering the south and the **USSR** the north. Two separate governments, North Korea and South Korea, were established in 1948; they have been officially at war since 1950.

Kosovo Partially recognized Balkan state with primarily Muslim Albanian population; became de facto independent from Serbia in 1999.

Kush Egyptian-influenced **Nubian** kingdom of the middle Nile, emerged c. 900 BC. Known as the kingdom of **Meroë** after 590 BC.

Kushans Central Asian nomad people. They originated as a tribe of the Yuezhi confederation, which they took over in the 1st century BC. Invaded **India** c. AD 46–50 and established an empire that survived until the 4th century.

Kuwait Country in northern Arabia. Kuwait developed in the 17th century as a trading centre under nominal **Ottoman** control. It became a British protectorate in 1899 and became independent in 1961.

Kyrgyz Traditionally nomadic Turkic people of Central Asia.

Laos Southeast Asian country, founded in 1354 though not securely united until the 16th century. The country is named for its main ethnic group, the Lao, a **Tai** people. Laos became part of **French Indochina** in 1893, becoming independent again in 1954.

Lapita culture (c. 1600–500 BC) Archaeological culture associated with the spread of **Austronesian** farming peoples from Southeast Asia to the archipelagos of the western Pacific Ocean.

Latins Ancient **Italic** peoples of present-day Lazio in central Italy.

Lebanon Middle Eastern country with a mainly **Arab** population. Lebanon was created as a French-administered League of Nations mandated territory in 1920 from former territory of the **Ottoman** empire. It declared independence in 1941, recognized in 1943.

Liao Khitan dynasty, established AD 915, which ruled much of **Mongolia** and northern China; overthrown by the **Jürchen Jin** dynasty in 1125.

Liberia West African country founded as a homeland for freed slaves by the American Colonization Society in 1821–22. It was the only African country never to come under European rule.

Libya In ancient times Libya was used in a general sense to describe all of Africa. The modern state of Libya originated when **Italy** conquered the **Ottoman** province of Tripoli in 1911–12. It was occupied by British forces in 1943 and came under joint British and French administration until independence in 1951.

Lithuania Baltic country. Lithuania became a unified state in 1253. In 1386 it entered a dynastic union with **Poland** in return for accepting Christianity (the last European country to do so), becoming a full political union in 1569. Following the partition of Poland in the 18th century, Lithuania became part of the Russian empire. Lithuania became independent of **Russia** in 1918 but was annexed by the **USSR**

in 1939. It became independent again on the fall of the USSR in 1991.

Lombards An early German people, first recorded in the 1st century AD. Invaded **Italy** in 568 and founded a number of states, the last of which fell to the **Normans** in the 11th century.

Longshan culture Later **Neolithic** culture of the Yellow river region, China, with walled proto-urban settlements, 3200–1800 BC.

Louisiana French-claimed territory in North America comprising the entire Mississippi river basin, established 1682. Ceded to **Spain** in 1763. Returned to **France** in 1800 and sold to the **USA** in 1803.

Luxembourg European Grand Duchy, which was recognized as an independent state in 1815.

Macedon Hellenized kingdom of the Balkans, founded c. 640 BC, with a mixed population of **Greeks**, Illyrians, and Thracians. Briefly a great power under Alexander the Great (r. 336–323 BC), it was conquered by Rome in 168 BC.

Magadha The most powerful of the early Hindu *mahajanapadas* (great realms) of northern **India**. Emerged in the 7th century BC; under the Mauryan dynasty (321–185 BC) and again under the Gupta dynasty (AD 320–550) it dominated India.

Magyars (Hungarians) A nomad people probably originating in northeast **Russia** or Siberia who invaded Central Europe in AD 896, founding the kingdom of **Hungary** in 1000.

Majapahit Javanese kingdom 1293–1527, the last major Hindu state in the East Indies; at its peak in the 14th century it created a maritime hegemony over much of Sumatra, Borneo and **Malaya**. Overthrown by the Muslim state of Demak.

Makuria (Makkura) Christian **Nubian** kingdom, a successor to the kingdom of **Meroë**, established *c.* AD 350. Civil war caused the kingdom to collapse in 1317.

Malacca City and sultanate commanding the Straits of Malacca between **Malaya** and Sumatra founded *c.* 1400. After the Portuguese captured Malacca in 1511 the sultanate was re-established at **Johor**.

Malaya British colony on the Malayan peninsula. Britain had brought all the Malay states on the peninsula under its control by the 1890s. Britain federated the Malay states in 1948; the federation became independent as Malaya in 1957, and a part of **Malaysia** in 1963.

Malays An ethnic group of the Malayan peninsula, but also, more generally, the **Austronesian** peoples inhabiting **Malaysia**, **Indonesia** and the **Philippines**.

Malaysia Southeast Asian country created in 1963 by the federation of **Malaya** with the former British colonies of Sarawak, North Borneo (Sabah) and **Singapore**. Singapore left Malaysia in 1965.

Mali 1. West African trading kingdom of the Mandinke (or Malinke) people; founded sometime in the late 1st millennium AD according to oral traditions, it was the dominant power in West Africa in the 13th–14th centuries, but was supplanted by **Songhay** in the 15th century. The kingdom finally collapsed in 1670. 2. Former French West African colony comprising much of the territory of the historical Mali state; became independent in 1960.

Mamluk sultanate Turkic slave (mamluk) dynasty, which ruled Egypt 1250–1517. The Mamluks inflicted the first serious defeat on the **Mongols** in 1260 and expelled the crusaders from **Palestine** in 1291.

Manchu See **Jürchen**.

Manzhouguo Japanese puppet state of Manchuria (northeast China) under the nominal rule of the deposed Chinese **Qing** dynasty Emperor Puyi 1932–45.

Maoris Polynesian people of **New Zealand**, descended from the first settlers of the islands who arrived *c.* 1200.

Marathas Hindu warrior clans of **India** united by Shivaji who founded an independent kingdom in 1674 that came to dominate central India in the 18th century. Broke up into a confederacy of allied states in 1761, most of which had been absorbed into British India by 1820.

Marquesas Islands See **French Polynesia**.

Masina (Macina) Much-disputed fertile inland delta of the Niger river, West Africa and centre of a Fulani jihadi state founded *c.* 1818; conquered by **Tukulor** in 1862.

Mauretania Berber kingdom in North Africa 3rd–1st centuries BC; Roman client kingdom in 46 BC, fully annexed by Rome AD 40–42.

Mauryan empire Ancient Indian empire founded by the Mauryan dynasty of **Magadha** (321–185 BC).

Maya Mayan-speaking native American peoples of southern **Mexico**, Belize, **Guatemala**, **El Salvador** and Honduras.

Medes Ancient **Iranian** people who entered present-day **Iran** in the early 1st millennium BC from the Eurasian steppes. They built a considerable empire in the late 7th century, but were conquered by the **Persians** in 546 BC.

Megalithic tomb cultures Neolithic cultures of Atlantic Europe characterized by the construction of tombs and ritual structures using megaliths (large stones) *c.* 4500–1500 BC. Megalithic construction was also a feature of many other prehistoric cultures across the world.

Melanesians An ethnic and cultural group of the western Pacific islands and New Guinea who speak mainly **Austronesian** languages.

Meroë Nubian kingdom on the middle Nile, 590 BC–*c.* AD 350, the successor to **Kush**. The kingdom fragmented after an invasion from **Axum**.

Mesoamerica Prehispanic cultural region of Central America, extending south from central **Mexico** to northern Honduras and **El Salvador**, the ancient civilizations of which (including the **Aztecs** and **Maya**) shared many cultural characteristics.

Mesolithic (Middle Stone Age) Term used to describe the period between the end of the Palaeolithic and the beginning of the Neolithic during which hunter-gatherers adapted to post-glacial conditions and began the transition to a farming way of life. The term is most commonly used with regard to European prehistory.

Mexico Central American country. The modern state of Mexico was founded when the Spanish viceroyalty of **New Spain** declared independence in 1821. In 1823 the **Federal Republic of Central America** seceded, Texas seceded in 1836 and vast territories, including California, were lost to the **USA** in 1848. Mexico is named for the Mexica, the most prominent **Aztec** tribe.

Middle Ages The period of European history between the fall of the western Roman empire in the 5th century AD and the Renaissance (roughly the 15th century).

Ming Chinese imperial dynasty 1368–1644.

Minoans Ancient people of Crete, probably of Anatolian origin. Disappeared after their conquest by the **Mycenaean** Greeks *c.* 1450 BC.

Mississippians Advanced maize-farming cultures of the Mississippi basin characterized by temple-mound construction, long-distance exchange and shared religious beliefs 8th–16th centuries AD.

Mitanni Hurrian kingdom of **Syria** *c.* 1500–1300 BC.

Mixtecs Native American people of southwest **Mexico**, formed a kingdom by the 12th century AD. They conquered the **Zapotecs** in the 14th–15th centuries, resisted the **Aztecs**, but were conquered by the Spanish in the 1520s.

Moche Kingdom, or group of kingdoms, of **Peru** that dominated the coastal lowlands *c.* 100 BC –*c.* AD 700.

Mongolia Central Asian country, historically at the heart of many nomad empires, including that of the **Mongols**. Following the **Qing** conquest of the Mongols in the 17th century AD, the area became the autonomous Chinese province of Outer Mongolia. The modern Mongolian state was created when Outer Mongolia declared independence from China on the fall of the Qing dynasty in 1911.

Mongols A group of nomadic peoples of Central Asia. The term is also used in a general sense to describe the many Mongolic and Turkic peoples united under the rule of Chinggis Khan in the 13th century AD.

Mons An **Austro-Asiatic** people of Southeast Asia, now largely assimilated by the Thais and **Burmese**.

Morocco North African kingdom with an **Arab** and **Berber** population. A Moroccan state has existed in some form since the country was first unified by the **Idrisid** dynasty in AD 789, but it was only permanently unified in the 17th century. Between 1912 and 1956 the country was divided into French and Spanish protectorates.

Moscow (Grand Duchy of Moscow) Russian state founded in 1283, a tributary of the **Golden Horde** until 1480. By 1521 Moscow had conquered all the other Russian principalities and formally became a unitary state when Ivan IV adopted the title Tsar of **Russia** in 1547.

Mozambique Southeast African country. Formerly a Portuguese colonial territory built up from 1508, it became independent in 1975.

Mughals Turkic Muslim dynasty of **Timurid** descent 1526–1857, which ruled most of northern **India** from the mid-16th to mid-18th centuries. The last ruler was deposed by the British in 1857.

Mutapa (Mwenemutapa) Shona successor kingdom to **Great Zimbabwe**, founded mid-15th century AD; conquered by Rozwi in 1695.

Mycenaeans Modern name given to the Late **Bronze Age** Greeks (*c.* 1650–1100 BC), named after the site of Mycenae.

Nanyue (Nam Viet) Kingdom in southern China and northern **Vietnam** with a primarily **Vietnamese** population founded by rebel Chinese general Zhao Tuo in 204 BC. Conquered by the **Han** in 111 BC.

Nanzhao Kingdom of Yunnan in southern China, with a Tibeto-Burman-speaking ruling class, founded in AD 729; it was succeeded by the kingdom of Dali after 902.

Nazca (Nasca) Culture of the southern coast of **Peru** *c.* 100 BC–AD 750, a successor to the Paracas culture. Famous for its geoglyphs, the culture was at its peak *c.* 1 BC–AD 400.

Neolithic (New Stone Age) Technological division of human prehistory covering the period in which people first began to practise agriculture, but were still reliant on stone tools. The dating of the Neolithic is variable because agriculture was developed at different times in different parts of the world. Originally defined on the basis of polished stone technology; pottery and agriculture were added later. The term is not used in **New World** archaeology.

Nepal South Asian country in the Himalaya mountains. The modern state of Nepal began with the unification of three rival Nepalese kingdoms in 1768. The country's modern borders were established following the Anglo-Nepalese War of 1814–16.

Netherlands The Netherlands was formed from the seven northern provinces of the **Spanish Netherlands** which formed a union as the Republic of the Seven United Netherlands in 1579 to fight their war of independence against **Spain**. The provinces formally declared independence from Spain in 1581. Spain formally recognized the independence of the Netherlands in 1648 after several attempts at reconquest had failed.

New England The modern US states of Maine, New Hampshire, Vermont, Massachusetts, Rhode Island and Connecticut. The name was first given to the region in 1614 and the first successful English colony in the area was founded at Plymouth, Massachusetts, by the Pilgrim Fathers in 1620.

New France The area of North America colonized or claimed by **France** in the 17th and 18th centuries. New France was ceded to Britain and Spain in 1763.

New South Wales Britain's first Australian colony founded in 1788. It became a state of the Commonwealth of **Australia** in 1901.

New Spain Spanish viceroyalty covering at its greatest extent Central America, much of the Caribbean and southwest North America, Florida and the Philippines. The viceroyalty was created following the conquest of the **Aztec** empire in 1521 and was dissolved in 1821.

New World The continents of North and South America and the associated islands.

New Zealand Island nation in the South Pacific Ocean. New Zealand was first settled by the Polynesian **Maoris** c. AD 1200. It was annexed by Britain in 1840, becoming a self-governing dominion in 1907 and fully independent in 1931.

Newfoundland English North American colony claimed in 1497, but not colonized until 1610. Newfoundland was a self-governing dominion of the British empire from 1907 until 1949 when it became part of **Canada**.

Nicaea, empire of Byzantine successor state created after the capture of Constantinople by the Fourth Crusade in 1204; it recaptured Constantinople in 1261, re-establishing a much diminished **Byzantine empire**.

Nicaragua Central American republic that became independent after seceding from the **Federal Republic of Central America** in 1838.

Nigeria West African country, formerly a British colony created from territories annexed between 1861 and 1900. It became independent in 1960.

Nobatia Nubian successor kingdom to **Meroë**, founded c. AD 350, conquered by **Makuria** c. 600.

Nok culture Early **Iron Age** culture of central **Nigeria** known almost entirely from its terracotta figurines of animals and stylized humans, c. 600 BC–c. AD 400.

Normans French-speaking people descended from **Scandinavians** (Northmen) who settled in the area of northern **France** known after them as Normandy c. AD 900 and went on to conquer **England**, southern **Italy** and **Sicily** in the 11th century.

Norse Early medieval **Scandinavians**.

Northern Circars Historic peoples of eastern **India**, now part of Orissa state, conquered by the British 1768.

Northern Wei Dynasty founded by the Tuoba clan of the Xianbei people, originally nomads, which ruled northern China AD 386–535. Divided following civil wars into Eastern Wei (534–50) and Western Wei (535–56).

Norway European kingdom, formed in the late 9th century AD. Norway was in union with **Denmark** from 1388 to 1814 when it was united with **Sweden**. It became independent of **Sweden** in 1905.

Nubians African peoples of southern **Egypt** and **Sudan**. A distinct Nubian culture emerged as early as 5000 BC.

Numidia Berber kingdom of North Africa, founded in 200 BC; annexed by the **Roman empire** in 46 BC.

Oguz (Oghuz) Turkic nomad confederation of Central Asia related to the Pechenegs and Kimeks 8th–early 13th century AD.

Oirats Confederation of nomadic Mongol peoples that dominated the eastern Eurasian steppes after the end of Mongol rule in China in 1368.

Old World The continents of Europe, Asia and Africa.

Olmecs Modern name for the people of Mexico's southern Gulf coast who founded the first Mesoamerican civilization c. 1200 BC.

Oman Country in southeast Arabia; emerged as a fully independent state in the 12th century AD. Its capital Muscat was occupied by the Portuguese from 1508 to 1648. It became a major naval and commercial power in the Indian Ocean, bringing the **Swahili** coast of East Africa under its control in 1690. Oman was a British protectorate from 1891 to 1971.

Orange Free State Boer republic of Southern Africa, founded 1854. Conquered by the British in 1899–1902, it became a province of **South Africa**.

Oregon Region of western North America between California and 54° 40' north. Disputed between Britain and the **USA**, it was divided along the 49th parallel in 1846.

Ostrogothic kingdom The Italian kingdom of the Ostrogothic branch of the **Goths** who invaded and conquered **Italy** in AD 489–93. The kingdom was conquered by the eastern Roman empire in 535–54.

Ottomans Turkish dynasty 1299–1923. At their peak in the 16th–17th centuries, the Ottomans ruled an empire which controlled most of the Middle East, North Africa and Southeast Europe. The empire declined steadily through the 18th and 19th centuries, and by 1918 it was reduced to Anatolia and part of Thrace in Southeast Europe. In 1923 the sultanate was legally abolished and what remained of the empire was proclaimed the Republic of **Turkey**.

Pakistan South Asian country that became independent in 1947. **Pakistan** was created as a Muslim homeland by the partitioning of British **India** and originally consisted of two geographically widely separated and ethnically distinct parts. The larger, West Pakistan, was centred on the Indus river valley, while East Pakistan comprised the eastern half of **Bengal**. East Pakistan became independent as **Bangladesh** in 1971.

Palaeolithic (Old Stone Age) Technological division of human prehistory extending from the first appearance of tool-using human ancestors *c*. 2.6 million years ago to the end of the last glaciation *c*. 11,500 years ago.

Palestine 1. Historic much-contested territory in the Middle East, often also known as the 'Holy Land'. 2. British-administered League of Nations mandated territory 1922–48.

Panama Central American country; became independent of **Colombia** in 1903.

Panama Canal Zone A ten-mile-wide zone ceded by **Panama** to the **USA** in 1903 for the purpose of building the Panama Canal. The zone came under joint US–Panamanian control in 1979 and full Panamanian control was restored in 1999.

Paracas Culture of the south coast of **Peru**, *c*. 800–100 BC, showing the influence of the religious centre at **Chavín**. The culture is notable for its fine textiles.

Paraguay South American country that became independent of **Spain** in 1811. The country's present borders were established in 1935.

Parhae (Balhae or Bohai) Korean kingdom founded AD 698, a successor to the kingdom of **Koguryo**. Parhae was destroyed by the **Khitans** in 926.

Parthia Middle Eastern kingdom founded by the Parni, an **Iranian** nomad people, in 238 BC, which at its peak comprised most of modern **Iran** and **Iraq**. The kingdom was overthrown by the **Sasanians** in AD 224–26.

Pegu (Bago) **Mon** kingdom of the lower Irrawaddy region, **Burma**. Conquered by the Burmese kingdom of **Bagan** in AD 1056, regained its independence after that kingdom was destroyed by the **Mongols** in 1287. Reconquered by the Burmese in 1539.

Pergamon Ancient Greek city state in Anatolia, became independent in 281 BC, bequeathed to Rome by its last ruler Attalus III in 133 BC.

Persian empire Major imperial state, also known as the Achaemenid empire after its ruling dynasty, created in the mid-6th century BC and conquered by Alexander the Great of **Macedon** in 334–330 BC. At its height in the 5th century BC, it controlled almost all of the Middle East as well as **Egypt** and parts of Southeast Europe, Central Asia and northern **India**.

Persians An **Iranian** people who settled in Fars **(Parsa)** in southwest **Iran** around the 9th century BC. The Persians have called themselves Iranians since around the 3rd century AD, but the name Persians remained in use by their neighbours into the 20th century.

Peru South American country that declared independence from **Spain** in 1821, secured following the defeat of Spanish loyalist forces at Ayacucho in 1824.

Peru, Viceroyalty of Spanish viceroyalty founded in 1542 to govern Spain's South American empire. Its northern territories were separated to form the viceroyalty of New Granada in 1717, and its southern territories to form the viceroyalty of **Rio de la Plata** in 1776. The viceroyalty was dissolved in 1824.

Philippines Southeast Asian country. The Philippines were conquered by **Spain** between 1521 and 1565. The Philippines were ceded to the **USA** in 1898 and became independent in 1946.

Phoenicians A seafaring Semitic people of the Levant, closely related to the **Canaanites**, late 2nd–late 1st millennium BC. The Phoenicians gradually lost their identity after their conquest by Alexander the Great in 332 BC.

Phrygians People of Anatolia, 13th century BC–4th century AD. The Phrygian kingdom dominated Anatolia in the early 1st millennium BC; it was destroyed by the **Cimmerians** in 690 BC.

Poland–Lithuania East European kingdom created by the union of crowns of Poland and **Lithuania** in 1386. Full political union under the name Poland came in 1568.

Polynesians Austronesian people of the central Pacific islands, including **Tonga**, **Tahiti**, Hawaii, **Easter Island** and **New Zealand**.

Portugal European country. Originated as a county of the Spanish kingdom of León and Castile and was proclaimed a kingdom in 1139. Achieved its present-day borders in 1249.

Poverty Point culture Complex hunter-gatherer culture of southeastern North America, 2nd–early 1st millennium BC, centred on a massive semi-circular earthwork ritual site.

Prussia Militaristic German kingdom created in 1701 when the elector of **Brandenburg–Prussia** was elevated to kingship. The kingdom was the leader of German unification in the 19th century.

Ptolemaic kingdom Greek-ruled kingdom of **Egypt** founded in 304 BC by Ptolemy I, one of Alexander the Great's generals. Annexed by Rome in 30 BC.

Puerto Rico US dependency in the Caribbean. Puerto Rico became a Spanish colony in 1508 and was ceded to the **USA** in 1898.

Qi Short-lived Chinese imperial dynasty AD 479–502.

Qin 1. Chinese state of the Spring and Autumn, and the Warring States periods (770–221 BC), which conquered China between 230 and 221 BC under King Zheng. 2. The first Chinese imperial dynasty 221–207 BC, founded by King Zheng of Qin who took the title Shi Huangdi.

Qing Manchu imperial dynasty of China, founded in 1644. Overthrown in 1911, the last Qing emperor formally abdicated in 1912.

Rajputs Aristocratic Hindu warrior clans of northern **India**, originating in the early **Middle Ages**.

Rashtrakutas Major dynasty of southern **India** AD 753–982; overthrown by the West **Chalukya** dynasty.

Rhodesia, Southern British colony in southern Africa, created in 1895. To prevent the introduction of majority rule, its white minority unilaterally declared independence as Rhodesia in 1965. British rule restored in 1979 to oversee the transition to majority rule and official independence as **Zimbabwe** in 1980.

Roman empire Roman state founded by Augustus in 27 BC following the collapse of the **Roman republic** into civil war in the mid-1st century BC; characterized by a monarchical form of government under emperors. The Roman empire was divided into western and eastern parts in the 4th century AD, each with its own emperor. The western Roman empire fell in 476; the eastern Roman empire, commonly known as the **Byzantine empire**, survived until 1453.

Roman republic The Roman state, governed by elected magistrates, from the abolition of the monarchy in 509 BC to the establishment of imperial government by Augustus in 27 BC.

Romans Originally inhabitants of the city of Rome. As Rome developed as an imperial power from the 4th century BC, Roman citizenship was gradually extended to conquered peoples as a reward for loyalty. In AD 312 citizenship was granted to all free inhabitants of the **Roman empire**.

Rus Swedish Vikings active in Eastern Europe in the 9th–10th centuries AD who imposed their rule on the indigenous **Slav** peoples and who were ultimately assimilated by them. They have given their name to **Russia**.

Russia Transcontinental country in Europe and Asia. The modern Russian state originated in the 16th century when the Grand Duchy of **Moscow** conquered the independent principalities into which **Kiev**, the first Russian state, had split by 1132. Russia began to expand into Asia in 1581–82. Following the 1917 revolution, the Russian empire was divided into ethnically based Soviet Socialist Republics. The Russian Soviet Federative Socialist Republic (RSFSR) was the dominant republic of the **USSR**, which was formally declared in 1922. The RSFSR became independent as the Russian Federation or Russia on the break-up of the USSR in 1991.

Rwanda Central African kingdom formed by the 17th century AD. Annexed by Germany in 1884. In 1923 it was united with Burundi by the League of Nations as the Belgian mandate territory of Ruanda–Urundi until independence in 1962.

Safavids Enormously influential Shi'ite Iranian dynasty, ruled **Iran** 1501–1736.

Saffarids Persian dynasty AD 861–1003 that ruled eastern **Iran**, **Afghanistan**, the Indus valley and parts of Central Asia under its founder Ya'qub bin Laith as-Saffar (*r.* 861–79); it quickly declined under his successors.

Saint-Domingue French Caribbean colony in western Hispaniola. **France** seized the territory from **Spain** in 1659; it became independent as **Haiti** in 1804.

Sakas Old Iranian name for the **Scythians**.

Samanids Persian Sunni dynasty of Central Asia AD 819–999.

Sardinia Kingdom of Sardinia and Piedmont in northwest **Italy** 1720–1861, generally known as Piedmont–Sardinia after 1815. The kingdom was the leader of Italian unification.

Sarmatians The last major Iranian nomad people of the Eurasian steppes, originated *c.* 6th century BC. They lost much of their lands to the **Goths** in the 3rd century AD; the remainder was conquered by the **Huns** in the 4th century.

Sasanians Major **Persian** dynasty that overthrew the **Parthians** in AD 224–26; conquered by the **Arabs** in 637–51.

Saudi Arabia Kingdom of the Saudi dynasty comprising the greater part of the Arabian peninsula; founded in 1924 after the Saudi state of Nejd annexed Hejaz.

Scandinavians North European peoples: the Danes, Swedes, Norwegians, Icelanders and Faroese. They were often referred to collectively as the **Norse** in the early **Middle Ages**.

Scotland Kingdom of northern Britain founded *c.* AD 843 with a mixed Celtic and, from the late 10th century, Anglo-Saxon population. United with **England** in 1707 to create the **United Kingdom**.

Scythians Iranian nomad people who dominated the Eurasian steppes 8th–1st centuries BC. Absorbed by the **Sarmatians** and other nomad peoples.

Seleucid empire Greek empire of the Middle East founded by Seleucos, one of Alexander the Great's generals, in 312 BC. The empire's history was one of steady decline, finally collapsing in 83 BC.

Seljuks (Seljuqs) A branch of the **Oguz** Turks who conquered most of the Middle East 1037–87 and established Turkish dominance in Anatolia. Their sultanate broke up into separate states in 1092.

Semites Ancient and modern peoples speaking Semitic languages, including the **Arabs**, **Hebrews**, **Canaanites**, **Phoenicians**, Assyrians, Babylonians, **Aramaeans**, **Chaldaeans** and Ethiopians.

Serbs Slav people of the Balkans, emerged in the early 7th century AD.

Shang Bronze Age dynasty in northern China c. 1600–1046 BC.

Siam Tai kingdom founded at Ayutthaya in 1351 (often called the Kingdom of Ayutthaya until 1767), renamed **Thailand** in 1939.

Sicily Norman kingdom of Sicily and southern **Italy** founded in 1130. The kingdom's southern Italian possessions became independent in 1282 as the kingdom of **Naples** after Sicily itself came under the rule of **Aragon**. Sicily was reunited with Naples in 1816 to form the **Kingdom of the Two Sicilies**.

Silla Early Korean kingdom, founded c. 57 BC. In the 9th century AD the kingdom suffered civil wars and peasant rebellions and in 935 it was overthrown by the Koryo dynasty, which unified **Korea**.

Singapore Southeast Asian island state, founded as a British colony in 1819. It became independent in 1965.

Slavs Major group of Eastern European peoples, including the Russians, Belorussians, Ukrainians, Poles, Czechs, Slovaks, Slovenes, **Serbs**, Croats and Bulgarians, who speak Slavonic languages.

Slovakia Central European country. Part of **Czechoslovakia** from 1918, it was a German puppet-state 1939–45 and became independent in 1993.

Solomon Islands Island nation in the western Pacific Ocean. Settled by **Melanesians**, the islands became a British protectorate in 1893. They became independent in 1978.

Song Chinese imperial dynasty that unified most of China in AD 979. Northern Song, 960–1126, had its capital at Kaifeng. Southern Song 1127–1279, following the loss of the north to the **Jin**, had its capital at Hangzhou. The dynasty was ended by the Mongol conquest.

Songhay (Songhai) Muslim kingdom of the Songhay people, which became independent of **Mali** in 1340 and expanded to control much of the West African Sahel. Its power was broken by the Moroccans in 1591.

South Africa Southern African country created by the union of the British colonies of **Cape Colony**, Natal, the **Orange Free State** and **Transvaal** (the last two former **Boer** republics) as a self-governing dominion in 1910. It became independent under white rule in 1931; majority rule was achieved in 1994.

Spain Western European country created in 1516 by the union of the kingdoms of **Aragon** and **Castile**.

Spanish Netherlands Wealthy territory approximating to the modern **Netherlands** and **Belgium**, which came under the Spanish crown in 1519. The northern provinces rebelled in 1568, becoming independent as the Republic of the Seven United Netherlands. The southern provinces were ceded to **Austria** in 1713.

Sri Lanka Island nation in South Asia, known as Ceylon until 1972. The first states in Sri Lanka formed in the 5th century BC. The Portuguese gained control of coastal areas in the 16th century AD, but were driven out by the Dutch in the mid-17th century. The British conquered the whole island in 1815; it became independent in 1948.

Srivijaya Indianized Malay kingdom of Sumatra, which dominated **Malaya** and Java from the 7th to 13th centuries AD. It was conquered by the short-lived Singhasari kingdom of Java in c. 1280 and was under the control of its successor state **Majapahit** by 1300.

Sudan North African country, formerly Anglo-Egyptian Sudan, which became independent in 1956. By a referendum in January 2011 the country's southern provinces voted to become independent as South Sudan.

Sueves (Suebi) Early German people first recorded in the 1st century BC. Invaded the **Roman empire** in the 5th century AD and founded a kingdom in northwest **Spain**; conquered by the Visigoths in 585.

Sumerians Ancient people of southern Mesopotamia who founded the first urban civilization in the 4th millennium BC. In the 2nd millennium BC they were gradually assimilated by neighbouring **Semitic** peoples.

Swahili People of the East African coast whose

culture and language have been greatly influenced by trading contacts with the Arab and **Persian** worlds.

Sweden Scandinavian country that was formed by the union of the Svear and Götar peoples in c. AD 995. Joined in a union of crowns with **Denmark** in 1397, Sweden regained full independence again in 1523.

Switzerland European federal state formed in 1848 by the Swiss Confederacy, a loose confederation of Swiss states formed in 1291 that gained independence from the **Holy Roman empire** in 1499.

Syria Middle Eastern, mainly Arab, country, created in 1922 as a French-administered League of Nations mandated territory from territory formerly ruled by the **Ottoman** empire; became independent in 1946.

Tahiti Archipelago in the South Pacific Ocean, settled by **Polynesians** c. 200 BC. The islands were annexed by **France** in 1842, along with the Marquesas Islands and the Tuamotu Archipelago. In 1946 the islands collectively became the French overseas department of **French Polynesia**.

Tais Peoples of southern China and Southeast Asia who speak Tai languages, including the modern Thais (i.e. the people of **Thailand**) and Laotians.

Taiwan See Republic of China.

Tang Chinese imperial dynasty AD 618–907.

Tanguts A pastoralist people of Tibetan origin 9th–13th centuries AD; founded the kingdom of **Xixia** c. 1038.

Tatars Turkic nomad people who originated in **Mongolia** c. 7th century AD. Conquered by the **Mongols** in the 13th century, they migrated west and settled on the Eastern European steppes as part of the **Golden Horde**.

Teotihuacán Ancient city state of the Valley of Mexico, founded c. 200 BC. In the early 1st millennium AD it became a major power whose influence spread throughout **Mesoamerica**. It was destroyed and abandoned c. 650.

Thailand Southeast Asian country, known as **Siam** until 1939.

Thirteen Colonies The British North American colonies of Connecticut, Delaware, Georgia, Maryland, Massachusetts, New Hampshire, New Jersey, New York, North Carolina, Pennsylvania, Rhode Island, South Carolina and **Virginia**, which became the founding states of the **United States of America**.

Thule Inuit culture The most sophisticated **Inuit** marine-mammal hunting culture, superbly adapted to Arctic conditions, it originated around the Bering Sea c. AD 1000 and spread west to Greenland, displacing the early Dorset Inuit culture.

Tibet High plateau in Central Asia and kingdom founded in the early 7th century AD. Tibet was under Mongol rule from 1251 to 1346–54. In 1751 Tibet was conquered by the Chinese **Qing** empire, regaining de facto independence on the fall of the Qing dynasty in 1911; reconquered by China in 1950.

Timurids Turkic dynasty of Central Asia 1370–1506, founded by Timur (Tamberlaine) (r. 1370–1405) who conquered an empire that stretched from the Indus to the Black Sea.

Tiwanaku (Tiahuanaco) Ancient city on Lake Titicaca in the Bolivian Andes, developed into a locally important cult centre by the early 1st millennium AD.

Toltecs People of central **Mexico** who emerged around the 8th century AD. They dominated **Mesoamerica** during the 11th century, but their state collapsed abruptly in 1168.

Tonga Island nation in the South Pacific Ocean. The archipelago was united into a single kingdom in 1845. Tonga was never formally colonized, but was a British protected state from 1900 to 1970.

Tongking Kingdom of northern **Vietnam** 1620–1802.

Transvaal Boer republic in southern Africa, established 1852, conquered by the British in 1899–1902. It became a province of **South Africa** in 1910.

Tunisia North African country with an **Arab** and **Berber** population. The modern country of **Tunisia** roughly corresponds to the former Ottoman beylik of Tunis, which became a French protectorate in 1881. Tunis became independent of France in 1956.

Turkey Middle Eastern and European country, the successor state to the **Ottoman** empire; founded in 1923.

Turkmen Traditionally nomadic Turkic people of western Central Asia descended from the **Oguz** Turks.

Turks A major group of peoples of Western, Central and Northern Asia including the Kazakhs, **Kyrgyz**, **Tatars**, Turkish (the people of modern Turkey), **Turkmen**, **Uighurs**, **Uzbeks** and Yakuts. Historical Turkic peoples included the Cumans, **Huns**, **Oguz**, **Ottomans**, **Seljuks**, Khazars and **Xiongnu**.

Two Sicilies, kingdom of the Kingdom of southern **Italy** and **Sicily** formed by the union of Naples and Sicily in 1816. Annexed by Piedmont–

Sardinia in 1860, which led to the creation of the kingdom of Italy in 1861.

Ubaid culture Complex farming culture of Mesopotamia practising irrigation agriculture with proto-urban settlements 5900–4200 BC.

Uighurs (Uyghur) Originally a Turkic nomad people who ruled a khanate centred in present-day **Mongolia** from the 740s until it was destroyed by the **Kyrgyz** in 840. Survivors migrated east to present day Xinjiang giving their name and language to the local settled population.

Ukraine Eastern European country with a **Slav** population. Formerly the Ukrainian Soviet Socialist Republic, Ukraine became independent on the collapse of the **USSR** in 1991.

Umayyads 1. The first major Islamic dynasty; ruled the **Arab** caliphate AD 661–750. 2. After the dynasty's overthrow by the **Abbasids**, a survivor founded an independent Umayyad emirate in **Spain** in 756 (also called the emirate of Córdoba). The emir Abd al-Rahman III adopted the title caliph in 929. The caliphate broke up into petty kingdoms in 1031.

USSR (Union of Soviet Socialist Republics) Communist state comprising most of the territory of the Russian empire, founded in 1922. It was a Russian-dominated federation of nominally autonomous ethnically based Soviet Socialist Republics. The USSR broke up in 1991 when its constituent republics declared independence.

United Kingdom The United Kingdom of Great Britain was created by the union of **England** and **Scotland** in 1707; it became the United Kingdom of Great Britain and **Ireland** in 1801, and the United Kingdom of Great Britain and Northern Ireland in 1921.

United States of America (USA) North American federal republic. Founded by the **Thirteen Colonies** that declared independence from Britain in 1776. Britain recognized the United States' independence in 1783. The United States' westward expansion across the North American continent began with the **Louisiana** Purchase in 1803; it achieved its modern borders with the annexation of Hawaii in 1898.

Urnfield cultures A complex of cultures of later **Bronze Age** and early **Iron Age** Europe, c. 1350–900 BC, characterized by cremation burials in urns in large open cemeteries. Originating in Central Europe, Urnfield practices had spread across much of Western Europe by 1000 BC.

Uruguay South American republic. Originally part of the Spanish viceroyalty of Rio de la Plata, Uruguay was occupied by Portuguese forces from **Brazil** in 1816. Uruguay declared independence from Brazil in 1825; recognized 1828.

Uzbeks Turkic-speaking people of Central Asia, emerged in the 15th century AD from the break-up of the **Golden Horde**.

Vakatakas Dynasty of central **India**, 3rd–6th centuries AD.

Vandals Early Germanic people, first recorded in the 1st century AD. They invaded the Roman empire in 406 and, after an epic migration through **Spain** and North Africa, founded a kingdom in present-day **Tunisia** in 439; conquered by the eastern Roman empire in 533–34.

Venezuela South American republic. Following a war of independence against **Spain** (1811–23), Venezuela became part of Gran Colombia, from which it seceded in 1830.

Venice Italian mercantile republic, became independent of the **Byzantine empire** in the early 9th century AD, at its peak from the 11th to 16th centuries. Conquered by **France** in 1797.

Vichy France Collaborationist French state, based at Vichy, formed after the German conquest of France in 1940. It ceased to exist with the liberation of France in 1944.

Vietnam Southeast Asian country, known as **Dai Viet** until 1802. Conquered by **France** between 1859 and 1885, it became part of **French Indochina**. On independence in 1954, Vietnam was partitioned along the 17th parallel into communist North Vietnam and US-backed South Vietnam. North Vietnam conquered the south in 1975, reuniting the country.

Vijayanagara Major Hindu kingdom of southern India, founded 1336, named after its capital Vijayanagara (city of victory). The capital was captured and destroyed by **Bijapur** in 1565; a much-diminished kingdom survived until 1646.

Vikings Early medieval **Scandinavian** pirates, active late 8th–11th centuries AD; often used to describe early medieval Scandinavians in general.

Virginia England's first colony in North America. The first English attempts to settle Virginia, in the 1580s, failed; the first successful settlement was founded at Jamestown in 1607. The name Virginia was originally applied to all of the North American coast between the 34th and 39th parallels. The present-day borders of the US state of Virginia were defined in 1863.

Visigothic kingdom Kingdom founded by the Visigothic branch of the **Goths** in AD 418. At its peak the kingdom controlled what is now **Spain**, **Portugal** and southwest **France**. It was conquered by the **Arabs** and their **Berber** allies (Moors) in 711–13.

Wari (Huari) Expansionist state of the Peruvian Andes and rival of **Tiwanaku**, *c*. AD 500–*c*. 1000.

Warsaw, Grand Duchy of French-dominated Polish state created by Napoleon in 1807 from Polish lands ceded by **Prussia**. In 1815 it was partitioned between Prussia and **Russia**.

Wessex Anglo-Saxon kingdom in southern Britain, founded in the early 6th century AD, that united all the **Anglo-Saxons** under its control by 927 to create the kingdom of **England**.

West Germany (Federal Republic of Germany) Federal republic formed in the US, British and French occupation zones of **Germany** in 1949. In 1990 it was reunited with the former communist state of **East Germany**.

Xiongnu A powerful confederation of nomad peoples, which dominated the eastern steppes from the 3rd to 1st centuries BC. Though often identified with the **Huns**, the evidence for this is inconclusive. The confederation broke up in the 1st century AD.

Xixia Kingdom of the **Tanguts**, in present-day Gansu, Shaanxi and Ningxia provinces, China, founded in AD 1038; conquered by the **Mongols** in 1227.

Yangshao culture Early Neolithic culture of China's Yellow river region based on millet farming *c*. 5000–3200 BC.

Yugoslavia Multi-ethnic Balkan federation founded in 1918 as the Kingdom of the Serbs, Croats and Slovenes; officially known as Yugoslavia since 1929. The federation broke up in a series of civil wars between 1991 and 1999. The last two members, Serbia and Montenegro, abandoned the name in 2003.

Zapotecs Indigenous people of southern **Mexico** and major pre-Columbian civilization of **Mesoamerica**, flourished *c*. 600 BC–AD 1500. By the time of the Spanish conquest of Mexico, most Zapotec lands had been occupied by the **Mixtecs** and the **Aztecs.**

Zhou Chinese dynasty 1046–256 BC. The dynasty is conventionally divided into two periods, Western Zhou (1046–771 BC), when the capital was near present-day Xi'an and the Zhou king ruled China through vassals, and Eastern Zhou (770–256 BC), when Zhou controlled only the royal domain around Luoyang and great powers struggled for control of China.

Zimbabwe Southern African country, formerly the British colony of **Southern Rhodesia**, which became independent in 1980. Named for the ancient site of **Great Zimbabwe**.

Zulu The largest ethnic group of **South Africa**; originated as a clan of the Nguni, *c*. 1709

FURTHER READING

General Books

Aldrich, Robert (ed.), *The Age of Empires* (London and New York, 2007)

Barker, Graeme, *The Agricultural Revolution in Prehistory* (Oxford and New York, 2007)

Bayly, Christopher A., *The Birth of the Modern World 1780–1914: Global Connections and Comparisons* (Oxford and Malden, 2004)

Bell, Julian, *Mirror of the World: A New History of Art* (London and New York, 2010)

Black, Jeremy (ed.), *Great Military Leaders and their Campaigns* (London and New York, 2008)

Chamberlain, Muriel E., *Decolonization: The Fall of the European Empires* (2nd edn, Oxford and Malden, 1999)

Diamond, Jared, *Guns, Germs and Steel* (New York and London, 2005)

Elliott, John H., *Empires of the Atlantic World: Britain and Spain in America (1492–1830)* (New Haven and London, 2007)

Fagan, Brian and Nadia Durrani, *People of the Earth: An Introduction to World Prehistory* (14th edn, London, 2013)

Harrison, Thomas (ed.), *The Great Empires of the Ancient World* (London and New York, 2009)

Haywood, John, *Great Migrations: From the Earliest Humans to the Age of Globalization* (London, 2008)

Headrick, Daniel R., *Power over Peoples: Technology, Environments and Western Imperialism, 1400 to the Present* (Princeton and Woodstock, 2010)

Livi-Bacci, Massimo, *A Concise History of World Population* (5th edn, Oxford and Malden, 2012)

MacGregor, Neil, *A History of the World in 100 Objects* (London, 2010)

Morris, Ian, *Why the West Rules – For Now* (New York and London, 2010)

Roberts, John M. and Odd Arne Westad, *The New Penguin History of the World* (6th edn, London, 2014)

Robinson, Andrew, *The Story of Writing* (2nd edn, London and New York, 2007)

Scarre, Chris (ed.), *The Human Past: World Prehistory and the Development of Human Societies* (4th edn, London and New York, 2018)

Strachan, Hew, *The First World War: A New Illustrated History* (London and New York, 2003)

Stringer, Chris and Peter Andrews, *The Complete World of Human Evolution* (rev. edn, London and New York, 2011)

30,000 Years of Art: The Story of Human Creativity Across Time and Space (rev. edn, London and New York, 2015)

Weinberg, Gerhard L., *A World at Arms: A Global History of World War II* (2nd edn, Cambridge and New York, 2005)

North America

Anderson, Fred and Andrew Cayton, *The Dominion of War: Empire and Liberty in North America, 1500–2000* (New York and London, 2005)

Berlin, Ira, *The Making of African America: Four Great Migrations* (New York and London, 2010)

Davis, David Brion, *Inhuman Bondage: The Rise and Fall of Slavery in the New World* (Oxford and New York, 2006)

Fagan, Brian, *The First North Americans: An Archaeological Journey* (London and New York, 2011)

Middleton, Richard, *Colonial America 1565–1776* (4th edn, Oxford and Malden, 2011)

Oberg, Michael L., *Native America: A History* (2nd edn, Chichester and Malden, 2017)

South and Central America

Chasteen, John C., *Born in Fire and Blood: A Concise History of Latin America* (3rd edn, New York and London, 2011)

Coe, Michael D., *The Maya* (9th edn, London and New York, 2015)

Evans, Susan Toby, *Ancient Mexico and Central America* (3rd edn, London and New York, 2013)

Lynch, John, *The Spanish American Revolutions 1808–26* (2nd edn, New York, 1986)

Morris, Craig and Adriana von Hagen, *The Incas* (London and New York, 2011)

Thomas, Hugh, *The Conquest of Mexico* (London, 2004)

Townsend, Richard F., *The Aztecs* (3rd edn, London and New York, 2010)

Europe

Anthony, David W., *The Horse, the Wheel and Language: How Bronze Age Riders from the Eurasian Steppes Shaped the Modern World* (Princeton and Woodstock, 2010)

Blanning, T. C. W., *The Oxford History of Modern Europe* (3rd edn, Oxford and New York, 2000)

Boardman, John, Jasper Griffin and Oswyn Murray (eds), *The Oxford History of Greece and the Hellenistic World* (Oxford and New York, 2001)

Broodbank, Cyprian, *The Making of the Middle Sea* (London and New York, 2013)

Cunliffe, Barry, *Europe between the Oceans: 9000 BC–AD 1000* (New Haven and London, 2008)

MacCulloch, Diarmaid, *Reformation: Europe's House Divided 1490–1700* (London and New York, 2004)

Mazower, Mark, *Dark Continent: Europe's Twentieth Century* (London and New York, 1998; new edn, London, 2008)

Osborne, Robin, *Greece in the Making* (2nd edn, London and New York, 2009)

Outram, Dorinda, *Panorama of the Enlightenment* (London and Los Angeles, 2006)

Potter, David, *Rome in the Ancient World* (3rd edn, London and New York, 2019)

Service, Robert, *The Penguin History of Modern Russia: From Tsarism to the Twenty-First Century* (London, 2009)

Spivey, Nigel and Michael Squire, *Panorama of the Classical World* (London and Los Angeles, 2008)

Tuchman, Barbara W., *A Distant Mirror: The Calamitous 14th Century* (new edn, New York 1987; London, 1991)

Wiesner-Hanks, Merry E., *Early Modern Europe 1450–1789* (Cambridge and New York, 2006)

Wickham, Chris, *The Inheritance of Rome: A History of Europe from 400 to 1000* (London and New York, 2010)

Middle East

Axelworthy, Michael, *A History of Iran: Empire of the Mind* (London and New York, 2008)

Gelvin, James L., *The Modern Middle East: A History* (3rd edn, New York and Oxford, 2011)

Kennedy, Hugh, *The Great Arab Conquests: How the Spread of Islam Changed the World We Live in* (London and Philadelphia, 2007)

Leick, Gwendolyn, *Mesopotamia: The Invention of the City* (London, 2001; New York, 2002)

Lewis, Bernard, *The Middle East* (London and New York, 1995)

McCarthy, Justin, *The Ottoman Turks: An Introductory History to 1923* (London, 1997)

Norwich, John Julius, *A Short History of Byzantium* (London and New York, 1997)

Van de Mieroop, Marc, *A History of the Ancient Near East ca. 3000–323 BC* (3rd edn, Oxford and Malden, 2015)

Africa

Davidson, Basil, *West Africa Before the Colonial Era: a History to 1850* (London, 1998)

Ehret, Christopher, *The Civilizations of Africa: A History to 1800* (2nd edn, Oxford and Charlottesville, 2016)

Fage, John D. and William Tordoff, *A History of Africa* (4th edn, London and New York, 2002)

Naylor, Phillip C., *North Africa: A History from Antiquity to the Present* (rev. edn, Austin, 2015)

Phillipson, David W., *African Archaeology* (3rd edn, Cambridge and New York, 2005)

Reid, Richard J., *A History of Modern Africa* (2nd edn, Oxford and Malden, 2012)

Ross, Robert, *A Concise History of South Africa* (2nd edn, Cambridge and New York, 2008)

Thomas, Hugh, *The Slave Trade: The History of the Atlantic Slave Trade 1440–1870* (London, 2006)

Wilkinson, Toby, *The Rise and Fall of Ancient Egypt* (London, 2010; New York, 2011)

South Asia

De Silva, K. M., *A History of Sri Lanka* (rev. edn, London and New York, 2005)

Judd, Denis, *The Lion and the Tiger: The Rise and Fall of the British Raj 1600–1947* (Oxford and New York, 2009)

Keay, John, *India: A History* (rev. edn, London and New York, 2010)

Kulke, Hermann and Dietmar Rothermund, *A History of India* (6th edn, London and New York, 2016)

Robinson, Francis, *The Mughal Emperors and the Islamic Dynasties of India, Iran and Central Asia 1206–1925* (London and New York, 2007)

Wynbrandt, James, *A Brief History of Pakistan* (New York, 2008)

East and Central Asia

Beckwith, Christopher I., *Empires of the Silk Road: A History of Central Eurasia from the Bronze Age to the Present* (Princeton and Woodstock, 2009)

Brook, Timothy, *Troubled Empire: China in the Yuan and Ming Dynasties* (Cambridge, Massachusetts, and London, 2010)

Cullen, Louis M., *A History of Japan 1582–1941: Internal and External Worlds* (Cambridge and New York, 2003)

Fenby, Jonathan, *The Penguin History of Modern China: The Fall and Rise of a Great Power 1850–2008* (2nd edn, London and New York, 2013)

Huffman, James L., *Japan in World History* (Oxford and New York, 2010)

Keay, John, *China: A History* (London and New York, 2009)

Lewis, Mark E., *The Early Chinese Empires: Qin and Han* (Cambridge, Massachusetts, and London, 2007)

Morgan, David, *The Mongols* (2nd edn, Oxford and Malden, 2007)

Pratt, Keith L., *Everlasting Flower: A History of Korea* (London, 2006)

Van Schaik, Sam, *Tibet: A History* (New Haven, 2011)

Southeast Asia and Australasia

Coe, Michael D. and D. Evans, *Angkor and the Khmer Civilization* (2nd edn, London and New York, 2018)

Denoon, Donald (ed.), *The Cambridge History of the Pacific Islanders* (Cambridge and New York, 1997)

Denoon, Donald and Philippa Mein-Smith, *A History of Australia, New Zealand and the Pacific* (Oxford and Malden, 2000)

Milner, Anthony, *The Malays* (Oxford and Malden, 2008)

IMAGE CREDITS

Timelines: The Events That Shaped History © 2019 Thames & Hudson Ltd, London

Maps by Dražen Tomic © 2019 Thames & Hudson Ltd, London

Designed by Ocky Murray

First published in 2011 in hardcover in the United States of America as *The New Atlas of World History* by Thames & Hudson Inc., 500 Fifth Avenue, New York, New York 10110

www.thamesandhudsonusa.com

This revised and updated edition 2019

Library of Congress Control Number 2019934253

ISBN 978-0-500-02257-3

Printed and bound in Slovenia by DZS-Grafik d.o.o.